IT'S ALL GOING
TERRIBLY WRONG

IT'S ALL GOING TERRIBLY WRONG

Organised Chaos
at Royal, National and Military
Celebrations over 45 years

Mainly the fault of
SIR MICHAEL PARKER KCVO CBE
The Accidental Showman

BENE FACTUM PUBLISHING

It's All Going Terribly Wrong
Published in 2012 by
Bene Factum Publishing Ltd
PO Box 58122
London
SW8 5WZ
Email: inquiries@bene-factum.co.uk
www.bene-factum.co.uk

ISBN: 978-1-903971-65-6

Cover and text design: www.mousematdesign.com

Printed and bound in Malta for Latitude Press

Picture Credits: *Inside Photographs:* René Burri/Magnum Photos, Henry Dallal, DIOMEDIA/Heritage Images, Richard Greenly, Guards Magazine, Le Maître Fireworks, Sampson Lloyd, Alasdair McDonald, Derry Moore, Ann Charlott Ommedal, Michael and Emma Parker, Press Association Photos, Royal Edinburgh Military Tattoo, Royal Tournament, Les Scriver, Louise Strickland, Tempest Photography, *and* Keith Waldegrave. *Front Cover Photograph:* Guards Magazine. *Inset:* Royal Edinburgh Military Tattoo, Royal Tournament, René Burri/Magnum Photos. *Author Photograph:* Emma Parker

Contents

The Rules

Over forty-five years I have made myself work to a list of masochistic, self-imposed, Rules for the Conception and Production of my Events.

Rule One: Have a very big idea in the first place - then double it.

Rule Two: If it's easy to do it's not worth doing.

Rule Three: If given more than one option, always choose the most difficult one – never take the easy way out.

Rule Four: If you're 100% certain that an event is going to work perfectly then you're probably doing the wrong thing and not being ambitious enough – make it more complicated immediately.

Rule Five: Never regard 'No' as an acceptable answer and always treat 'Experts' with considerable caution.

Rule Six: Try never to tell people what is supposed to happen. Then they won't know when it hasn't.

Rule Seven: Always stand as close to the Principle Guest as possible, so that you will be the first person in with your excuses when things go wrong.

Rule Eight: It must be as much fun for as many people as possible.

Author's Note

To avoid confusion between the two Queens Elizabeth, the late Queen Mother is referred to as Queen Elizabeth, while her daughter is simply 'the Queen'.

As there are so many of them spread over such a long time I have described events by category rather than chronologically. I hope readers will not find it too confusing.

Foreword March!

One of the regrets of my life is that I didn't get to work with Michael on the show "About Time" that I was asked to put together for the Labour Government to celebrate the Millennium at that famous white elephant, the Dome (now the prosperous privately-run 02). A segment of that aborted (and unlamented) production was to be devoted to the extraordinary achievements of our wonderful Armed Forces and Michael, whom I have the pleasure of knowing a little, was a positive font of hilarious excess, offering to recreate anything from the Charge of the Light Brigade to the bombing of Dresden (he thinks 'PC' is an abbreviation for an Officer of the Law).

His organisational skills are legendary. If necessary, he will open doors with a barrage of artillery, and there is no detail that escapes his beady searching eye – except perhaps the word 'no'! If there are fireworks involved – and there usually are – he will light the blue touch paper himself to make sure things go off with a bang.

America may have given us P.T. Barnum and Florenz Ziegfeld, but Michael Parker in full military flood makes Andrew Lloyd Webber and me feel like wallflowers.

I have no doubt that *It's All Going Terribly Wrong* will be a Major success, and have rank and file falling about with uncontrollable laughter.

Sir Cameron Mackintosh
September, 2012

If Something Can Go Wrong...

It was a fine early June evening in 1977. I was standing by the Copper Horse, the great equestrian statue of George III, at the top of the Long Walk in Windsor Great Park. And I was feeling absolutely sick with fright.

'Don't worry; not many people will come,' the experts had said. 'They'll all be at home watching it on television.' Well, that turned out to be a very false prophecy indeed. But it was one that I was to hear repeatedly during the next thirty-five years.

People were surging towards me, tens of thousands of them. As the dusk deepened, the hordes began to resemble the waves of an incoming tide. I was feeling sicker than ever because, although I had been working on this day for over a year, I had suddenly realised that I was going to be held totally to blame for whatever went wrong. Live television coverage would ensure that every last detail was sent around the Commonwealth and the world – there would be no second takes, no question of 'We'll sort that out in the editing later'. This was It!

The main problem was that we were running very late. Poor Raymond Baxter, the BBC commentator, was well into his second book of background detail and there was still no sign of the Royal party.

The massive crowds had also delayed the three thousand members of the Sealed Knot Society who were to march – the New Model Army in buff coats and steel breastplates, the Royalist officers resplendent in brocade, lace and wigs – from their campsite in the Home Park. A thousand members of the Lewes Bonfire Society, all bearing flaming torches, were struggling to get through the throng. Both groups were there because I'd thought their numbers would be needed to make the evening work – nothing could now be further from the truth.

Somewhere beyond the crowds, we knew, the Queen and the Royal Family were making their way towards us in order to light the first in a chain of beacons stretching the length of Britain. Such a chain had originally been devised to blaze a warning the length of Britain in the event of invasion.

These few stirring lines from Macaulay's 'The Armada' describe it perfectly:

For swift to east and swift to west the ghastly war-flame spread,
High on St. Michael's Mount it shone: it shone on Beachy Head
Till Skiddaw saw the fire that burned on Gaunt's embattled pile,
And the red glare on Skiddaw roused the burghers of Carlisle.

Now it was being used in a celebration that would join every corner of the kingdom on the eve of the Queen's Silver Jubilee celebrations in London.

In the distance we could hear cheering, so that was promising. At the very moment that I spied the royal Land Rovers, a stage manager from the BBC tapped me on the shoulder. 'Sir, one of our generators has just blown up,' he said. 'Can we please have one of yours?'

I obviously had to say yes, knowing that the BBC needed the light more than I did. But it meant at least half of my site would now be in darkness. Amongst many other problems, the Massed Bands of the Household Cavalry, splendid in Gold State Dress, would now be sunk in gloom which would be a challenge for the musicians. Fortunately the Director of Music had on white gloves, which might show up a bit in the dark.

Fortunately, too, I had brought four World War II searchlights from Hounslow which I thought would add to the jollity of the occasion. Enthusiastic, if not very skilful, TA operators had been playing the powerful beams on the clouds and trees, not to mention the odd aircraft trying to land at Heathrow (we had already had one complaint from Air Traffic Control). They were now re-tasked and moved around by the TV producer, Michael Begg, to illuminate some of the areas left dark by the missing generator.

Then I caught sight of the Queen, standing up in the State Land Rover and waving happily to a hugely enthusiastic crowd. A note of optimism crept into Raymond Baxter's running commentary, and the cold sinking feeling in my stomach lessened slightly – surely nothing else could go wrong now?

The Royal party started at the top end of the line-up of the 'great and good' who were to be presented to them. I was at the other end of the line, ready to escort Her Majesty to the actual beacon lighting. I had only met the Queen once before, for about thirty seconds when she gave me an MBE in 1967, so I was doubly nervous.

At last she arrived at the other end of the line. I bowed. 'Ma'am, it might be a good idea if we got a bit of a move on,' I suggested. The Queen smiled, and off we went in the direction of the beacon. As we rounded a slight corner

I saw that the 1948 London Olympic torch, which was to be used to light it, had gone out, and British Olympic Committee officials were madly trying to relight it. I gave a little cough. 'Er, Ma'am, it might be a good idea if we were to slow down a bit.'

'Do make up your mind!' (with another smile).

At last the torch was lit. The little boy who was to hand it to the Queen was obviously upset by all the hoo-hah, and started to cry. 'You should be in bed!' the Queen told him cheerfully, as she took the torch.

I had been worried that the vast beacon wouldn't light quickly enough, so I'd got the pyrotechnics boys to stuff it with electrically ignited fireworks and had asked a Royal Signals major, who I thought looked like a sensible sort, to be on the ignition button.

The Queen went forward and lit the fuse, which fizzed up spectacularly. Unfortunately, the gallant Royal Signals major, having seen the fuse flare up, pressed the button. The Queen's fuse was burning nicely along the ground when suddenly the beacon, some sixty feet away, prematurely and very obviously caught fire.

'Can't think why you bothered to ask me!' the Queen joked. I groaned. Everybody else thought it was hugely funny.

At last, the two sources of fire were conjoined and the beacon burst into very impressive flames – ah well, better early than never.

Then we heard, way over to one side of us, the sound of a firework mortar being fired.

'What on earth is that?' the Queen asked.

'Well, Ma'am,' I explained, 'we've given each of the beacon sites a very bright flare to use when lighting their beacon, in case visibility is bad.'

But instead of a flare, the firework men had put a maroon into the tube; after a few seconds there was a very loud bang a hundred feet above us.

'What are they meant to do with that – listen to it?'

I gave a deep sigh, and decided that I would have to come clean. 'Your Majesty, I'm afraid it's all going terribly wrong...'

It's a well-worn cliché that silences of a few seconds can stretch out until they feel like an eternity, but that's exactly what happened. Being chained up in the Tower for life was the gentlest of the possible fates that flashed through my mind.

But then the Queen's face lit up in her famously glorious smile.

'Oh, *good!*' she said. 'What fun!'

CHAPTER ONE

❧

An Unpromising Beginning

The Battle of Britain had been won. Hitler had just made his single biggest mistake and was invading Russia. London was reeling in the aftermath of the Blitz. Amongst these huge events a very insignificant one occurred. On Sunday 21 September 1941, I was born at Fulmer Chase, the officers' maternity home in Buckinghamshire. My parents were Vera Wilkins (née Parker) and Captain John Wilkins of the Intelligence Corps.

My mother had already been deserted by my father and was living with her parents. She had tuberculosis and was not around very much; in fact, the whole of her side of the family had TB and it was to plague me too. So I was looked after by a series of people, most of whom I did not know. Looking back now, I feel that I had a very strange upbringing but at the time I knew no better so was quite content. I was well looked after, well fed – probably *too* well fed – and wanted for nothing.

I had no friends of my own age. I imagined that no one wanted to mix with a family that had TB. Various aunts came and went, mainly moving from King Edward VII Sanatorium in Midhurst to Switzerland and back again. I thought none of this at all unusual and supposed that all families were the same. It was not until I joined my regiment some twenty years later that I discovered what real families were actually like.

I never blamed my father for leaving my mother – she was, like her sisters, an impossible woman – however, I did blame him for deserting me. I would see him probably about once a year, and he would take me out for totally inappropriate 'treats'. I was given oysters at a very young age, and it took me years to get to like them.

* * *

When I was six I was sent to Dulwich College Pre-Preparatory School in Coursehorn, near Cranbrook in Kent. There were about thirty boarders and thirty day boys, housed in a lovely Georgian house with a wing of Nissen huts surrounded by rolling fields. Recently I was asked to go back to do Speech Day Prize Giving; it has grown enormously and is now much in demand locally, though no longer attached to the London school. Every Sunday we would walk, hand in hand, to the village church. During the interminable sermons I would gaze up at the medieval shields and helmets, mentally re-fighting the jousts and battles of the Wars of the Roses, little thinking that in twenty years' time I would be producing battles of my own.

From Coursehorn we all went to the proper prep school at Dulwich in south east London. We had heard rumours that life was rather different there, and it certainly turned out to be. The boarders were housed at Brightlands, a large Edwardian house with about forty pupils living in. The house master was a 'dirty old man', who enjoyed beating boys and would do so for the flimsiest of reasons. We got used to it but it was not much fun.

My mother was in hospital again, and every few months I had to go for a check-up in Brompton Hospital, where I would wait in a dark brown cubicle with about thirty old and emaciated men. Never once, in all those times, did any of the other patients say a word to me; they just ignored me. I was by far the youngest and the nurse had to find me a box to stand on. Then I had to wait to see the specialist, Dr Todd. I came to believe that doctors ruled the world, so my first ambition was to become one. I changed my mind quickly when I first saw large quantities of blood, and passed out cold.

One day the death of King George VI was announced over the internal loud speakers, and that day a boy was beaten for sticking a stamp on an envelope upside down. The following year the Coronation came round, and I was thrilled to be taken to see it from seats in The Mall. I was enthralled by the epic pageant, and by the way the whole Mall changed colour as the Navy in dark blue and white, the Army in khaki and scarlet, and the Air Force in crab blue marched past. It all seemed endless and wonderful. Not long before the Gold Coach appeared it was announced that Everest had been conquered, and the cheers were deafening. The crowd on the ground had simple cardboard periscopes through which they tried to see what was going on. I felt very sorry for them. I cannot claim that I determined then to make it easier in future for people on the ground to see, but I remembered it, and when I could do something I did, by installing giant TV screens for the Golden Jubilee. It also never occurred to me as I watched the Gold Coach go by that fifty years later I would play a leading role in that celebration or use the coach for the finale of 'All The Queen's Horses' at Windsor. But the wonder of that day lit a small flame inside me which was to grow into a passion.

For the time being, my move to public school was far more on my mind. I think originally I had been meant to go to Dulwich College, but I wanted to get out of London and as far away as possible from home. Money was not in great supply so the only possibility seemed to be the Hereford Cathedral School. I loved the idea of this, and had visions of singing like a nightingale dressed in cassock, surplice and ruff. The only trouble was that I had not taken the precaution of being able to sing.

First impressions were not brilliant. The school was dirty, cold and brutal, but probably no different from any other school at that time. Our introductory talk by an older boy centred mainly around who could beat us and with what. House monitors could beat us with a gym shoe or hair brush; school monitors could use a cane. Life seemed to be divided into three phases: being bullied and beaten by older boys; bullying younger boys but still being beaten by older boys; and beating younger boys yourself.

We lived in long bleak dormitories with not many blankets. Someone suggested that we should join the Combined Cadet Corps because then we got thick greatcoats which we could put on our beds. This I did immediately. I suppose it was as good a reason as any to start a military career!

In spite of this regime I still volunteered not to have to go home at half terms. Normally we were only allowed into four buildings in town – the Cathedral, the post office, the library and the tuck shop. But at half term we could go anywhere. We had pocket money of two shillings a week (10p), then half a crown (12½p). Threepence bought a large bag of chips which was luxury beyond our dreams.

Shortly after arriving I went to the Cloisters for an audition to join the Cathedral choir. The Master of Choristers sat at the piano and I stood beside him. With his left hand he played chords on the piano, which I was supposed to follow, and with his right hand he stroked my bottom. Sadly, both my voice and my bottom failed the audition. I was not surprised about my voice – I was tone deaf and could not sing a note – but rather disappointed about my bottom. I was to find my tone-deafness very useful later on when producing large-scale musical shows – I once had a band of nearly two thousand – as I was not distracted by musical technicalities.

Some thirty years later, when I was producing a large event in the Royal Albert Hall with massed choirs, massed bands, and singers and stars galore, one of the many conductors was the very same Master of Choristers. I issued my instructions, longing to finish by asking, 'And finally, would you like to come and try my bottom again to see if it has improved over the years?' Sadly, I chickened out.

Thwarted in my ambition to become a chorister and wear a ruff, I volunteered as Cross Bearer. I wore a smart blue cassock and surplice and carried a wonderful medieval cross. I spent a lot of time reading during the service or breaking bits off the Victorian choir screen. We all thought it hideous at the time but it was later sold to the Victoria and Albert Museum and magnificently restored. It is now in pride of place above the main entrance to the museum. I have never had the nerve to tell them that I still have a few bits from it.

The only taxing part of being a cross bearer was when there was a processional litany, and all the priests and the Dean, and the choir led by me, processed singing around the cathedral. Apart from remembering the very complicated route, the biggest problem was to get the timings right. I would always arrive at the final stop either far too early or, worse, far too late with a silent procession behind me. I thought that there must be some way around this, and 'invented' a technique that I was to use thirty years later at national events for the Queen and Queen Elizabeth the Queen Mother. I paced out the route, and one of the choir boys walked with me singing the litany. This also gave me the tempo of the paces. I then worked out how many paces there were and how long each one should be to enable me to arrive at the correct moment. The next time we had a processional litany we arrived at the finish point exactly as the music ended. I was very impressed and so was the Dean, who gave me a glass of sweet sherry afterwards.

* * *

In order not to have to go home during the holidays I volunteered to go on a Combined Cadet Force course to become an instructor. This was quite fun as we were introduced to beer by the regular soldiers. We didn't like it at all at first, but we persevered. On returning to school I discovered that an unforeseen benefit of having been on the course was promotion to Lance Corporal. I was thrilled – it was the first 'preferment' I had ever had. I eventually rose to the dizzy heights of Sergeant which involved wearing a very smart red sash.

One day I was called up for yet another beating for some trivial offence, and decided to rebel. I demanded to see the Headmaster. Mr Hopewell was a nice gentle man, who with his small head and very large shoulders looked a bit like a tortoise as he sat behind his desk. I put my case, which was admittedly rather flimsy, and he let me off. Never again would anyone try to punish me.

I was hopeless at games but tried a little acting. I was cast as the female lead in Gogol's *The Government Inspector* with Alec Rowe, later a playwright, as my suitor. I think my only qualification for this part was a squeaky voice because I was about a foot taller than my 'mother', who later became a judge.

I had turned into a great lump of a thing by this time, so I was tried out for the rugger team, where my lack of talent or fitness was made up for by my bulk. I was in the second row and would just about catch up with the scrum by the time it had broken up and gone. To my surprise I had advanced quite well in rowing, again I think because of my size, and ended up being the bow in the first eight. I was very pleased with my Colours – very smart piped blazer and boater – though I don't think we ever won a single race.

*   *   *

I had been thinking seriously about my future career, the main prerequisite of which was that I should be as far away from home as possible. I was finding the Corps more and more fun and, much to the surprise of my friends and teachers, I decided that I would try and join the Army. It seemed ideal – I would be away from home, doing something useful and exciting, and joining a group of people. I think subconsciously I wanted to find a real family, and also that I wanted to join a 'something' rather than just be a 'somebody'.

I went to my Regular Commissions Board (RCB) at Westbury with no preparation at all. I had no idea what to expect: the only hint we were given was that they would watch how we used our knives and forks. This left me completely mystified as I had no idea there was more than one way that you could.

At Westbury we were given a series of tests and tasks, such as moving barrels and logs and people over various chasms. One task was to get a large oil barrel, and ourselves, over a real stream with two platforms on either side. 'You're the tallest, Number 14,' the team leader said. 'So you've got to lie down with your head over the edge of the platform.' He then put the oil drum on my chest. 'Right, the rest of you, push him out across the stream.' Of course the inevitable happened; my knees hinged and down I went into the water, oil barrel and all. 'I'd really like to try that again,' the team leader announced. Fortunately the instructor intervened.

We each had to give a short talk on any subject we wanted. I stood up and said I was going to talk about 'campanology'. I had done some bell-ringing at Hereford, mainly because the noise of our practices annoyed all the others who wanted to get on with their prep. The officer said that there was no such word. I was somewhat nonplussed and protested that there was. 'Rubbish,' he said, and left the room. The others sniggered. After what seemed like an age he returned with a dictionary, leafed through it, and said, 'Fine, carry on'. I imagine he had done it to try and put me off; he very nearly succeeded.

The Board finished and we all went home. I received a letter a week later telling me that I had passed. I was amazed but was more intrigued by the fact that it ended 'I have the honour to be, Sir, your obedient servant,' and was signed by a Major General, which seemed to me to be overly polite.

I went for my medical to Chester. The doctor said that I was fine though I had a slight murmur on my heart but it was nothing to worry about. Thirty years later, that murmur would turn into something very much to worry about and almost proved a disaster.

* * *

It was at about this time that I first met Gordon Fairley. My mother introduced me to him in Ramsgate, of all places. He became a friend to both of us and was to fill, in many respects, the role that my father should have played. He had many cosmopolitan and colourful friends who were great fun and very generous, and he was later to play an important part in my choice of regiment.

* * *

For years my mother had been talking about reverting to her maiden name. We had not seen or heard of my father for at least ten years and she wanted to break all links with the past. So did I, and now, just as I was about to start what I was always to refer to later as my 'real life', seemed a perfect time to do it. Accordingly, the deed poll was signed and I was now Michael John Parker.

CHAPTER TWO

The Fledgling 'Professional Killer'

What I call my 'real life' started on a warm September day in 1959. I was nearly 18, I had a new name and I was longing to put my earlier life behind me and start my new one. In my new grey flannels, sports jacket and brown shoes – which I was soon to discover were very much 'beyond the pale' – I drove up in a taxi to the huge pillared portico of a very grand Georgian building. This, I was told, was called the Grand Entrance, and if I survived the course I would, in two years' time, be slow marching up these very steps to be commissioned. It was all very exciting.

Unknowingly I was immediately the recipient of three pieces of very good luck. Firstly, I was to join Old College, which we soon discovered was much more laid back than the other two rather keen colleges. Secondly, I was to be in Dettingen Company which prided itself on coming twelfth out of twelve in all Academy competitions. Thirdly, our Permanent Staff were to be Company Sergeant Major Bill Preston, Grenadier Guards, and Colour Sergeant Johnny Hallett, Coldstream Guards. Both of them were firm but fair and not inclined to make one's life unnecessary hell. Later we were to hear scary stories of how petty and vindictive some of the staff in the other Colleges could be. We remained very smug. I was also lucky enough to be sharing a room with Charlie Radford, a very gassy and jolly fellow with a marvellous sense of humour. He later went into the 16th/5th Lancers and won a very good Military Cross in Northern Ireland.

It was slightly weird being called 'Sir' by virtually everybody, although we were soon to discover that it could be said in so many different ways that it could mean everything from, 'You are a bloody fool, Sir' to 'Well done, Sir'. The Company Sergeant Major explained. 'I call you Sir, you call me Sir. The only difference is that you mean it!' On my very first parade Sergeant Major Preston looked me pityingly up and down, and said, 'Do you know, Sir, you've got the best childbearing hips in the Academy!'

We were incredulous when we were told we were to do 'bicycle drill'. Surely that wasn't what becoming a 'professional killer' entailed. We were issued with heavy duty khaki bikes, for which we had to sign (you could get virtually anything in the army, from a mess tin to a tank, if you signed for it) and formed into pairs. My pair was a delightful Nigerian called Murtala Mohammed, who was what was known as 'an overseas gentleman'.

'I've never ridden a bicycle before,' he told me apprehensively.

'Never mind, just hang on to me,' I said. So he did, and off we went, wobbling uncertainly down the road, until we and several others ended up in a pile of spinning wheels and dusty flannel trousers, all laughing our heads off. This was of course the whole point – the ice had been broken, and over the next two years our journey of 'shared adversity' would make us all friends for life. Murtala, or Myrtle as we always called him, was later to become President of Nigeria, but sadly was assassinated soon afterwards for being too honest.

Each day started at 0630 hours with a senior cadet crashing into our rooms and turning the lights on. We had to bound out of bed immediately and shout out our names and army numbers – I could never remember my number – then go down to the side of the Parade Square for BRC (Breakfast Roll-Call). The first time we did it we were told to 'Size!' which meant tallest on the right, shortest on the left. I decided that it would be better to be the tallest. Being the tallest meant that I was going to be the Right Marker, the person everybody else had to keep 'in dressing' (lined up) with. The second tallest ended up on the far left and had to struggle keeping in dressing.

We were issued with our uniforms, Hairy Battle Dress for everyday wear and very smart Blues – Number One Dress – for parades and evening wear, all with white gorgets to proclaim our status. The blues were tailored, the battle dress fitted where it touched. We at Old College had smart red lanyards and a brown leather belt. The boots were heavy and knobbly and many happy hours would be spent trying to smooth them with hot spoons and then 'bulling' them to a high gloss. Why they couldn't be made smooth in the first place was beyond us. In fact the cadet in the next room, Michael Westmacott, being well off, bought himself some special smooth boots. This did not go down well with Colour Sergeant Hallett, who gave him a hard time from then on.

Lights had to be turned off at 2200 hours but we were supposed to keep on bulling in the dark. Bulling was literally a mixture of spit and polish which was worked in circles all over the surface to be cleaned, which in our case was virtually everything. In order to see in the dark most of us took up smoking so we could see a bit from the glow of the cigarette. It also made us feel very grown up.

My brother cadets were all great fun. I also had many friends in other Companies who we met whilst doing Academic Studies. Martin Carver was one such. He made an unlikely soldier, being almost horizontally laid back and endearingly scruffy; he was later to become a professor and author. I think the only reason he had joined the Army was because his step-grandfather was Field Marshal Montgomery. He once asked me to go and have tea with the great man. It was rather like meeting an elderly vulture. Stooped and bird-like, he pecked at everything one said. It was certainly quite an experience watching the famous victor of so many battles trying to decide how to eat a cream bun.

Paul Cordle, who was going into the Grenadiers, became a great chum; I later became godfather to his eldest son George who has always been a delight. Charles Messenger was to become an excellent historian and has helped me enormously. Jeremy Mackenzie became a four-star general and Governor of the Royal Hospital Chelsea. Many of the others I do not see so often, but when we do meet it is as though we had last seen each other only yesterday.

Each term had its carefully chosen 'unpleasantness'. The first term was the Juniors' Steeplechase. This involved a cross country run, wading through the Wish stream, clambering over walls and running through mud. Each platoon was allowed two 'swingers' – runners who did not count towards the competition score. Naturally I was elected to be a swinger, and I finished so far behind the rest of my platoon that I almost won the next race.

The second term had boxing, when all the intake throughout the academy would be paired off and invited to thump the living daylights out of each other. After this I had only just recovered consciousness when I was helped into my blues and led down to the dining room where I tried to carry on a conversation with one of the officer instructors. Amazingly, Intake 27 of Dettingen Company won the second term boxing competition, with zero help from me.

Once past our second term, things eased up a bit. By this time we had met most of the rest of the intake in the other companies and had made friends. The chap I got on with best was Jeremy Bastin of Waterloo Company, also in Old College. He had acquired quite a name for himself by doing his bulling in his father's full brigadier's uniform, which did not amuse the drill staff one bit. In fact, after the first term we did little bulling as we all had our own servants who did it for us. Mine was a lovely white-haired gentleman called George; he was quite old enough to be my grandfather but seemed content to clean up after us and make certain that we were fit for parade and so on. We had to pay him 2/6 a week, and if we forgot or thought we were broke he would stand sorrowfully blocking the door until such time as we handed over the required silver coin.

We were paid eighteen shillings a day which seemed like riches at the time. Now that we were allowed out of the Academy we started on the serious business of learning how to drink. Actually I did not like alcohol at first so had to disguise its taste with lime or orange juice so that lager-and-lime and gin-and-orange were our normal tipples. I realised that it would take considerable willpower to overcome this problem but I was determined to succeed – and did.

We had to fill in a sports book every day with what we had done during the afternoon period. I rode quite a bit and enjoyed it, but I don't think my horse did; I parted company with him fairly frequently. Also, Jeremy Bastin and I 'played squash' every day for about four months or, to be precise, we went down to the squash courts and had a long chat and a cigarette or two. To this day I still don't know the rules of squash.

As we progressed through the various terms, we did more and more interesting things. We were taught sciences, languages, military history and Modern Subjects i.e. politics and the Commonwealth. In 2011, the fiftieth anniversary of our commissioning, we were able to see some of our Sandhurst reports of the time. Mine make mixed reading – 'He must guard against having a too high opinion of himself.' And 'He has plenty of moral determination but his apparent wetness makes others unwilling to follow him'!

Our cap badge carried the Sandhurst motto *Serve to lead* and this was the one thing they drummed into us continually – you must look after your 'boys'. This is a lesson that I have tried to carry out in real life ever since. As it happened, I never had the opportunity to experience real active service, so I will never know how I would have coped under fire. I hope that I would have been rather more worried about letting my boys down and getting them injured or killed through my own stupidity than about my own safety.

Little by little all the strands of leadership and competence were being drawn together and I appeared to be making some progress. In our intermediate term a new rank of Cadet Lance Corporal was introduced, and I was amazed to be promoted to it together with my friend James Cassels.

Had I given it a little more thought I would have noticed that James and I were actually about the same height and that the cadet lance corporals were going to be commandants or 'stick orderlies'. This meant that on Sunday we would march in our full finery, complete with silver sticks, to Government House where the Commandant lived. We would have breakfast with him and his wife and then march him to chapel. The Commandant, Major General 'Geordie' Gordon Lennox, was a Grenadier of – to us – huge age, though now I realise he could not have been more than fifty. As we sat to attention trying to control our self-destructing fried bread which would in an instant snap and fly across the room, it became clear why we were there – James Cassels' father was the Commander in Chief of the British Army of the Rhine and was shortly to become Chief of the Imperial General Staff i.e. the boss of the whole army. The General's ADC, Captain Michael Hobbs, Grenadier Guards, was huge fun and became a friend in later life. He went on to become a Major General himself and a Knight of the Royal Victorian Order looking after the Military Knights of Windsor.

*　　*　　*

A very big decision had to be taken about this time, about which regiment we would like to join. Before I arrived at Sandhurst I had wanted to join the Royal Horse Artillery – the King's Troop, in fact. I did not allow my inability to ride to affect my judgement. But I was told that I couldn't join the RHA on commissioning, so I had to put myself down for the Gunners, the Royal Artillery. However, I soon went off that idea. Quite a few of my friends – Paul Cordle, John O'Connell, Conway Seymour and Mike Westmacott – were joining the Grenadier Guards, which seemed a good idea, until I suddenly woke up to the fact that they would all be marching everywhere. I didn't think this was a very good idea. I needed to be driven!

Daily we were bombarded by the regiments and corps trying to persuade us to join them. Demonstrations were laid on on Barossa – our local training area – where they would lay out all their toys and tanks and guns and things, and talk enthusiastically about the joys of being a Gunner, a Signaller, an Infantryman or whatever. The best by far was a young officer in the Royal Army Service Corps, who stood in front of a whole load of canvas tents with sounds of running water and steam hissing out of the top. 'There is nothing more exciting and rewarding,' he said, 'than being in command of a Mobile Laundry and Bath Unit.' Little did I realise that, when producing the Royal Tournament some twenty years later, I would be delighted to have one of these contraptions posted to us at Earls Court, which meant the boys could at least have an approximation of a decent shower.

Looking at my old reports I discovered that I must have applied to join the Household Cavalry, although I have no recollection of doing so. But my College Commander wrote to them saying, 'I don't know whether he could afford to come to your regiment. My own view is that he's not the type of boy you want. I feel you could do better.' So there!

By chance, at that key moment, a friend of my mother and Gordon Fairley came on the scene – Major Delmé Seymour-Evans, late of the 7th Hussars, a lovely kind gentleman who poured a very good gin and tonic. He suggested that I might like to try to join his old regiment, which had just amalgamated with the 3rd Hussars to become the Queen's Own Hussars.

I now made what I believe to be one of the two best decisions I have ever made in my whole life; I asked to join the Queen's Own Hussars. It would be forty years before I would make the second, possibly even more important, decision.

About this time we had a new adjutant at Sandhurst. My first adjutant was Lieutenant Colonel David Toller of the Coldstream Guards, a 'god' who rode around on a large grey charger being saluted by everything that moved. He was never ever known to have spoken to a cadet at any time. One day someone ran into the accommodation block saying, 'The Adjutant has just spoken to me!' We couldn't believe it, but it was true – not because Toller had softened but because we had a new adjutant. Lieutenant Colonel Philip Ward, Welsh Guards, had taken over and he was completely different. He was very approachable and made a point of getting to know as many as the cadets as possible. In fact, he became a friend and someone I could confide in. I was worried that I might not be able to afford to go into such a splendid regiment as the Queen's Own Hussars. In those days there was a lot of talk about having to have a private income to go into a smart regiment, and I did not have one. 'Don't worry about that,' he said. 'I didn't have one. Anyway, when you're in London you can always go home and play the gramophone!' I wasn't quite certain what he meant by that but I knew he was trying to be helpful and kind. By an extraordinary series of coincidences Philip Ward was to play a pivotal role in my later life. He became the Major General Commanding the Household Division and as such Chairman of the Royal Tournament. So when, some thirteen years later, my name was put forward as producer, he was very receptive. Once I had become producer, he then put my name forward to help with the Queen's Silver Jubilee. Both events started my entire later career. It is strange what can happen if someone takes the trouble to talk to a lowly cadet.

*   *   *

In the middle of my course I suddenly decided that I was going to write, direct and produce the 'Sandhurst Revue'. Mr Osborne, the tiny owl-like civilian instructor in charge of amateur dramatics, asked me suspiciously what experience I had had. 'None,' I said blithely, 'but I've got a few ideas.' So I got the job. I then spent the whole of the term writing the revue. *Oliver!* was the new hit musical in London and I decided to steal the tunes from that and other Lionel Bart musicals and rewrite the lyrics. One of my reports later said, 'His abilities must be well above average as, to my certain knowledge, the RMAS Revue took every spare moment of his time this term!'

My friends joined in and helped with ideas for scenes and lyrics. Charles Messenger was always a fount of useless background information, the weirder the better. Ray Pett, who later became a general, was also a great comedian. Ross Mallock was a talented musician who could play a hosepipe and a saw amongst other things, and later set up a marvellous air tattoo at Middle Wallop. The cast was over fifty strong and included girls from Paddock Wood, a smart finishing school nearby. The music was provided by Denis Lever, a civilian lecturer who very kindly did all the arrangements I requested, which were played by long-suffering musicians from the Sandhurst Band.

In the opening scene, a statue of Queen Victoria – a cadet in drag – sang *Fings ain't wot they used to be*. Another scene featured a chorus line of sergeant majors doing a burlesque dance led by an equally pantomime academy sergeant major. Here I must explain a bit. The rank of Academy Sergeant Major had just been invented for the legendary RSM Jackie Lord, making him the most senior warrant officer in the whole army. Jackie Lord had an extraordinary history. During the war, amongst other things, he had whipped a lax POW camp into parade ground shape, and after the war held a long and benign reign over many years of cadets, including King Hussein of Jordan. One evening in our third term we were all doing 'Monkey Hill Guard', to give us an experience of what soldiers' guard duty was like. Monkey Hill overlooked the theatre, where we could see television vans and masses of cable, a lot of to-ing and fro-ing and great excitement. Unknown to any of us, Eamonn Andrews was about to record the programme 'This is Your Life' featuring Academy Sergeant Major Lord. Suddenly a large convoy of Mercedes pulled up and out got a very small man surrounded by bodyguards. It was King Hussein, who had come to pay tribute to Jackie Lord in person, a huge compliment to him.

Every Saturday morning, we would have an Academy Parade, with over a thousand cadets. One such parade followed the last performance of my revue. I suddenly heard my name being called out. I marched the very long distance to the rostrum, expecting the worst. When I eventually arrived in front of the AcSM, he looked me up and down a few times and eventually said, 'I don't know what you think you were doing last night, Sir... (long pause)... but I thought it was very funny. Fall in!'

Lieutenant Colonel Pat Howard-Dobson, an instructor at the Staff College Camberley just down the road, and the senior Queen's Own Hussar in the area, was asked to interview me to see whether I was suitable to join the Regiment. By chance he came to the last night of my revue, after which the whole cast gathered on stage. To my huge embarrassment Mr Osborne launched into a paean of praise for me, saying how brilliantly I had done it all – completely over the top, I thought. I was extremely reluctant when called onto the stage to receive the applause – for one terrible moment I thought he might be about to kiss me. Next day I met Colonel Pat – he had loved the show, and was very impressed with Mr Osborne's impassioned speech. He asked me whether that happened every night. I told him, 'No, thank goodness!' That was that. I was accepted!

I did not fully appreciate at the time how very, very lucky I was. The Regiment was about to become my first real family, and I would not have missed my time with them for the whole world. There was one other cadet who was joining the Regiment, Ian McConnell, who until then I had not really known. Amazingly, we had been born on the same day, 21 September 1941, but he always made out that he was older than I because he had been born in India and the sun comes up earlier there!

I decided that it would probably be a good idea if I were to learn to drive. After weeks of lessons I took my first test. Unfortunately, the first thing I did was to drive into the back of a car just outside the Sandhurst Gate. The invigilator told me to drive back home immediately.

'Oh, have I failed?' I asked.

'Of course you've bloody failed! You're not supposed to hit other vehicles!'

On my next test I drove into the side of a car, and went on fail my third, fourth, fifth and sixth tests.

*   *   *

Our responsibilities became greater and greater as we became more senior. At the end of the term James Cassels and I, as stick orderlies, were chosen to be the Commandant's Orderlies for the Sovereign's Parade. I was thrilled, until I discovered that the officer taking the salute on behalf of the Queen was James's father – and there was me thinking I had been chosen on merit! The photograph of the event seemed to suggest that we did it quite well although I looked as if I had a red hot poker stuck up my backside.

Shortly before the parade my Company Commander, a lovely 16th/5th Lancer called Peter Holland, took me aside and told me that I was not going to become an Under Officer as everyone had expected. He said that I had spent far too much time on the revue and not nearly enough on my military duties. He kept muttering that 'Revues don't help to win wars'. Well, he was quite right but revues did help me recognise where my true talents possibly lay.

Our senior and last term started with me being promoted to the dizzy heights of Cadet Sergeant. This meant that I and my Junior Under Officer became responsible for being nasty to the junior cadets. We didn't really put our hearts into it – it all seemed a little petty – so we would take them for a drink instead.

The Sandhurst tailors Hobsons were rushed off their feet trying to get our new uniforms ready. Those who were rich enough went to London for theirs. In those days tailors didn't seem particularly fussed about customers paying their bills. Four pounds a month seemed to allow one to buy as many suits as one wanted. Similarly, two pounds a month to Poulsen, Skone & Co meant you could have as many pairs of handmade shoes as you wanted. Our uniform shirts and ties came from Coles, whilst our smart civilian shirts came from Harvie and Hudson in Jermyn Street. At that time they were the only shop in London making boldly striped shirts and we all used to save up to treat ourselves to them.

At about this time, I had a bash at trying to play polo. The best I could manage was to hit the ball and fall off the horse, or miss the ball and stay on the horse. I could never combine the two things at once.

As our Commissioning Parade drew nearer we were given our last physical fitness test, or 'battle fitness test'. I failed miserably and was told by Staff Haylett, with a certain amount of sadness, that I could not be commissioned. My immediate thought was, 'What a waste of two years'; my second was to go and drown my sorrows. In fact, James Cassels also had some trouble with his test, but as his father was shortly to be Chief of the Imperial General Staff it suddenly did not seem to matter. When I joined the Regiment I never once passed the annual fitness test but managed to gloss over the fact successfully for ten years.

The day of our commissioning came. Her Royal Highness Princess Marina, Duchess of Kent, on behalf of the Queen, took our Sovereign's Parade and at the conclusion we slow-marched up the steps, the only thing we hadn't rehearsed minutely; that symbolic rite of passage could only be done once. The Adjutant followed on his horse but we were all celebrating so hard in the hallway that the horse had nowhere to go and got very annoyed. My mother, for once not in hospital, came with Gordon Fairley to see the parade, and was thrilled by it. Extraordinarily, my father, whom I barely recognised, also turned up. I hadn't seen him for ten years and had no idea how he found out that I was to be commissioned. We spent about two minutes with him and then went off for the celebration lunch in New College.

At last I was a Second Lieutenant in the Queen's Own Hussars – hurrah! Yet even as I sewed the two single pips onto my epaulets I had a sneaking suspicion that I might not be a 'professional killer' for very long.

*   *   *

As soon as I left Sandhurst I went down to the South of France to stay in my Aunt Iris's flat in Juan-les-Pins with Gordon Fairley and my mother. It was to be the last holiday I ever had with her. Soon after our return she went into hospital yet again, and this time never came out. Later we all reported to the Royal Armoured Corps headquarters at Bovington in Dorset to start on our Young Officers' course. This was where we were to learn for the first time about our new toys – tanks!

The first course was Driving and Maintenance. The fact that I had failed my driving test five times didn't prevent me from driving a fifty-ton Centurion tank. In fact, I found it quite easy, as you didn't have to worry too much about steering; you could just crunch over things. The next course was Signals, learning about radios. We rushed around Dorset in our Land Rovers and quickly learnt the art of running an extension lead out from the Land Rover into a pub so that we could continue the exercise whilst being refreshed.

Then came Gunnery, easily the most fun. Apart from the bore of having to hump the very heavy ammunition everywhere you had the immense satisfaction of blowing up old tank hulks on the range.

The powers that be were still fussed by the fact that I hadn't passed my driving test, so I had extra tuition on one-ton Bedford lorries. This involved 'double de-clutching' which I never mastered, but I was still quite good at hitting things – once I almost got an old lady on a zebra crossing in Bournemouth. Believe it or not, my driving instructor was one Corporal Driver of the 16th/5th Lancers. On the last day of the course, in pouring rain, he gave up and passed me. When I did get my licence, I discovered that I was allowed to drive not only a car, but also a 'vehicle steered by its tracks', in other words a tank. The opportunities for mayhem seemed endless.

Our Young Officers' course completed, we set off to join our regiments.

CHAPTER THREE

More Nero Than Hero – My Military Career

Ian McConnell and I flew by plane to RAF Gütersloh in West Germany. We were one of the first groups not to have to go by ferry. We arrived in Münster, weighed down by all our new kit including, in my case, a ceremonial sword, not something that would be allowed on a 'plane nowadays. When we got to the Mess David Cannon looked at it and said, 'I'm so glad that you fence'. The next morning I went to meet my troop – First Troop of A Squadron. My Troop Sergeant was a Sergeant Allen who was Polish and had fought with the regiment in the war. He was old enough to be my father and had changed his name from something beginning with Z to something beginning with A so he could be first in the pay parade.

I looked apprehensively at my troop and they looked bleakly at me. I realised that while I knew pretty well exactly how Wellington had fought the Peninsular Campaign in the Napoleonic wars, I had no idea what to say to my men when meeting them for the first time. Sergeant Allen did all the talking for me. The men were a wonderful bunch of Brummies with a great sense of humour but with slightly impenetrable accents which took a bit of getting used to. I met my driver, operator and gunner, with whom I would be sharing a relatively small metal box which made a lot of noise and smelt dodgy. But it had an electric kettle for brew-ups and plenty of room for beer in the barrel.

There was a wager book in the Mess, where bets were written down and accounts kept of payments, which went back for at least twenty years. Ian and I were bet that we couldn't eat fifty eggs in an hour. I didn't think this would be much of a problem as I loved eggs. We could have them cooked however we liked so I chose lightly scrambled. The first plate of ten eggs was delicious. The second plate was less so. The third was a problem. The taste had become disgusting and we had to drink champagne and eat strawberries to take it away.

About ten officers and several wives had put their names in the book with their bets so a lot of money was at stake. The Officers' Mess had been a Luftwaffe one in the war and was therefore very well appointed. In the loo there was a large porcelain vomitorium with two handles to grip onto whilst being sick, or – as we called it – 'shooting a cat'. I had to take up residence in the loo as the plates kept coming, and the paymaster, Jack Turnbull, kept count of the eggs going in and the 'cats' coming out.

Poor Ian gave up after about forty eggs but I managed to stagger on and ended up winning the equivalent of a month's wages.

*   *   *

From Münster, the Regiment moved to Detmold, where we had a lovely mess with a huge garden which I was going to use to good effect in the near future. But as for the military situation, one of my troopers summed it up rather well: 'We're just farting against thunder, aren't we, Sir?'

We were indeed. Just over the border there were hundreds of Russian tanks to every one of ours. We made ourselves as battle ready as possible, but unlike some armies we were not forced to prove ourselves every moment of the day. If the boys had done their work, they went off and played sport; there was no clock watching. If, however, something went wrong, we were all more than ready to work all day and all night if necessary.

In the meantime we gave parties. Once we decorated the whole garden with lights and I produced the effect of swans swimming on a lake – don't ask me why. All equipment and material were acquired from the Ministry of Public Building and Works on the basis that 'the Queen will pay', i.e. it was done on the fiddle. Our wiring in the garden was a bit dodgy and we had some new fangled sort of circuit breakers in the fuse box which I had never seen before, and which kept popping out. So I armed two members of the mess staff with pencils to keep them pushed in. The box got very hot but we got through the evening without a fire.

The next dance would obviously have to be better so I came up with the idea of building the Taj Mahal at the end of the garden. Our wonderful Quarter Master was Major A S C Blackshaw MBE, who had lost an eye in the war. But his one eye noticed more than ten pairs of anybody else's. 'Blackie' took me under his wing and gave me all the help I needed.

In my troop I had a very tall soldier called Trooper Child, who was almost seven feet tall and couldn't fit into any tank – he had even had to have a special bed made for him, and his shoes would have made very good dinghies. But he was such a nice fellow that we couldn't possibly get rid of him, so I told him that although he couldn't come on an exercise with us, he could paint my Taj Mahal while we were away. He muttered, 'I didn't join the effin' Army to paint an effin' Taja-whatever it is.'

The exercise went quite well. It certainly proved beyond any doubt that I was completely useless at map reading, so Sergeant Allen sensibly put the troop corporal in the lead whenever we had to go anywhere important. At night we would sleep on the warm back decks of the tank and I always embarrassed my crew hugely by insisting on changing into pyjamas every night. And when we got back to barracks there was my lovely Taj Mahal, over forty feet high, at the end of the garden! We went to the stores and nicked every bit of polythene we could find and had it laid on the lawn to form a 'lake' leading to the Taj.

The dance was deemed a great success, although I had a slight hiccup the following day. For all our dances we used to bring out a plane full of our girlfriends from England and as they were all there anyway we laid on a jolly lunch party for about sixty people in the mess on the Sunday. I had reckoned without the President of the Mess Committee, who came down just before lunch to find the mess full of women!

'It's all very well to have them for a dance, but not for lunch,' he said very loudly. Out in the hall he started berating me, and every time the mess staff walked past with trays full of Pimms he would take a couple of glasses and throw them over me. It all got rather sticky and I ordered the next waiter to find another way round. The PMC then put me under close arrest and sent me to my room in disgrace. As he couldn't find two officers either willing or sober enough to escort me I went on my own. Just as I was thinking that my military career was probably over, the door burst open and in came two brother officers, Peter Steveney and David Pipe with his wife-to-be Patricia, with many bottles of champagne. I was fairly horizontal by the time a letter arrived releasing me from my arrest. The Colonel had told the PMC not to be so silly.

*   *   *

Building on the success of the Taj Mahal party, I decided we would do a production of Anouilh's *Becket*. I had recently seen it on the London stage and also the film with Peter O'Toole and Richard Burton which had just come out.

When I look back on it now I am somewhat surprised at my cheek in getting the production on the road at all. I got Blackie on board, closed the gym to the rest of the Brigade for a month, and got the workshops to stop doing what they were supposed to do and make me four scaffolding seating stands. I thought it would be fun to have the audience on wheels, formed in a circle for 'theatre in the round' or wheeled out into a shallow V for the open air scenes. So I had the dolly wheels taken off all the half-tracks in the regiment to go under the scaffolding, which of course meant that the workshop vehicles could no longer go to war. I asked the Regimental Sergeant Major if I could have some prisoners to get under the stands and push them around during the performance. Prisoners (soldiers who had been found guilty of minor misdemeanours and locked up for a few days) were always a ready source of 'slave labour'.

I went to London and asked for, and got, all the costumes from the film, and to the theatre to borrow the realistic life-size hobby horses they had used in the original play. As if this were not enough I then persuaded the commanding officer to dress up as a monk and lead a team of senior ranks in plainchant.

Naturally, I had decided to play Becket myself, even though my previous acting experience was close to zero, and I persuaded ten officers and a number of other ranks to play the other roles. The prettiest lady in the garrison, Catherine Vivian, had agreed to play my on-stage lover, and with her taking part there was a queue of people for every other role.

The parts of the four barons, who were to kill me, were much in demand as word had got around that they entailed a lot of eating and drinking. On the opening night all four decided that acting was too difficult so they decided to get drunk for real and happily threw all their partly-eaten chicken legs into the startled German audience.

Even so, the first performance earned a standing ovation which tested the strength of the wheeled stands somewhat. Afterwards the RSM came up and said he was worried about using prisoners to move them.

'Surely it's safe enough?' I asked.

'That's not the problem, Sir,' came the reply. 'The trouble is they're enjoying it, which is not acceptable!'

I thought I cut quite a dash in Richard Burton's beautiful cope and mitre, and I even got some fan mail!

*   *   *

The Regiment was planning its new move. We were going to be split, with one enlarged squadron going to Berlin and the remainder to Catterick. I really wanted to go to Berlin as I didn't want to be in England. Next to my office was a very small room, one wall of which was covered with the 'manning chart' for the split. After a good lunch one day I crept in and filled in the blanks with my name and the name of my troop. Nobody ever queried it, so we were all set to go off Berlin.

However, just before that, we heard that the Regiment was to play host to an enormous annual NATO get-together called the Prix Leclerc, a shooting competition in which all NATO's armies would compete. Virtually every general in Western Europe was going to be there. All the officers of the Brigade were briefed because masses of temporary ADCs would be needed to look after them all.

The Supreme Allied Commander Europe was General Lemnitzer, who was to be looked after by John Stanier, one of our squadron leaders who was later to become the Chief of the General Staff and a Field Marshal himself.

To my surprise and delight I was chosen to look after the second most senior officer in NATO, Commander Land Forces Central Europe, General Hans Speidel, who had been Field Marshal Rommel's chief of staff at the time of D-Day. He was one of the very few German generals involved to survive the aftermath of the bomb attempt on Hitler's life; even his boss Rommel had to commit suicide when he was implicated.

I was given an extremely large American staff car and, better still, an American Military Police escort car. We could rush around the countryside with blue lights flashing and sirens wailing, knocking everything out of our way as we went. It was great fun.

I took to General Speidel immediately. He was very amusing and self-deprecating. When I arrived to pick him up for his first engagement in full mess kit, all scarlet and gold, he looked down ruefully at his grey Wehrmacht uniform and said, 'You can't stand anywhere near me, you look far too beautiful!' My American policemen thought I looked 'swell' and well worth a few extra blasts on the siren even when we didn't need them.

At first I stared at the General with some awe; here was a man who actually knew Hitler and had worked with Rommel. Later I had some fascinating chats with him, and if I teased him he would say, 'Now, don't you be cheeky to me – I won D-Day for you!'

'Really, General?'

'Yes, Rommel was away at the time, but I telephoned him and told him not to worry, Normandy was just a feint, the real invasion was to be in the

Pas de Calais. So I won D-Day for you!'

On the evening before the competition we laid on a very grand dinner for everyone in the mess, and a massed bands and pipes and drums display on our large lawn. It all made a fantastic sight and sound, and as I watched it I knew that running just this sort of event was what I really wanted to do. Speidel loved every minute and when I drove him back to the hotel that night I asked him what he thought of it all. He smiled. 'I have only one complaint – everybody looked more beautiful than me!'

At the shooting competition, John Stanier and I sat behind our respective generals The competition was designed so that everybody would win a prize but the Americans seemed to be trying very hard not to. They had a series of mishaps and got more and more flustered, until finally their main machine-gun packed up altogether.

'Bring me the man responsible!' General Lemnitzer ordered. A quaking sergeant was brought forward. 'No – I said, bring me the man responsible. Bring me the divisional commander!' John and I looked on in amazement as a major general crawled on hands and knees towards his commander for a tongue lashing.

I was sorry not to have had more time with General Speidel. As we said goodbye I told him that I had come that day trying to look as scruffy as possible. I asked him, 'General, are you still glad that you 'won' D-Day for us?'

He laughed and slapped me on the back. A few days later I received a lovely signed photograph from him, inscribed *To my friend Michael Parker, from Hans Speidel.* I later discovered that he was one of the generals who, at considerable personal risk, countermanded Hitler's specific order to destroy the whole of Paris before the retreat.

* * *

On a creative level, my thoughts moved from one tyrant – Hitler – to another – Napoleon. I found it interesting that two such evil regimes were both so beautifully designed. Napoleon's personal and national ambitions, seen by some as rather romantic, had subjected most of Europe to widespread destruction and caused hundreds of thousands of deaths. But he did it all with great panache, and with some very impressively designed uniforms, ciphers and flags most of which still influence our military uniforms to this day. Hitler's evil was, of course, infinitely worse but was also accompanied by arresting designs and the simple but strong use of red, white and black. If you compare the neatness, precision and spectacle of the Germans' uniforms and parades of the 1930s with the British 'Dad's Army' look, the difference is striking. Fortunately that bad design did not stop us winning the war!

For our next dance I decided on a Napoleonic theme. We would decorate the whole mess to look like the Duchess of Richmond's ball on the eve of Waterloo, and we would invite the guests to come in full dress uniform or mess kit and get the regimental band to play the 1812 Overture whilst we 'burnt' Moscow at the end of the garden, just in front of the Colonel's house. I was becoming very keen on French defeats.

Blackie thought there would be no problem at all and started building Moscow immediately. It was two hundred feet long and forty feet high. The workshops made replica cannon which would be manned by our troopers in full dress uniform which, from a distance, looked similar to the Gunners'. The guns were placed facing each other down the lawn.

At midnight the guests were invited outside and the band started to play. The cannon-fire was actually army thunder flashes wired to fire electrically. Towards the end, Moscow started to burn, unfortunately rather too enthusiastically, so it was not long before the trees around it also caught light. The Colonel's house was next and was badly singed. However, the local fire brigade had been stationed quietly behind the house; in those days one could still tell the German authorities what to do.

The fireworks filled the sky and the music ended. There was thunderous applause and shouts of 'Encore!' But I had to point out that we only had one Colonel's house so we could hardly do it again.

I went to thank the troopers who had stood behind the guns, to find their faces covered with blood. The thunder flashes in front of the guns had been throwing up stones from the lawn into their faces. So I gave them a very large drink, our answer to most problems in those days, and thanked them profusely. And I heard, for the first time but by no means the last, 'I didn't join the effin' army to stand behind an effin' cardboard gun and be effin' blown up for effing' officers!'

However, that party is still well remembered some forty-eight years later.

*   *   *

Most of the Regiment moved to England and I went with A Squadron to Berlin. To us, at that time, it was a very exciting city, although not very pleasant for the Berliners. The West German parliament had decided to meet in Berlin at the Reichstag to which the Russians took great exception. They started 'dive bombing' the city, pulling the aircraft up at the last moment and breaking the sound barrier. The resultant noise and shockwaves were very frightening, and broke windows all around us. Their timing was not very good, though, and they broke more windows in East Berlin than in West Berlin.

We drove through the streets in our Centurion tanks waving to the locals, presumably in an effort to raise their morale. I suspect any sensible Berliner would have been more than aware that there were more than a thousand Russian tanks just over the border. Our tanks were always fully 'bombed-up' with ammunition, ready for World War III. This had two immediate disadvantages: firstly, it was almost certainly not a good idea to smoke inside the tank, and secondly, all the space that we had used in the past to store creature comforts like drink and goodies was taken up with boring shell cases.

Our barracks were on the Herrstrasse, which ran through West Berlin in a straight line almost up to the Brandenburg Gate and the Wall. Right next door was Spandau prison where Rudolf Hess was guarded on a rotational basis by contingents from the four powers – Britain, the United States, France and Russia. It was one of Russia's only toeholds in West Berlin, which is presumably why it continued.

The barbed-wire border, with its watch towers, search lights and minefields, was just along the road. At night from time to time we would hear machine gun fire and the occasional mine going off as some poor desperate East Berliner tried to escape. The Wall proper, between the Russian sector and the other three, had many small shrines with flowers and photographs where scores of hopeful refugees had been mown down, often in full view of the relatives waiting to greet them. The whole city had the air of a bad B-movie, the relative opulence of the smugly-cocooned West surrounded by the deprivation and poverty of the East.

We, the Allies, had free access to the East and were encouraged to go there as often as possible. Official 'flag tours', where we showed the flag, were organised by Brigade Headquarters every day. We always had to go through Checkpoint Charlie in an official car and in uniform. For us the East Germany border guards did not exist; we could only deal with Russians, preferably officers. Few if any of them spoke English or were able to read it, so very often our papers would be carefully scrutinised whilst being held upside down.

Once through the multiple layers of concrete, barbed wire and obvious minefields, we found ourselves in the deserted streets of the Russian sector. There was no need to look around when crossing the road as there was so little traffic. The few people wandering around looked miserable and scruffy, and would never look you in the eye. Before the war the most attractive part of the city was in what was now the East. But the Kaiser's Palace had not been restored and neither had the baroque cathedral, which was exactly as it was when the bombs fell. Smashed pews and chairs lay everywhere, and the hymn numbers were still in their broken boards. The only buildings which had been fully restored were government offices, the Opera House and some of the museums. The Tomb of the Unknown Russian Warrior was just across from the Opera House. Great entertainment was afforded when the guard changed. Their exaggerated goose-stepping was presumably meant to impress – it failed totally, and we found it all very funny.

The magnificent East German State Opera House had been returned to its original splendour. The rate of exchange between Ostmarks and Deutsche marks, if obtained on the black market, meant that the best seats cost about £2, and with a bottle of filthy Russian 'champagne' and the only meal available in the East the total cost of the evening was about £5. In the evenings we had to go in our mess kit of scarlet and gold which emphasised even more the huge difference between the two sectors. Sitting in the Royal Box, with our spurred wellingtons up on the velvet handrail and some ghastly East German fizzy vinegar by our side, we were not a very good advertisement for capitalism. But the operas were always magnificent, with no money spared on the production or props; there was even a real elephant in one.

One evening, when leaving the Opera House, I was accosted by a very old German grandmother, shabbily dressed and with her feet literally bound in rags. She spoke no English and her German accent was difficult to understand, but the gist of it seemed to be that she wanted us to take her granddaughter back to the West in the boot of our car. This, in theory, we could have done because the border guards were not allowed to stop us, but had we come across a Russian officer we would have caused an international incident. I must admit I had a tear in my eye as we drove away leaving the wretched old woman sad and disappointed.

Each troop in turn was the 'Alert Troop', which meant we were on thirty minutes' notice to move anywhere. Berlin was full of waterways, and was reputed to have more bridges than Venice, so we stationed one troop of tanks at the Olympic Stadium which was the British Sector Headquarters; this was in case the bridges had been blown up. One day we went out to view our war positions. For security reasons, we were all dressed in sports jackets and flannels and trilby hats so we did not look at all British. Harry Dalzell-Payne, our Squadron Leader, showed me my troop position and where my tank would be – right on top of a BP petrol station.

I asked, 'Do you really think it's a good idea for me to be sitting on top of thousands of gallons of petrol?'

He just laughed. 'You won't survive long enough to worry about it!'

I discovered that one could sell one's blood for DM20 a pint, a good sum in those days. So every so often I had my troop driven to the hospital to give a pint each and then give me the money. The first time we all went in uniform, a big mistake, as most of the soldiers fainted – not a very good advertisement for the British Army! With the money I then hired the Royal Engineers' motorboat which took my whole troop, and filled it with beer. Then we motored up the Havel to the French Officers Club – in spite of its name it was actually open to all ranks. I insisted on choosing what we were to eat. Snails, frogs' legs and other such delicacies always featured, much to the annoyance of my boys – and of the staff when the boys started smashing the carefully-preserved snail shells. But it was always a good trip, all for the price of a pint of blood.

Berlin's nightlife was notorious and fascinating. There were reputed to be over three hundred nightclubs and our boys did their best to try them all. The officers mainly went to Chez Nous, a very decadent 1930s transvestite club run by one of Goering's ex-boyfriends. Any guests, and there were many, always wanted to go there so we became rather well known and were always greeted with our Regimental March when we walked in.

One of the joys of Berlin was meeting a fascinating cross-section of people. The officers of the Squadron were befriended by the great Wertenbaker clan. Colonel George Wertenbaker, who ran Tempelhof Airport, was a marvellous Southern gentleman, and he and his wife Betty were the epitome of American hospitality. Every Sunday they would ask us to a barbecue, a word we had never heard before. They had four lovely daughters, the eldest of whom, Liz, I took out for a while. Liz married my fellow officer Jeremy Mackenzie, and two of her sisters also married officers in the British Army. Only the youngest, Page, married an American.

In 1965, the Queen came on her first State visit to Germany. Huge excitement was generated by her deciding to come to Berlin, which was still regarded in those days as somewhat risky. My troop was chosen to fire the twenty-one gun salute whilst the whole Brigade fired *feux de joie* interspersed with bars of the National Anthem. Our guns were twenty-pounders, and the blank rounds for them were notoriously fickle and liable to misfire. But all went well, and I became the first and possibly only tank troop leader ever to fire a twenty-one gun Royal Salute in front of the Sovereign. One of my shell-cases is in the Regimental Museum, suitably engraved with the fact.

The whole of Berlin had gone 'British crazy' and anyone in British uniform got free drinks in most bars. I even got a free haircut. Telefunken made a huge Union Flag to cover one side of their building, and later I asked to borrow it for my first tattoo. They were more than willing but the American general, very sensibly, refused to lend us a helicopter to fly it.

Every year each of the Allies put on a special event for the Berliners. The Americans ran a large fair, the French provided a food market and the British did a military tattoo. This tattoo had started in the woods near the Brandenburg Gate in the 1950s and had grown and grown until now it was held in the magnificent Olympic Stadium. This was a classic oval sunk into the ground, much larger than it looked from outside, with amazing acoustics, and which seated a hundred thousand people. At one end was the Marathontor, which led out onto the vast Maifeld where we mounted our Queen's Birthday Parade and where Hitler had once paraded a million Storm Troopers.

The staff officer who was to run the tattoo was suddenly posted and his successor, a lovely man in the 15th/19th Hussars called John Inglis, was none too pleased at taking it on, on top of his proper job. Encouraged by Harry Dalzell-Payne, the Brigadier, Alan Taylor, asked if I would help produce it. It was to involve well over a thousand men.

'But, Brigadier,' I said, 'I'm only a very junior lieutenant.'

'Well,' he replied, 'you can't go any lower than you are at the moment, so you've nothing to lose!'

So with the arrogance of complete ignorance I set about devising a huge show. I had absolutely no experience in anything of this sort, but I still had a vision of the impressive display which had been put on in Detmold for the Prix Leclerc. Everything in Berlin was heavily subsidised for the Allies. Basically, Berlin was still supported by 'occupation costs' and the Berlin Budget was a marvellous arrangement of which I was to make full use. To all intents and purposes money was unlimited and, as I thought of more and more ideas, it was no longer 'the Queen will pay'; the Berlin Budget would pay.

I told the Brigade Headquarters that if I was going to do the job I had to have all the trappings. To the fury of my brother troop leaders I was given a large Opel staff car with a driver and an orderly. I swished around looking frightfully important but still not having the faintest idea what I was supposed to do.

As I was to discover in the future, not being an expert was a very good thing, as you were therefore not constrained or confused by the facts. The number of times I have been told by 'experts' that something could not be done are legion. I would always reply, 'Don't confuse me with facts; we're doing it anyway', and nine times out of ten I got away with it.

Fireworks were obviously going to be vital. I had the idea of making a ring of fire around the top of the arena seating using electrically ignited army flares, through which we would fire our main fireworks. We did a trial of about a quarter of the circumference of the stadium, and the General and many senior officers came to watch. There was a blinding flash, and for a brief moment the partial ring of fire looked brilliant. Then smoke completely filled the arena and we had to retreat quickly to avoid being suffocated. The senior officers went away shaking their heads, but I persevered and we got our ring of fire in the end, but this time using proper fireworks.

Ten days before the first performance, eight hundred bandsmen turned up at RAF Gatow. They had come from all over Germany and some from England. It was the first time I had met that extraordinary species, the 'military musician'. Long-suffering and resilient, with an excellent sense of humour, they seemed impervious to being mucked around all day long and were still able to produce excellent music at the end of it all.

The Senior Director of Music seemed not to have made any plans, so eight hundred of them lay on the ground smoking and drinking tea whilst he and the drum majors marched up and down working out what to do. This seemed strange but I let it go for a couple of days, reasoning that this must be the way it was always done. By the end of day two we had still not got anywhere. The SDM now decided that the band was too big so he stood down two hundred and fifty of them. I thought it was quite extraordinary, to bring them all the way to Berlin and then tell them that they were not needed. The band masters, most of whom would later become Senior Directors of Music, told me that this was actually most unusual; it was not normally like this.

So we sent the Director off in my smart staff car for a tour of East and West Berlin, and I took the band masters to the Brigade Officers Mess and got them all plastered. Afterwards, not being capable of standing, we lay on the grass outside the Mess and decided what we were actually going to do. The SDM got back to find the whole thing had been organised; he just stood there and watched it, probably believing that he had done it all.

The Finale was going to be the splendid march 'Crown Imperial' by William Walton. The two hundred and fifty spare musicians would form a huge crown behind the massed bands all carrying torches and the base drummers would have lights inside their drums to make the jewels of the Crown. I also asked for two hundred Light Division soldiers to form an E and an R on either side. The whole effect looked great and the hundred thousand-strong audience seemed to like it. Sadly, when the show was over I had to give up my staff car, driver and orderly and go back to being a junior subaltern again. But I had definitely been bitten by the bug.

*   *   *

The following year I decided, unilaterally, that we would put on a large-scale production of Shakespeare's *Richard III*. I took over the Kuppelsaal, where pre-war German television shows had been made, and sent a four-ton truck to London to collect all the costumes used in Laurence Olivier's film. We got wigs from the Berlin Opera House and Ordnance Services built me a Tower of London, and a Whitehall Palace which could convert into a battlefield. I was to play Richard, naturally, and was delighted to find that I could fit into Olivier's original costumes.

Casting the three bishops was more difficult. The Head Padre said that he ought to be the Archbishop of Canterbury, and the Restitution Court Judge wanted to be another. I scoured the garrison for the third, but the only person I could find that looked like a bishop was a serial offender in the Irish Fusiliers, who had to be brought from the guardroom to rehearsals by regimental policemen and then locked up again afterwards. The entire cast took part in the Battle of Bosworth, but on the last night the Irish Fusilier bishop got completely plastered and started laying into everybody using the sharp side of his sword. It was probably the only re-enactment of that battle that had two red-capped military policemen come on and arrest one of the participants. The German audience was mystified.

That occasion was the first time since the war that Germans had been allowed into the old Olympic Games Headquarters (then the Headquarters of the British Sector and Military Government). One evening I was outside the back of the stage in full costume and wig having a quick cigarette, when I came across an elderly German couple who had managed to get around the security. The woman was crying and, incongruous though I must have looked in Laurence Olivier's red velvet tunic and black wig, I tried to comfort her. They told me that the last time they had been on this site was just as Berlin was falling at the end of the war. The hillside then was covered with dead children from the Hitler Youth. They had looked for their son, but never found him. That made my 'stage fright' seem rather pathetic.

Whilst we were rehearsing, the latest Russian fighter crashed into the Havel in our sector. The Russians threatened to come with an armoured heavy ferry to recover it, so the squadron was put on alert and we took up positions on the bridges in our sector. The fuselage was quickly recovered with the body of the pilot still in it, and was brought ashore on one of the Royal Engineers' ferries with a piper playing a lament as Russian generals watched impassively. What they really wanted was the top secret engines and computer system. These were found by frogmen, brought up and secured under one of the boats, and taken quietly down to RAF Gatow, where our boffins dissected them and learnt all they needed to know. They were then taken back to the crash site where, with great fanfare, they were 'discovered' and handed over to the Russians. But I was too busy fighting a fifteenth-century war to worry about a possible Third World War.

During my stint in Berlin I had been back and done a gunnery course for which, surprisingly, I had received very high marks and a recommendation that I should become a Schools Instructor. So shortly afterwards I left Berlin to go back to Lulworth in Dorset to become a gunnery instructor.

Before going to the Gunnery School at Lulworth, I did a signals course which was where I met Francis Gradidge, who was to become my best friend. He had taken to playing his gramophone at parties – gone were the days when people could afford bands – and these 'discotheques' were much in demand. I didn't think this was a particularly good 'cavalry officer' thing to do until I discovered how much money he was making. I became keen immediately and started to help him with scenery for his parties.

When I got to Lulworth Francis went back to his regiment, so I decided to set up in the discotheque business with Roseanne (Zannie) Cordle, daughter of the Member of Parliament John Cordle. I knew nothing about pop records so she chose them all. Our first parties went very well but I thought they were lacking something. So I designed a mobile frame which when decorated could be put in a room of any size. We also invented most of the lighting effects that you can now buy so easily. I had to chat up the workshops a bit to help with my Heath Robinson inventions, but they found them more interesting than mending tanks.

Now a fully-fledged gunnery instructor, I would quite often appear on the range in the morning with my dinner jacket under my greatcoat having got back from the previous night's party at about seven am. But I did not allow my gunnery instructing to get in the way of putting on parties. We staged another 1812. The oil tanker *Torrey Cannon* had grounded in the Channel and was leaking oil badly, so it was decided to set fire to her. Hundreds of gallons of napalm were made up. When the ship had been completely burnt out there was quite a lot of napalm left, and as it did not store well I persuaded them to give to me. On the high steep hill on the ranges opposite the Mess we set out a hundred high-explosive rounds, modified to be fired electrically, in a two-hundred-foot high '1812' surrounded by hundreds of drums of napalm. At midnight, as the band played the Finale, they were ignited. It was a serious and very impressive explosion but unfortunately the top half of the 8 failed to go off. So we celebrated the Battle of 1o12. The next morning during lessons the top half of the 8 suddenly went off, to great cheers from the bored students.

My next dance was no more successful. We built Pompeii, and Mount Vesuvius which was supposed to erupt on cue. Prisoners were brought over from the guardroom to pump kerosene to the top of the thirty-foot-foot high 'mountain'. Stupidly, I decided to have a quick rehearsal which set light to, and completely destroyed, Vesuvius and most of Pompeii. The prisoners were singed but glad of the fresh air. Later the guests at the dance were too 'relaxed' to notice the absence of the key features.

In the midst of all of this Berlin asked if I might be prepared to go back and do another tattoo. This would happen during our block leave period, so I said yes. I now knew a little about how to do these things, so I decided to be more ambitious. We would do the 1812 Overture again – I do like French defeats – and asked for Moscow to be built in the Marathontor in the arena. It would be some sixty feet high and two hundred and fifty feet across and would be built by the Royal Engineers. We had cannon brought over from England and fireworks from Denmark.

This time my Senior Director of Music was the brilliant Lieutenant Colonel 'Jiggs' Jaeger of the Irish Guards, a small and very enthusiastic man with whom I got on very well immediately. Every time I arrived for rehearsal he would bring the eight hundred musicians to attention, salute me and ask permission to carry on. I was extremely embarrassed and begged him not to do it, but he insisted that I was the 'Producer' and so had to be acknowledged.

I had decided that the show would start off with the biggest Union Flag in the world and that it would be pulled up by an American helicopter. We brought World War II searchlights over from England to illuminate it as it flew over the arena.

I was getting suspicious that things were going too well when the General, Sir John Nelson, rang to say there had been an official complaint from the Russians that we were going to be burning their capital city in our show. So I told him to tell them that it had been a Russian victory and a French defeat, and they were happy with that.

Then the French complained. We agreed there was nothing relevant that we could say to them, so they boycotted the show.

Just when we thought we were clear we suddenly had a complaint from a number of Berliners saying it was very insensitive of us to be showing another city in flames while Berlin suffered so much on a daily basis. I pointed out that this was just an entertainment, but that did not placate them.

Then the Foreign Office came in on the act and decreed that we could only burn Moscow if it appeared to be a firework and not a city in flames. Some civil servant, with the high intelligence of the breed, suggested that thirty seconds should be the maximum time that Moscow could burn. So I got the local fire brigade to spray the whole structure with kerosene and the Engineers fixed electrically ignited fireworks all over the inside of it. Because of Moscow's now-explosive nature, we set aside a safety cordon on either side which would normally have held about fifteen thousand people.

The helicopter and flag went up at the beginning of the show and looked splendid. Unfortunately the wind speed a hundred feet up was rather stronger than we anticipated and the helicopter and flag were being blown into the arena. The pilot was beginning to lose control so he had only one option, which was to release the flag. This he did, and everybody said how pretty it looked as it fluttered down. However, it had a one-ton rolled steel joist at the bottom of it to weigh it down. Only afterwards did we discover that it had fallen into the safety area where, unknown to us, some people had moved illegally across the safety barriers into the danger zone. It had seriously injured the grandfather of a Berlin family, who sadly died the next morning. He had fought the British in two world wars and survived, only to be killed by the Union Flag at the British Tattoo in Berlin. I was devastated.

Afterwards there was a British Court of Enquiry which found that the American pilot, Jim Stottler, had not been to blame and that the accident was an Act of God. The Supreme Allied Commander Europe disagreed; he maintained there was no such thing as an Act of God, and that somebody had to be to blame. He blamed the pilot, who was sent to Vietnam immediately. Many years later, when looking at the impressive Vietnam Memorial in Washington, I found a very similar name, and fervently prayed that it wasn't his.

As the Finale was about to start I received a telephone call in the control box from the General – he and the British Minister were sitting there with their stopwatches, ready to time the burning of Moscow. The music played, the guns fired, the fireworks started to go up. I cued Moscow, and there was a blinding flash of light and a thunderclap of an explosion. The massed bands stopped playing in amazement – Moscow had completely disappeared. The General and the Foreign Office were thrilled; it had taken about five seconds, they said. Everybody in the control box clapped and cheered except for a little man sitting in the corner who was looking very glum. He was the Engineer who would have to build Moscow all over again for the next night's performance.

* * *

I went back to Lulworth a happy man. One morning, one of the other instructors, Barrie McCombe, came rushing in to my room waving the newspaper. The letter had been sent to Bovington by mistake, so I had no idea that – to my huge surprise – I had been awarded the MBE in the Queen's Birthday Honours List.

A couple of months later I went to the Palace for my investiture. It was the first time I had been there and I was mesmerised. There were about thirty military MBEs of whom I was easily the youngest, and I was really nervous as I had not met the Queen before. We all lined up and our names were read out. The tension was greatly relieved by the discovery that the two squadron leaders after me were called William Shakespeare and John Thomas.

* * *

After the second Berlin Tattoo Lieutenant Colonel 'Jiggs' Jaeger and I produced the Wembley Musical Pageant to raise money for the Army Benevolent Fund. We conceived the largest band show ever held, with over a thousand musicians on parade. They almost filled the football pitch and had some difficulty playing together as the distance from the front rank to the rear was so great.

Over the years I did four musical pageants, all remarkable for one reason or another. Vera Lynn took part in one of them. She was later to become a good friend but we did not start off on the right foot, through no fault of hers. When she heard the music she was to sing to she said it was in the wrong key. To me a key was something that you locked a door with. The Director of Music was horrified because he had no time to get the music rewritten.

'I'll just have to try to get the musicians to transpose it into the correct key as they go along,' he said resignedly. Apparently this was a rather difficult thing to do, but the boys did not let us down. I was to work many times in the future with Vera over the years, and have never ceased to wonder at her generosity and kindness.

My job as a gunnery instructor at Lulworth continued with most of my time being taken up with my discotheque. Whenever I could, I went to visit my mother at Midhurst but one day I received a telephone call to say that she had died. She was only fifty-six. She had had a very sad life and unfortunately never had the chance to enjoy my later success. I like to think she would have been proud of me, which might have been a little compensation for all her sacrifices and pain. My last letter to her was returned unopened.

*   *   *

My Regiment said it was about bloody time that I came back and did some real work for a change. They had already become my 'real' family and I was very fond of them all.

I received a letter from the Commanding Officer, Robin Carnegie, later to become a general, telling me that poor Ian McConnell, who had joined the Regiment with me, had had to leave the army because he had asthma, and 'therefore unfortunately you will have to become Adjutant'. Robin was a great person whose military intellect was in direct and opposite proportion to his handwriting, which was minuscule. I've always had great difficulty in reading it, but I'm sure that it did say 'unfortunately'.

Lieutenant Colonel Mike Pritchard was about to take over from Robin so I went up to Stanmore to meet him. The Regiment then had a main headquarters in Maresfield and an advanced regimental headquarters in Singapore with three independent squadrons, one in Cyprus, one in Singapore and one in Hong Kong – a series of dream postings. Colonel Mike never gave any indication that he was disappointed that I was about to become his right-hand man and was always very supportive and understanding of my lack of military virtues.

I was going to take over from Hugh Sandars who had very kindly looked after me when I first joined the Regiment. He was extremely thorough and competent and I was nervous about how I would match up to him. I might have been quite good at organising two thousand men in a show, but was uncertain how I would get on with staff work and regimental duties. However, I had excellent Chief Clerks in both headquarters, Sergeant Gibson in England and Corporal Hubbard in the Far East, and they did most of my work for me.

There was, surprisingly, no problem in moving freely between the squadrons. Rumour had it that the Chief of the General Staff, Mike Carver, had written a thank-you letter to the Commanding Officer after having dinner at Maresfield, saying, 'I hope you will take every opportunity to visit your squadrons.' This was quoted as authority for moving around the world for almost three years and was never queried!

I went first to Cyprus where we were part of the United Nations Force and had a great time with B Squadron under Peter Steveney. We were right on the sea at Zigi, a tiny village on the south coast where no one could ever find us, so we were not much troubled. I then went to Singapore with Mike where I took over from Hugh. Mike was an excellent Staff Officer and actually did most of my work for me so I just about kept my head above water. The excellent Corporal Hubbard really ran our HQ and was able to sort out or fiddle anything.

Part of my duties as Adjutant, the person responsible for discipline in the regiment, was to go on 'anti-vice tours' with the military police. The idea, I think, was to make certain that the various dens of iniquity that our boys went to use were disease-free. It was a fascinating eye-opener. The tour would start at the official American Services brothel (though it wasn't called that). The Vietnam War was in full swing and thousands of GIs were coming over to places like Singapore for R and R. The sixteen-storey hotel was like any other except that it was surrounded by barbed wire and each room came with a girl. The whole set-up was run by a colonel who used to mutter that he hoped that nobody at home realised what his real job was.

By three o'clock in the morning, having visited about twenty venues in descending order of quality, we would come to the sort of places that our boys could afford. I dreaded that a door would open and a trooper would come out, saying, 'OK, Sir, your turn now!' Bugis Street was always full of highly decorative and entertaining transvestites and literally piles of drunken soldiers and sailors. It was great fun, but of course totally dodgy. We did not get to check many of the medical certificates there!

In Hong Kong we lived with the Gurkhas at Sekong Barracks in the New Territories. They were a good lot but somewhat disconcertingly they ate curry for breakfast. Forays into the jungle in Malaya were fun and made more so by the services of Gurkha soldiers who would cut a path in front of you through the thick undergrowth and put it all back when you had passed. If you stopped for a rest or a cup of tea they would chop a little seat for you. They were wonderfully friendly, but even so I was glad that they were on our side.

I was asked by the Gurkhas' Brigadier if I would like to come to the ceremony of Desira, when scores of animals would be sacrificed to bring good fortune to the Regiment in the coming year. It took place on a double tennis court in the barracks. We, the officers, sat in large brown leather armchairs on one side with the rest of the battalion on the other three sides. All the arms of the battalion were piled at one end. I had come in a lightweight white suit; it soon became apparent that this was not a good choice.

A large bullock was led in, and a soldier stroked its nether regions to relax it. The Regimental Sergeant Major, his head bound with a white scarf, came forward with an extra-large kukri and with one stroke cut off its head. The head was then dragged around the pile of rifles. A second bullock was likewise decapitated, followed by scores of goats and finally hundreds of chickens.

I was completely horrified but tried not to show it. We were served very large glasses of Pimms throughout the ceremony, and there would occasionally be cries of 'Ah, good cut!' from all around me. When the nightmare finished I stood up to find the front of my trousers splattered in blood from the knees down.

*   *   *

I was beginning to have some serious doubts about my future in the army. I loved it very much, and the Regiment in particular, but I recognised that I was not very good at staff work and all the other boring bits. In many ways the super-efficiency of Colonel Mike highlighted my own inadequacies. I should at this stage have been doing the Staff College entry exam, but I was enjoying travelling far too much to want to do any real work. Also Pat Howard-Dobson, now the Colonel of the Regiment, who had been so supportive of me in the past, told me I was most likely to become a general. Well, I did not want to become a general. I thought generals were old and smelly – they are now, of course, all young and fragrant – so I put my papers in to resign my commission. I'm not certain whether Colonel Mike was relieved or sad!

The whole Regiment moved to Hohne, next door to the remains of the Belsen concentration camp. Our officer's mess was Schloss Bredebeck, easily the best mess in Germany. A grand nineteenth-century hunting lodge, it was set in lovely grounds with a large and a small lake, a stable block and piggeries, and ornamental gardens. It was completely refurbished for us and as soon as we were back in it we held a thank-you party for all those who had helped in the restoration. As usual, the German guests turned up well before the allotted time, while we were all still in the bath. The party went well, probably too well, as later that evening the roof of the Schloss caught fire. The German fire brigade arrived but had to contend with a lot of very 'relaxed' officers who were trying to rescue our regimental pictures and treasures. There was a wonderful confrontation on the main staircase when the burly German firemen with their hoses were pushed back down by a posse of officers carrying a huge tiger skin in a frame. The tiger won.

Colonel Mike never ceased to surprise me with his different take on things. Once we were told that seven shots of rare anti-flu vaccine were available for each regiment, and that we had to send our nominated names to the medical centre. I put down Colonel, 2I/C, Adjutant and four squadron leaders. Colonel Mike crossed them all out. 'The regiment could survive happily for weeks without any of us,' he said, and of course he was quite right. So we nominated the Pig Man, the Officers Mess barman and cook, the Sergeants Mess barman and cook, the head groom and two cookhouse cooks. When they went for their jabs I got a rude telephone call from the medics, asking what the hell 'all these Other Ranks' were doing with all the officers from the other units.

The end of my time both as Adjutant and in the army was coming nearer and nearer. We decided to give a large ball as my swan song. I wanted to stage the Battle of Trafalgar (another French defeat!) on one of the lakes, so we borrowed army assault craft from the Engineers which we turned into the English and French fleets, fitting them with mini-cannon. I decided the best way of moving them around would be to use frogmen, and told all my clerks that they were to be the frogmen. We compiled the music, and had a short rehearsal.

All the guests came in Full Dress or Mess Kit and the ladies in Trafalgar period dresses. At midnight the – by now very 'relaxed' – guests made their way out to the smaller lake. The music started and the fleets began the engagement. Unfortunately, the very first broadside was fired into the band, who spluttered and stopped playing. But the cheers of the audience brought them back to life and the battle continued. I had arranged for the French fleet to burn spectacularly as it was defeated. I had also had the English fleet made ready in the same way which I intended to use as an encore. I was certain we would be asked for one.

The battle progressed well, with broadsides crashing across the lake, until it became apparent that the British fleet had prematurely caught light. It looked very much as though the French were going to win. I shouted across to my clerks to burn everything at once so that no one would realise the mistake. With all the ships burning the trees caught light and, much to my surprise, the assault craft started to melt and sink. The water was obviously getting extremely hot, so my clerks/frogmen abandoned the ships and struggled out of the water elbowing the finely dressed guests aside, muttering, 'We didn't join the effin' army to push effin' boats around in effin' hot water for effin' officers...'

It was all very spectacular, if not totally planned, and as the inferno raged the General Officer Commanding our Division, General Jackie Harman, said to Colonel Mike, 'I have a horrible feeling I'm the senior officer present!'

The assault craft were complete write-offs, so I had them taken up to the tank park and had tanks run over them a few times. We made certain that the registered numbers did not get damaged. We then handed them back to the Royal Engineers saying we had had a terrible accident on the tank park and were very sorry, but was it not interesting that the boats were inflammable?

Unfortunately, the commanding officer of the Royal Engineers was very wet and refused to 'write them off' so we had to have a Court of Enquiry. This was convened just as I was packing to leave the Regiment so my successor, Hugh Lovett, had to pick up the pieces.

Much to our amazement and embarrassment, we discovered later that, unknown to us, the General had written to all the regiments that were guests, asking them to contribute to our massive damage bill. But by this time I was on my way to civilian life. I stopped off in Bavaria to see mad King Ludwig's theatrically fantastical castles. I think he and I would have got on rather well together.

*   *   *

However, my Battle of Trafalgar swan song in 1970 wasn't by any means the last show I would stage in West Germany. Every two years from 1977 to 1992 I produced a major tattoo in Berlin. The show had moved indoors to the Deutschlandhalle, part of Hitler's exhibition centre, where the excellent facilities made my fanciful ideas easier to achieve. With the help of Ordnance Services and the REME workshop, the 'Berlin Budget' could perform miracles.

For the first indoor tattoo the Welsh Guards Band and their Director of Music Derek Taylor joined all the bands from Germany. I asked Derek if he knew of a Welsh male voice choir and he sent me to Morriston, just outside Swansea. The chapel where they were rehearsing seemed full but the stage was empty and I wondered where the choir was. It turned out the congregation *was* the choir. It was a rather wet and miserable evening but the moment they started singing it was as though the sun had come out. We repaired to a nearby pub afterwards which they cleared of other customers before beginning to sing again. As the evening wore on they got better and better. I wondered how they were going to cope with the duty-free drink in Berlin. In the event, they came out, sang, and proceeded to drink us dry! I am honoured still to be one of their Vice Presidents.

Over the years we made sets of Windsor Castle, the Tower of London, Holyrood Palace, and Edinburgh Castle. Holyrood Palace caused a bit of a problem because Herr Kaiser of Ordnance Services went over to Scotland and started measuring up the real Palace. We received a very irate call from their security asking who the hell he was and who was this Major Parker who had sent him? The final result did look rather splendid though.

The great thing about Berlin was that money was never a problem. One year I decided to use 'The Princes of Wales' as a theme. The Morriston Orpheus Choir came over again to drink and sing, both of which they did brilliantly. I also thought we should have massed harps. Harps do not 'mass' very often, in fact hardly ever, which is why I wanted them. Twenty-one seemed a good number so Headquarters of the Army in Wales scoured the country for them, and sent trucks padded with old and questionably-stained mattresses up and down the valleys to collect the twenty-one sizeable, fragile and very valuable concert harps and transport them to Germany. The harpists were all, with the exception of a single man, very pretty young girls. They spoke to each other in Welsh and I formed the impression that they hadn't quite understood that they were to be part of a military tattoo run by the dreaded English, and English soldiers at that. But the girls soon discovered that the soldiers weren't ogres; in fact, one of them even ended up marrying the Chief Petty Officer of the Royal Navy Display Team.

Another year I decided on 'Chivalry' as a theme. Ordnance Services made a hundred robes of the various chivalric orders: the Order of the Thistle, of the Garter and of the Bath, as well as replicas of their gold and enamel collars. I included the patron saints of our four nations. Saint George was easy – the workshops made a huge articulated dragon which breathed fire and was killed by a Household Cavalry Mounted Duty Saint George. Saint Andrew was tied to his cross, while Saint David was a bishop with a daffodil.

I thought I would have some fun with Saint Patrick. He is said to have rid Ireland of snakes, so I hired a snake charmer from England. She brought with her a large steel chest full of snakes including an enormously heavy python, and a burly male partner who played the saint. The snakes were stored in the cellar of one of the barrack blocks. Unfortunately, one night some soldiers released them from their chest – 'to let them have a walk', they explained afterwards. The python and some of the other very large snakes found the central heating pipes and wrapped themselves round them. The pipes broke under the weight and flooded the cellar with very hot water. The soldiers, hoping to save the situation, swam around trying to catch the snakes. They did not succeed. The snake charmer was furious – her snakes would all catch cold, she said. She berated the soldiers far more fiercely than any sergeant major could have done, so the matter was closed.

In 1982 it was decided to lay on a very large band concert in the Waldbühne, where the Hitler Youth used to perform. It was that year that I discovered a new tune, 'Highland Cathedral', which we played for the first time at a major show. It had been written by a Berliner, Michael Korb, and offered to me as a slow march. I thought it was wonderful and asked the Senior Director of Music, Derek Kimberley, to arrange it for military bands and pipes. The result was stunning and the tune has now become just about the most popular pipe tune in the world.

At the same show we did a skit on 'Tam O'Shanter'. For the dream sequence a piper was to come down a 'death slide', playing. To my surprise the Pipe Major seemed to think it a good idea. When I saw who he had chosen to do it I knew why. The poor lad had just joined the Army and this was to be his first-ever show. He was fitted with a harness, taken up sixty feet to the top of the rope and pushed off the platform. As he slid down, piping, at some speed it became quite clear that Scotsmen do not wear anything under their kilts. He was supposed to be caught at the end of the slide by a member of the arena party. Inevitably one day they missed him and he crashed to the ground, where his flattened pipes wailed like tortured animals. And on subsequent slides a safety-pin guarded his modesty.

Cliff Richard, who had taken part in many of my charity shows in the intervening years, came and sang, as did Leo Sayer. Cliff is always very generous with his time, and his presence was responsible for a considerable extra contribution to service charities.

One year I thought it would be rather fun to have an elephant battle. My friend Bobby Roberts, whose elephants had performed at the Great Children's Parties which I had organised, said I could have his troop of six so we arranged for them to be shipped over. The Russians, being rather keen on circuses, speeded their journey through the corridor from West Germany. They did not, as one helpful staff officer had feared, think we were trying to reinforce the British garrison and therefore stop them. The boys at the Royal Anglian Battalion, near the wire at Gatow, thought it was an elaborate joke as news came that the elephants had got through Checkpoint Bravo. Virtually the whole battalion gathered round as the enormous pantechnicons arrived on the square. The door opened from inside, the elephants having been trained to do this and to roll out one of circular stands used in the act. One by one six huge beasts came out. The look on the boys' faces was wonderful. But once out, the elephants all relieved themselves, with a tidal wave in one direction and ten wheelbarrow loads at the other. The boys retreated fast.

Rehearsals went well. The elephants got used to lying on their sides with ten infantrymen with rifles lying across their stomachs firing blank ammunition. The long-suffering look in their eyes seemed to say, 'I didn't join the effin' circus...'

One day, however, one of them – whose name was Maureen – obviously had a sense of humour failure, threw off her soldiers and went charging towards the border barbed wire. The East German border guard had the fright of his life as the great beast came lumbering towards his watch tower. Although Maureen would probably have coped with the wire, she most certainly could not have survived the mine-field beyond. Bobby Roberts managed to get his Land Rover between the elephant and the wire and put up his hand. At this she came to a skidding halt and looked bashful. Bobby led her back to the battle rehearsal, giving the startled border guard a two-fingered salute as he did so. I was later to ride Maureen down the Kurfürstendamm in full Number One Dress, and later still, when I had elephants at the Royal Tournament, I rode her down the Mall.

The practical problems were considerable, but with the willing help of our – mainly German – technical team, 'elephant lines' with very strong tethering points and ample drainage were built into the Deutschlandhalle, which pop groups playing there since may have found useful.

It was in Berlin that I first developed the idea of 'wise virgin' meetings, where we would try to second-guess what might possibly go wrong, on the principle that if you're prepared for everything then nothing will happen. I was worried about what we would do if an elephant died or was injured. Bobby said we needed to make a 'strop' (a fixing to go round something), which could be attached to a powerful Land Rover so the beast could be pulled out of the way. The workshops did not bat an eyelid when I told them what I wanted, and within a few days a fine mahogany plaque, five feet by two, appeared with the leather and rope strop displayed on it, and the words 'Dead Elephant Strop' in large brass letters. We never used it and when British troops eventually left Berlin for good it was presented to the incoming German unit and is probably still hanging in the workshops, prized as an example of British eccentricity.

Talking of eccentrics, some of the GOCs (General Officer Commanding) came well into that category. David Scott-Barrett, known to everybody as Wobbly, was quite a handful. He bounded everywhere but I told his terrified Staff that I preferred someone to be too enthusiastic; it was easier to rein someone back than to egg them on. He asked if I had considered flying a real helicopter indoors at the show. I said I had but had dismissed it as being rather silly. We both knew that before the war Hitler's personal pilot, Hanna Reitsch, had flown an auto-gyro inside the hall.

'If Hitler could do it,' Wobbly announced, 'so can I. And,' he added, 'as Military Governor I can do whatever I like!'

So I arranged for a small helicopter, a Sioux, to be brought from RAF Gatow. Wobbly, beside himself with excitement, decreed that only he and I would be there to watch. It was wheeled in and the blades opened up. The pilot started the engine, which was deafening indoors. As the Sioux rose slowly from the ground considerable quantities of dust blew everywhere and the roof tiles started to flap. The pilot, obviously enjoying himself, saluted as he flew past; Wobbly jumped up to return the salute and lost his hat. We found the biggest problem, apart from the obvious ones, was that the helicopter needed to cool down for at least three minutes before the engine could be switched off.

When our test flight had finished and the helicopter had been pushed out we notice someone hiding in a doorway. Wobbly shouted, 'What the hell are you doing there?'

'Sir, I'm the Air Safety Officer from Bielefeld, and I'm afraid I can't possibly allow this helicopter to be used indoors.'

'Well, you can just bugger off!' Wobbly roared. 'As Military Governor, I make the rules in Berlin!' Fortunately this assumption never had to be tested in a Court of Law. And Wobbly got his indoor helicopter flight, which worked to perfection.

In 1992, on another state visit, the Queen came to the Last Tattoo, which marked the end of twenty-eight years of performances. Each year we had made it bigger and better, until someone commented, 'We might as well do it on ice.' What a splendid idea, I thought! So for the second part of the show, half the arena became an ice rink.

The Finale, which was set on the frozen River Thames in the eighteenth century, had Royal barges entering through London Bridge and indoor fireworks. There was a skating cast of about sixty in period costume, plus a skating band and four hundred non-skating musicians. I gave the skating band lessons every morning, even though I could only skate in an anti-clockwise direction which rather limited what they learnt to do.

When the Queen arrived I explained what was going to happen during the show. A pop group was making a guest appearance. 'You might not care for the music, Ma'am,' I told her, 'but you might like their name – Status Quo.'

The band had difficulty skating and playing simultaneously and a number of instruments got bent in rehearsal. But the boys quickly learnt that running over concrete blunted their skates so they would go much more slowly. Unfortunately for the Queen's Performance, some kind member of the German arena staff had noticed that the band's skates were blunt and had sharpened them. The entry of the band was disastrous, with loud mutterings of, 'I didn't join the effing Army...'

'Perhaps it would have been better if they had marched rather than skated,' the Queen observed afterwards.

The Staff Officer in charge was Tweedie Brown, a remarkable entrepreneur who made a fortune for charity out of the Last Tattoo. So all our efforts over the years have a permanent memorial in a trust fund, which is still distributing money.

I have only been back to Berlin once since then. In 1999, I was asked to the fiftieth anniversary celebrations for the Berlin Air Lift, which took place in the Olympic Stadium. As I sat there watching the Allied bands performing, it felt very strange being back where my whole career had started thirty-four years before.

CHAPTER FOUR

Chicken Dinners and Chippendale
– Civilian Life

After my trip round Bavaria I had no idea what I wanted to do; all I knew was that I wanted to leave the Army. So I went on the dole – about £13 a week. I had my gratuity of about £2,000, and that was the sum total of my wealth.

I went to stay with great friends in Dorset. Keith Hubbard had been in the Regiment with me and now ran a small farm at Frampton, outside Dorchester. His wife Oonagh and her friend Sally Inchbald had started a business making pre-cooked frozen meals, which in those days was a highly original idea. They were both very good cooks and it all tasted delicious. I immediately saw opportunities in this and agreed to help them. We rebuilt one of the cow sheds into a proper kitchen and had a large walk-in blast freezer fitted. We redesigned the labels, and a hundred foil containers of chicken Vallée d'Auge and I set off for London. I went to the frozen food department at Harrods and bearded the manager.

'Oh no,' he said. 'This will never catch on; people would much prefer to cook their own meals.'

I persisted and he bought half of them to try. I then went to Fortnum and Mason and sold the remainder. Both buyers seemed to be more interested in my new electronic pocket calculator than in the food I was selling.

I returned to Dorset elated, and we set about creating different dishes. The whole enterprise nearly came to a sticky end one day when I was hanging some shelves in the freezer and pulled the door closed by mistake. The light went off and a blast of freezing air hit me full in the face. I pushed the safety release but it was frozen solid so I felt around in the dark, in some panic, for something to hit the door with. I found what I later discovered to be a left-over frozen turkey with which I pounded the release bar. Eventually it gave and I staggered out into the brilliant sunshine covered with my own frozen blood. My interest in frozen food waned rapidly.

At the time I was living mainly with my Aunt Maggie in Brompton Square. She was an accomplished antique dealer, with a very good eye for furniture and decorative items and an excellent sense of colour. She was running the antiques side of Colefax and Fowler, the famous interior decorators in Brooke Street. John Fowler, one of the founders, was brilliant at decorating but not so good at accounting, so Tom Parr had been brought in to sort out the finances.

John, a very civilised old 'queen', took a shine to Maggie and later to me, and we used to go and stay with him in his lovely hunting lodge near Odiham. There we would have tea with the Redgraves who lived at the end of the garden. Nancy Lancaster, then living in the magnificent rear part of the Brooke Street building, also became a kindly friend. She had immaculate taste and had turned two very large country houses, Ditchley and Haseley, into masterpieces. Winston Churchill used to go to Ditchley to rest at weekends during the war. By the time I knew her well, Nancy had moved into the garden room at Haseley where we used to stay on occasions. Her butler lived in a mobile home in the walled garden and every morning at breakfast he would play us a cassette tape of the dawn chorus that he had recorded earlier that morning.

John was taking more and more of a back seat at Brooke Street and Maggie was not getting on well with Tom Parr at all. In fact, she was constantly complaining.

'Why the hell don't you leave Colefax and Fowler?' I suggested. 'We could set up our own antique shop.'

I had always been interested in antiques and had collected a number of pieces of good Meissen and Dresden china when I was in Berlin. So we started off selling small items from Maggie's flat. We made quite a lot of money, mainly because my aunt had a good following of old customers from Colefax. One evening, just behind her flat in Cheval Place, we found a small shop with a For Sale sign on it. Maggie was reluctant to make any decision so I made it for her and bought the lease with my gratuity. We decorated the shop with scarlet felt and brown and white floor tiles and it looked wonderful.

Most of the top dealers in London came to the opening party including Mallets, very grand dealers in Bond Street and at Bourdon House, and even John Fowler himself came. We sold everything in the shop immediately. Restocking was easier in those days and we would go on buying trips each week. Maggie could not drive so I was left to do that, and each day when we returned dealers would be waiting and would often buy everything straight out of the car.

One day Jenny McLean, a decorator friend of mine, telephoned to say that she had won a Jaeger competition for two people to go around the world, and would I like to go with her? I was still on the dole, for which in those days you had to physically sign in every week. The week before I went, I asked if could sign in for the next few weeks because I would be away.

'Where?' they asked.

'Bermuda, New York, Moscow, Rome and Paris.' I was not surprised to be told, more or less, to eff off.

So we set off for Bermuda – Jenny and I and the other two winners, a speech therapist with a tooth-grinding boyfriend – and our mentor from Jaeger, Erica Frie. The speech therapist and her friend spent most of the next two weeks in bed whilst we thoroughly explored all the sights and nightlife everywhere we went.

New York came next, with a stay at the Plaza Hotel on Fifth Avenue. I introduced the group to the joys of the Scorpion, a delicious drink which the Regiment had first found in Trader Vic's under the Hilton Hotel. Then off to Rome. We were supposed to have gone to Moscow but Sir Alec Douglas-Home had just expelled a number of Russian diplomats/spies from London so it was thought not a good idea, so we just went to Paris and stayed in the Hotel George V.

*   *   *

In this smart part of London, our neighbours were rather fun. Sir Lew Grade lived just across the road and his huge Rolls Royce, reputed to have been owned by Queen Elizabeth the Queen Mother, waited while he drew a couple of puffs on a huge cigar, threw it away, and was driven off.

Ava Gardner lived in Ennismore Gardens and would frequently walk her corgi past the shop. She always used to dress in a nondescript tracksuit and woolly hat so no one would recognise her. No one would have guessed that she was once described as the most beautiful woman in the world. She would frequently come in for a glass of water and a chat, and would be fascinating about her early life. She used to buy things from us and I would deliver them to her flat. One day she bought a pair of painted commodes for her bedroom and asked if I would go round to see if they looked all right. So she and I lay on her bed together to judge what they looked like from there. If my friends could have seen me then! I said that she had probably had far more exciting people than I lying on this bed, and she laughed and gave me a very large drink.

Jack Hawkins would march by, always immaculate and ramrod stiff, and sometimes come in for a chat. His voicebox had gone by this stage, but it was still recognisable, if only in gulps.

Charles Grey, famous as the James Bond villain Blofeld, was also a neighbour; he too would stroll past, needing only a white cat to be back in character.

Maggie and I were beginning to make a good profit at the shop, so I began to spend more time doing other things that I really wanted to do, as I never really saw myself as a shop keeper.

Each year on the first weekend of May we used to have a Regimental Officers' dinner on the Friday, followed by an Old Comrades' dinner on the Saturday and the Cavalry Memorial Parade on the Sunday. When we bought the shop I had taken the house next door which also had a garage. This was very useful for keeping stock in and, more importantly, for giving a large party for all my friends in the Regiment after the Cavalry Memorial Parade. About fifty of us would gather in the street if it was dry and in the house and garage if it was wet. The food was always the same, Coronation Chicken and salad and a huge cheesecake in the shape of the Regimental cap badge. Serious quantities of drink were consumed and often the police would arrive, having been called out by an irate neighbour. But Philippa Cannon, who was married to my brother officer 'Shorty', was expert at dealing with them, and very soon they too were having a glass of wine. This exhausting combination ensured that the Monday morning would be extremely well hung over.

In 1973 Colonel Dan Reade, our Second in Command in Detmold, was at the Regimental dinner as usual. We had just heard to our amazement that he was going to take over as Vice-Chairman of the Royal Tournament at Earls Court. He was a very good chap with a dry sense of humour and a much better brain than he would like to admit, but not perhaps an obvious choice for that job.

I congratulated him and he asked if I would like to come and see the Tournament in July that year; he thought he might be able to get me tickets to the last night. It turned out that Earls Court was only half full on the last night, and on every other night for that matter. Dan was shadowing his predecessor and learning the ropes. He showed me the office set-up, which I thought was rather quaint to say the least, but they did have very pretty secretaries.

That night I sat in splendid isolation in the Royal Enclosure. The evening started with a mean fanfare of about ten trumpets. Very small jumps had been set up all over the arena floor and the Tournament actually started with an Army horseman coming in and clearing most of them easily. The show then staggered on from act to act. All were quite unmemorable except for the King's Troop, Royal Horse Artillery who were immaculate as usual, and the Royal Navy Field Gun Competition which was as baffling as usual. A Caribbean band, clearly very drunk, swayed on and attempted a few tunes. It was apparently a tradition that most acts played the fool on the last night, but they did so without being in the least bit funny. Field Marshall Montgomery took the salute, bobbing up and down like a Jack-in-the-box; not surprisingly, he did not remember meeting me at Sandhurst. After the Finale, which was just the Massed Bands display, the show came to an inconclusive end.

I met Dan for a drink afterwards, and he asked what I thought of the show. 'What I mean is – could you do any better?' was what he actually said.

I said I certainly couldn't do any worse, and so began my career as producer of the Royal Tournament. I never thought at the time that I would do it for as long as I did, but I was to do it – as well as many other things – for the next twenty-six years.

CHAPTER FIVE

❧

Challenges and Unwelcome Change – The Royal Tournament

The Royal Tournament was the oldest running Tattoo in the world. It started in 1880 as a Skill at Arms competition in aid of the Duke of Cambridge's Military Charity for Soldiers' Widows. It was originally called The Grand Military Tournament and Assault-at-Arms. The first show, held on Wimbledon Common, attracted a very small audience as it was obviously as boring as hell. Watching fifty horsemen tent-pegging one after another gets rather tiresome after the first few. As was the Massed Fencing, given that no blood would be drawn. Cleaving the Turk's Head sounded excellent but, again, sadly there were no real heads. The first show made a thumping great loss.

So in 1881 they introduced the first act of military entertainment to go with the competitions. This was a Musical Ride by the Household Calvary. Over the years more and more acts were added to the programme. The Tournament was responsible for everything that we now know as tattoo acts, like massed military marching bands, massed pipes and drums, gymnastics, continuity drill, mock battles and so on. In 1882 it was moved to the Royal Agricultural Hall in Islington which had four thousand seats and ten thousand standing places, a huge number for those days, and very soon it became the most popular show in town. The arena, two hundred feet by eighty, was shortly to prove too small. The Tournament moved to Olympia in 1906.

Now named more simply The Royal Military Tournament, it went from strength to strength. Cavalry mêlées (an excuse for a good fight with wooden swords on horseback), massed cavalry charges and the introduction of acts from the Empire, such as Zulu battles and the Camel Corps, became very popular indeed.

1896 saw the first Royal Naval event, with parades of guns and cutlass drills. The guns were taken over small obstacles but it was not until 1900, when the Navy brought in a 4.7 inch gun hauled by oxen, that the crowds really began to get enthusiastic. The gun had actually been used at the Relief of Ladysmith and was of huge patriotic interest. It fired one round, but as an early history of the Tournament by Lieutenant Colonel Binns states: 'As an entertainment this was perhaps rather on the meagre side.'

The obstacles became larger and more difficult until in 1907 the Royal Naval Field Gun Competition that millions of people were to know and enjoy over the next ninety-two years came into being.

The event's name had been changed to The Royal Navy and Military Tournament in 1905, when the centenary of the Battle of Trafalgar was marked by a naval pageant.

Not surprisingly the Tournament was not performed during the Great War (1914-18) but in 1919 it started up again and moved to Olympia. The newly formed Royal Air Force joined in and for one year it was called The Royal Navy, Military and Air Force Tournament. In 1920 this rather cumbersome title was shortened to The Royal Tournament and so it remained until the final show in 1999.

Over the years more and more acts were devised and virtually every country in the Empire and later the Commonwealth took part. As the Tournament's popularity continued to grow an even larger venue was required, so in 1950 it moved to Earls Court.

Royal patronage was, from the early days, very enthusiastic and almost every member of the Royal Family came each year. However, gradually over the years the show lost its unique appeal. It had failed to keep up with the times and from being the only way to see exciting live entertainment it became just one of many. By 1973 it was looking pretty sick and in need of resuscitation. I was appointed producer at the end of that year. I discovered that I was actually the first proper producer that the show had ever had and was in fact also sadly to be the last. Until then the show had been put together by the Committee and the Arena Master, and the Services produced whatever displays they wanted to.

The lighting was basic, either 'on' or 'off'. The sound system was rudimentary, and would have been thought bad even in a railway station. I looked rather glumly at all this and thought hard about what I could do. At every turn I was met with entrenched opposition – 'It's always been done like this', 'We can't/won't do that', and so forth. It got very boring. Both Dan and I fought our own corners, he on the administrative side and in the box office – a huge task – and me about the show itself.

In all the twenty-six years that I produced the show I never once had a contract or a letter saying that I was the Producer; it was just a gentlemen's agreement. After Colonel Iain Ferguson took over from Dan Reade in 1980 he would kindly write to me each year and ask if I would like to go on. It occurs to me now that he might have hoped I would say no!

Having left the Regiment and the Regular Army I was part of the AER (Auxiliary Emergency Reserve), one of the duties of which was to visit the Regiment each year for two or three weeks and 'train' with them, for which we were paid the going rate per day for our rank. My 'training' seemed to centre around giving parties for the Regiment, which I suppose is as good a way of doing it as any. I remained in the rank that I had on leaving the army i.e. Captain, and donned my uniform when convenient. I had a very good arrangement: if I needed to be rude to a general then I was a civilian; if I needed to be rude to a sailor, soldier or airman then I was an officer.

For the first couple of years I was not paid anything at all for producing the Tournament (it was in fact about four months' work), as it was considered that my AER pay, some £300, was adequate. Our antique shop was doing very well by this time and I did not worry too much about money. In year three I was commiserating with the Earls Court lift man about the late hours that he had to put in each day. He said he didn't mind as he was getting very good overtime. I thus discovered that the lift man was paid more than I was! Dan kindly agreed that I should at least be better off than the lift man so reasonable rates of pay were agreed. They were always below market rate but I wasn't worried at all. In order to try to sort out the inertia Dan and I had many good lunches together – I love doing work over lunch; I find a few glasses of wine extremely helpful to the Creative Process.

The three Services took it in turn to lead each year. 1974, my first year, was a Royal Navy year so it was with the Senior Service that I first started to do battle. My main suggestions were:

1. The show should have a theme, and a beginning and a proper Finale, and should be in the same order at every performance.

2. The control box must be on the same side of the arena as the Royal Box as one always tends to design things to look good from where one is watching.

3. The lighting must be improved and special effects used.

4. The sound must be improved.

5. The backcloth should be different and distinctive each year – until then it had usually been some sort of rock face as climbing was usually part of the show.

Needless to say, all these suggestions hit a brick wall. The Royal Marines Massed Bands would hear none of it – 'We've always done it like this and we're not going to change!' Their Director of Music was a very talented musician, Lieutenant Colonel Paul Neville, and of course the bands themselves were immaculate and played wonderfully so I persevered in the hope that they would see how much better it could be.

I wanted to have a large band fanfare to start the show, a massed bands display in the middle somewhere, and everybody on for the Grand Finale. The bands refused. I was told that they would only play once during the show. Clearly a lot of very alcoholic lunches were called for.

I chipped away at Paul and, with the support of Dan Reade and of the Major General (Philip Ward – an old friend), I gradually got him to agree to most of what I wanted. We got the Fanfare and the massed bands display but they were not keen on my idea that we should stage the Battle of Trafalgar by way of a Finale. I thought of having the English and French fleets on Land Rovers with thirty-foot high models of ships on top, with 'sea level' at about seven feet. The white helmets of the band, properly lit, would be the 'sea' through which the ships would 'sail'. But they categorically refused to do that. Dan and I got extremely browned off and at one stage even discussed resigning together. Another lunch was organised, and I outlined my main idea which was to commission a new piece of music called The Battle of Trafalgar (funnily enough) which I hoped would become the naval equivalent of the 1812 Overture.

Paul Neville suggested a composer who had been a Royal Marine musician and had written a number of scores for films. His name was Albert Elms, and we got on well immediately. I outlined to him the shape of the piece of music I had in mind, i.e. arrival of the French fleet – arrival of the British fleet – first part of the battle – death of Nelson – second part of the Battle – victory followed by celebrations, all with pyrotechnics and indoor fireworks.

Whilst he was writing the piece I went to 40 Command Workshops at Mill Hill and sold them my secondary idea, which was to have two huge ships lowered from the roof with sails unfolding as they came down. The finished ships would be about eighty feet long and eighty feet high. The workshops agreed immediately. I asked how much it would cost. 'Nothing,' they said. 'Her Majesty will pay,' which was the code word in those days for getting things on the fiddle.

In the past the Tournament had pulled things up and down using balloon winches left over from the Second World War, which lived in one of the huge R101 hangars at Cardington that the Royal Tournament owned and where kept all their spare kit. They also used it for rehearsals for the Royal Marine battles and the wall climbing and death slides and so on.

Another leftover from previous times was 'the Roof Master', retired Squadron Leader John Read, who in his spare time would sort out all the technical side. He was a very important man to have on side, so another good lunch was arranged and agreement was forthcoming. We could not afford proper pyrotechnics so, amazingly, the workshops bodged up some blank 0.76mm shell cases with detonators in them and the plan was for a man to go round under the skirts of the ship hitting the end of the caps with a hammer and nail; as it happened the shells were aimed straight at the bands! Had 'Ealth'n'Safety been in existence then they would have had a fit, but we did it and amazingly no one was hurt. And it looked rather good.

The more I become involved in the Tournament the more amazed I was by what went on behinds the scenes. Earls Court is a huge cavernous building designed to be used for trade fairs, concert and shows. What many people do not realise is that the centre part of the floor area is actually an Olympic-size swimming pool – Johnny Weissmuller and Esther Williams used to do water shows there in the 1950s. So the amount of weight we could safely put on it or drive over it was an annually recurring problem. Our arena was three hundred feet long by one hundred feet wide and the pool beneath was about two hundred and fifty feet by ninety feet, so most of our arena was pool. One of the main problems was that we had to fix shackles for the Royal Navy Field Gun Race, which had to take very heavy loads as the walls had to be winched down tightly. The Royal Navy riggers would arrive a week before anyone else and beaver away in the chasm of the pool on tall ladders, taking out plates and fixing all the support points.

As with so much else at Earls Court, the requirements of the Tournament had been designed into the building in the first place. Dormitories for over a thousand men were built up on the balcony level and later in Earls Court 2.

When I first took over there was a medium-size hall behind our backcloth, called the Chair Store, where the seating blocks for all the seats below balcony level were stored. When the seats were put into the arena the King's Troop stables were built in their place. Visiting them daily was a joy; it was like going back to the nineteenth century with all the immaculate guns and limbers, and the boys bulling their harnesses to within an inch of their lives. If the Household Cavalry were taking part extra stables would be built for their horses as well. Together, the horses were responsible for a considerable amount of 'midden' which was piled up in steaming mounds outside. In the early days we were able to sell it for good money, which we gave to the boys for a party, but once the EU imposed its pathetic regulations we had to actually pay for it to be taken away.

Changing the position of the control box was more difficult. I was determined that I had to be able to see the acts from as near the VIP angle as possible in order to design and direct them properly. This meant taking out some of the seats near the Royal Box area and building an enclosure on three levels to house some very tatty Heath Robinson electrical gubbins that had always been used to run the show. Even though by then a man had been put on the moon, high-tech control for the Tournament was three light sockets, red, orange and green (I was surprised that they weren't gas lights). Green meant the commentator could give the cue so the act would enter, orange meant a slight delay, while red indicated a huge problem. Only the control of these lights had moved from the nineteenth to the twentieth century.

The Arena Master was a splendid cavalryman retired from the 9th Lancers called Lieutenant Colonel Jumbo Preston, who lived the rest of the year in Ibiza. He was smallish with a totally round head and a huge grey moustache and sideburns crammed under his scarlet Number One dress hat. He would stand behind the main doors and shout at the performers and order the two terrified door orderlies to open and close the doors as quickly as possible.

He did not welcome my arrival on the scene at all. 'What do you think you're going to do, boy? I run this show.'

'Well...' I said, and so started a pitched battle which was to go on for a number of years. His wife, a substantial ex-Regimental Sergeant Major in the Women's Royal Army Corps, also had a go at me, growling that I was 'messing up Jumbo's show'. All in all she was rather terrifying.

Not only was Jumbo used to doing what he wanted to do, he was used to using a telephone which went through an old-fashioned plug exchange run by two naval ratings.

'Number please, Sir.'

'Give me the stables!'

'Just a minute, Sir.' And you would be put through. I had had the antiquated contraption changed for an Automatic Exchange the previous year but Jumbo did not like dialing, so he shouted instead. He most certainly did not like the acts to be in the same order each day. It actually took me three years to get the huge order board to the right of the main door that said, 'Today the Acts will be in the following order' taken down. Earls Court would only take orders from Jumbo. But when I explained to them that I was paying their wages the sign came down immediately!

The build-up to the first show was exhausting, with everything having to come together over a period of only a couple of days. I was being much more ambitious than they had ever been before and that would have been difficult enough without the constant 'We don't do it like that' refrain.

All the participants moved into Earls Court on the Saturday and settled in. The cookhouse started to provide some three thousand meals a day. The horses arrived and their fodder with them. Space had to be found for the arena equipment, not the least of which was the Field Gun kit.

On the Sunday there was a publicity parade from Horse Guards, down the Mall and back again. Rehearsals started at 0500 hours on the Monday morning with the Field Gun 'lynch in' i.e. getting all the walls and ramps into position, which would be followed by the training rehearsals. The acts came on continuously from then until about nine o'clock in the evening. To Jumbo's annoyance I had produced a programme for all this and he became more and more annoyed when I would insist on stopping acts to correct them and send them off to do it again. He seemed to be of the opinion that all displays came fully rehearsed. The Royal Marine Massed Bands came up trumps in the end and played beautifully. The Fanfare and massed bands rehearsals went well but the Finale was being rather difficult. We had trouble getting the ships down from the roof so we had to send the bands away while the riggers worked overnight to sort it out.

My fascination for flags has been lifelong. I cannot look at any Union Flag without checking that it is the correct way up. I decided to make the largest White Ensign in the world for the finale. The largest flying union flag is the one on Victoria Tower at The Palace of Westminster (18 feet by 36 feet). I telephoned the Clerk of Works at the Palace and asked for one which to my surprise he agreed to immediately and sent it down to the Hubbard's farm in Dorset. Here Oonagh and Sally Inchbald sewed it into an Ensign 100 feet by 60 feet! Later another Regimental friend Quintin Ambler, then a school master, and his class made us the largest Union Flag in the world, 300 feet by 150, again on a tiny machine. When made it was too heavy for even the whole class to carry.

The manpower for the Tournament was provided from a Tri-Service Manning Table which had not changed for forty years. So on the first day of the build-up two young naval ratings came up, saluted, and said, 'We're the telephone operators, Sir. Where do we go?'

I explained there that we had cancelled their requirement months ago – it actually took me three full years to persuade the Navy not to send telephone operators again – but said I was sure I could find something for them to do. They became unofficial Control Box Orderlies and sat at the back enjoying the chaos and running errands for me. Fighting off over a thousand participants was beginning to wear me down and a deep gloom took me over. There was no way this show was ever going to work. I decided the only answer was to pretend that everything was going really well, and told everybody just to keep going. In Berlin I had discovered that, left to their own devices, the common sense of officers and men somehow made it all work. Things were normally not helped by my interference the whole time. The secret, apparently, was to have a good idea in the first place and then let them get on with it. Even so there was a continual queue of all ranks asking me what to do. At one stage, one of the young naval 'telephone operators' tapped me on the shoulder, and said, 'You know, Sir, it's very unfair that someone as young as you should have to go through all this.'

I bought him a drink immediately!

At the end of the torturous Tuesday we had what we called a dress rehearsal. Basil Reitz, who had been Commentator of the Tournament for about fifteen years (he ended up doing it for over forty years), had been watching, bemused, as the 'new' Royal Tournament staggered through its birth pangs, and now proceeded to link everything together immaculately. We hadn't written a script, but he had picked up enough background and information as we rehearsed to make it sound as though he had been working on it for days. The ships came down, the cannons fired, no one was shot – so it was really quite a success. Everything seemed to be going rather well. So well that I decided to follow one of my self-imposed Rules – namely: 'If you're 100% certain that an event is going to work perfectly you're not being ambitious enough. If it's easy to do it's not worth doing – make it more complicated immediately.' We would augment the show, the Finale in particular. It seemed to me that we needed a Lord Nelson to be shot, and that he should die in a suitably sad and impressive way. At the key moment in Albert Elms' *Trafalgar* a single 0.303 blank round would be fired from a rifle up in the roof to represent the French sailor in the rigging.

The Royal Naval Display Team of young sailors was already performing the Window Ladder Display – which meant they had to climb ropes twenty-five feet up into the 'ladder' in time with music. As someone who, at Sandhurst, had never been able to get more than ten feet off the ground on the ropes, I suggested that the ladders might look better if they were ten feet higher. Their commanding officer, the splendid Lieutenant Commander Lawrence Jay, gave me a rather old-fashioned look. He was very jolly, rotund and rather scruffy, in many ways more like an army officer than a naval one. He clearly, like me, had never got too far up a rope either, but with the certainty of ignorance commanded them to raise the ladders. The boys got used to it after a bit and it was clearly very tiring, but it did look much better I suggested to Lawrence that we needed a tableau of Nelson, Captain Hardy, a surgeon and one or two sailors, all in period costume, to re-enact the shooting and death of Nelson. He got the costumes from Bermans and Nathans by taxi and acquired a platform on wheels with a life-size replica Trafalgar cannon on it. A key moment in the music was when Hardy had to take off his hat, lean forward and kiss Nelson, who would promptly die. At the first performance they couldn't get it right, so we marched them up afterwards and briefed them again. The next performance was no better, so we marched them up again and re-briefed them again, and again, and again. After the next performance I even got one of the musicians to come and play the key piece of music for them to listen to.

'What is the problem?' I demanded irately. 'All you have to do is take off your hat, lean forward and kiss Nelson, who then dies.'

There was a shuffling in the ranks and a little voice at the back said, 'He can't kiss him, Sir – he's someone else's boyfriend.'

The whole tableau was arrested immediately and disappeared to Portsmouth, to be replaced a few days later by a group of sailors who did not mind kissing. I couldn't see what all the fuss was about – I had always thought that sort of thing was compulsory in the Navy anyway!

My first Tournament progressed well, but I was finding it both physically and mentally exhausting. I was shattered at the end of each performance and knew that I had to rest. Never having dreamed that this might be a problem, I had not even asked for a room of my own and we all used the same changing room.

Robert Corbett, a friend I had first met when we did the British week in Brussels in 1967, had been appointed Commandant of the Royal Tournament and was there with his company of the Irish Guards, the administrative troops who looked after everybody else. He had a room of his own and I begged him to allow me to use it for a short kip between the shows. He kindly agreed, and would tiptoe around me whilst I slept. I also now had to start taking tranquillisers – one before the afternoon show, one in between to help me sleep and one before every evening performance. The tension was difficult to deal with. So many things could, and did, go wrong and one could never relax for a moment. My major concern was to do my best to ensure that no men or horses were injured during the performance. Of course, I was not actually personally responsible for them but I felt as though I was. I had told them what to do and I felt it would be partly my fault if it all went wrong. Almost the worst part of the strain was having to hide my thoughts the whole time. On the old principle of 'never do anything to frighten the horses', I could not let on that I was worried. I knew that I had to appear extremely calm, as if nothing was going to go wrong. I had discovered how infectious panic was, and for that reason I very seldom lost my temper; I had discovered early on that it was almost always completely counterproductive to do so.

I think in the whole of my twenty-seven years in the tournament I only lost my temper on three occasions and those were all for effect only.

Smoking played an important role in my calming-down strategy, but as I didn't like smoking very much I had to drink at the same time to take the taste away! It was normally canned orange juice but on occasions Bloody Marys, which cheered me up enormously!

The highlight of any Royal Tournament was the day the Queen came to take the salute. Everybody from the youngest sailor to the most hard-bitten old field gunner was so thrilled to be performing for the Queen herself, and as a consequence became more and more nervous. So there was a tendency for things always to go wrong on the Queen's day. I mentioned this to her some twenty years later, and she jokingly said, 'Would you prefer me not to come then?'

*   *   *

I didn't know what to expect in my first year. Firstly, we had moved the control box to the Royal Box side of the arena, just to one side and slightly below it. This had the unintended effect of my being able to see into the box and therefore to be seen by them.

For the Queen's visit a flag pole was fitted above the box, and on her arrival a Royal Naval yeoman would 'break' the standard which was carefully folded at the top of the pole. In the arena were a Royal Guard of a hundred and a band from the lead service, in this case the Royal Navy and the Royal Marines. At the rehearsals the yeoman had had difficultly 'breaking' the standard properly and we rehearsed a number of times, much to the annoyance of the band and guard. Eventually we were ready for the Arrival. The other noticeable thing that always happened on the Queen's day was the appearance, out of the woodwork, of scores of senior officers of all three services, who stood around looking proprietorial as though they were responsible for everything. I once asked Dan Reade who the hell they all were. He said he could only guess, but he thought they must be members of the Committee who had never turned up to any meetings.

The guard and band were now in place, and the Queen and the Duke of Edinburgh were about to arrive. I glanced at the yeoman, who looked bleak. The Queen and the Duke of Edinburgh came into the Royal Box and the guard gave a 'Royal Salute – Present Arms!' The band played the National Anthem. The yeoman 'broke' his standard perfectly. I rather stupidly turned to congratulate him; with a huge smile he saluted and took a step backwards, straight into the amplifier for the public address system which promptly blew up.

The Queen sat down, the guard and band marched off. I was about to burst; there was no power for the commentator to give his introductory cues so nothing happened for what seemed like an age. A little man rushed round with a new amplifier and fitted it in record time – fast, but it still seemed an age to wait in total silence. Basil spoke and away we went. The Queen had been looking down at us with quiet amusement during all this rushing around and said to me, when I apologised afterwards, 'I noticed your intake of cigarettes went up considerably.'

CHAPTER SIX

❧

Mud Men and Mechanical Dragons
– The Royal Tournament staggers on With Tears

In that first year, 1974, we made a bit of progress on the quality of the show and the new type of Finale, which was welcomed by most. We had much improved the public relations and publicity for the event, and we were definitely attracting more people. The BBC also seemed to be delighted as well because they had had much difficulty in the past trying to make something out of very little. Over the ensuing years, I came to the conclusion I was really a masochist at heart as I forced myself and everybody else to do more and more ambitious things. I worked on the principle that if I was 100% certain something would work then I obviously was not being ambitious enough, so I would change everything. This did not endear me to my performers or technical crew, but it was the only way I knew.

The two key acts, the King's Troop, Royal Horse Artillery and the Royal Navy Field Gun Competition, were the only ones that were in the programme every year. I had enormous respect for the King's Troop. Their skill and courage in galloping flat out in such a small arena was remarkable. However, I did feel that it was a pity that they never fired the guns nor, for that matter, had an officer and a trumpeter on parade. I badgered the commanding officer about this but was told that the space was too small to deploy the guns and that they could not spare an officer to be on parade. I thought this was quite strange considering that the ratio of officers to men in the King's Troop was much higher than in any other part of the army!

It was not until the arrival of Major Mike Webster as commanding officer in 1976 that I made any progress. He was very keen to do anything to improve the Drive and said he would look into it. We did trials up at the barracks at St John's Wood, and he worked out a way of bringing four guns into action with the other two leaving the arena at the end of the Drive. An officer and trumpeter were made available and our only outstanding problem was what ammunition to fire. The Ordnance Corps did various trials and came up with a two-ounce charge which seemed to fit the bill. We took the gun to Earls Court and fired off a few rounds so that the safety people could see it. They did not seem to notice that the wads from in front of the rounds were hitting the backcloth with some force. I pointed this out to them but assured them that it would not be a problem because there would be no one behind the backcloth at that stage. Not totally true as the Arena Master, Major George Douglas, was there the whole time, and in later years would complain that I had made him deaf. George Douglas had taken over as Arena Master in 1981. I had been much against having another officer to do the job; in all my other shows the job was done by a Warrant Officer. Iain Ferguson was keen to have him so I relented, which turned out to be very fortunate indeed as 'Uncle George', as he became known by everyone, was absolutely wonderful. Nothing fazed him: elephants, camels, fifty vehicles, a cast of two thousand – no problem. Always cheerful even when he wasn't, he was brilliant at remembering names, and going deaf never stopped him from answering questions that he had never been asked.

1977, the Queen's Silver Jubilee, saw the debut of the new Drive and everybody agreed that it was much better. The officer and trumpeter galloped in and halted in the centre of the arena, the trumpeter sounded the advance and the six teams galloped on. The officer then took post in the Warwick Road north entrance of the arena and watched the Drive until they formed up for the march past when he rode to the front and led the salute. Those in the audience who knew their stuff would stand up as the guns passed because they were the 'colours' of the Royal Artillery.

I was not quite as successful with the field guns. In those days the whole thing was very protracted. At a specified time in the programme the crews would 'lynch in' i.e. bring on the walls and ramps and other bits and pieces. This took at least fifteen minutes. Then the teams for the day would march on and do the race but with long pauses between each of the 'actions' so the whole pace of the thing was spoiled. Having finished the race and taken the salute the kit was then 'lynched out', taking another several minutes. The whole thing took over half an hour, which was almost a third of the show. I felt we had to do something about making it slicker.

I made a great error in asking to address all the teams and lynch-in parties. I explained that we were all in the entertainment business and that we had to keep up the pace and excitement. It was immediately clear from the mutterings that they were not on my side. It was at this stage that I noticed how very large they all were, and that they seemed to be moving towards me. The officer took me aside and explained that the men were not in the least bit interested in the audience or in being an 'entertainment'. In fact, they wouldn't care if there was no audience there at all. It was the race and the competition that mattered and everything else could get knotted. It was six years before we got Earls Court to agree to us having an interval during which we could lynch in and save valuable show time.

The Field Gunners were a law unto themselves. They got up at about five o'clock in the morning and did their first training rounds, which was not very popular with those who were trying to sleep in the other areas of Earls Court. After the run-throughs they went off to have a special breakfast large enough for four normal men. Any injuries were treated with contempt. Although we always had medics and a doctor on duty, they very seldom got a look in. The injured person would be spirited away and dealt with by their own 'witch doctors'. They seemed to be of the opinion that a lost finger ('a minor amputation') was barely worth bandaging. Anyone with a badly damaged hand was told, 'You've got another one, so just get on with it!' Olympic levels of adrenalin masked virtually any damage. Having seen what looked like a bad accident, the doctor would scour the building looking for the victim. He seldom found him, and would come back complaining that he could not do his job. I in turn would get hold of the Field Gun officer who would shrug and say that he was sure it was going to be all right.

Fortunately, really bad accidents were few and far between. On one training session at *HMS Excellent* a young man lost a leg. That was considered worth stopping for. On another very sad occasion, the sheer legs – the two huge trunks of wood used to support the twenty-eight-foot spire for the crossing of the chasm – fell on a rating and killed him. But by and large, in spite of the danger of the race, it was relatively accident-free. Fortunately any injuries were very minor. At the end of the race, when the two teams knelt in front of the box to hear the unofficial timings, a number could always be seen to have their shirts covered with blood. On the march off I would see the doctor dash from his seat in the front row by the 'wicket gate' to try and catch up with the men before they disappeared forever. More often than not he would return having failed in his purpose.

The Navy were having a little difficulty with my rank. When 'Captain Michael Parker' went to visit a naval ship or station as the producer of the Royal Tournament, they naturally assumed that I was a naval captain. All the officers would turn out, and would be disappointed and annoyed when a young(ish) army officer got out of the car. The navy asked that I should be promoted to Major to avoid confusion. This the AER Headquarters agreed to, but forgot to do the paper work. As no money was involved, nobody ever queried it until twenty years later when Iain Ferguson had to pick up the pieces. I think I must be the only army officer ever to have been promoted by the Navy Board!

Having survived my first year I watched for the first time the 'breakdown and pull-out' on the last night. Within moments of the show finishing, bulldozers would be in the arena scraping up the eight hundred tonnes of soil. The backdrop was ripped down, and all the scenery was smashed and carted away. It was profoundly sad, and I would sit up in the gods with a tear in my eye seeing 'my show' disappearing.

Backcloths had normally been paintings of bland landscapes or rock faces for the Royal Marines to climb. I decided they needed to be much stronger, much more heraldic and bold, so I took to designing them myself. I would paint to scale on a board about thirty inches by ten, which would be scaled up to about two hundred feet by eighty – the largest backcloth in the world. Initially they were painted by Earls Court painters and then for twenty years or more by the great Mervyn Harridence. Now I'm amazed by how ambitious and complicated they were, and they all had to be put up, rigged and made to work in three days maximum.

From my very first show I was determined to improve the lighting, which was appalling. Twelve square boxes hung at about thirty-five feet and threw slightly amber light all over the arena. No colour changes were possible, no subtlety, and no areas could be highlighted. It was either ON or OFF. I brought in experts, all of whom shook their heads. The roof was too high, the arena too large, the backcloth too wide; oh no, they couldn't put a proper lighting rig up.

Then one day two people from Theatre Projects, one of the biggest lighting companies in the country, turned up. They were Robert Ornbo and Roger Straker. A few weeks later they came back with a plan for a modern lighting rig that would perform more like a professional theatrical one. The only trouble was that it was going to be very expensive. Money was not exactly abundant; although audience numbers were going up, they weren't going up that quickly. We were still in dire financial straits.

I had an idea. The BBC, who televised the show each year, had been begging for better lighting for ages. So I went to them with a proposition – if they would increase the facility fee by two-thirds of the extra cost of the lighting, we would do the rest. They reluctantly agreed to and continued to do so until the end.

It was all such fun – I had a brand new 'toy set' to play with and it improved everything enormously. The sound was more difficult and it was some time before I was able to bring in a really good sound designer. Gary Withers of Imagination, who had become a friend of mine after I had organised a Great Children's party in 1979, lent me John Del'Nero who was also brilliant. He too became a great friend and the three of us, with Alan Jacobi of Unusual Rigging, went on to do a series of huge events around the world.

The new lighting rig required proper rigging. Until then, Earls Court riggers had hung everything. They were a very bloody-minded lot, heavily unionised and happy to hold us to ransom as show time came nearer. It took a great deal of pressure to get them to agree to Unusual Rigging coming in to do the specialist rigging. In the end we had to pay Earls Court for doing no work and then pay Unusual for doing their work for them.

For my second year, in which the army was to be the lead service, I decided to do one of my favourite pieces for the Finale – the 1812 Overture. I had always been very keen on French defeats, and this was a classic one!

Having 'burnt' Moscow so successfully in Berlin I was determined to do even better in Earls Court. I designed a Moscow backcloth that would be revealed out of a huge army crossed-swords logo. The Senior Director was Major Brian Keeling, who did a number of really good arrangements for both the massed bands act and the Finale. One of the highlights was when thirty musicians formed a circle and played the Post Horn Gallop on .303 World War II rifles with brass mouthpieces fitted to their barrels. When they finished, they were supposed to remove the mouthpiece, load a blank round and all fire together into the air. The Roof Party would then drop masses of feathers (this was high art!). One day, of course, the inevitable happened. One chap forgot to take out the mouthpiece and fired it with great velocity into the cheap seats. I was surprised that we didn't get a complaint but I think the lucky recipient wanted to keep it as a souvenir.

For the Finale I decided the Royal Military Police riding display team should gallop round the massed bands dressed as Cossacks with huge yellow Tsarist banners. The guns of the King's Troop would be the cannon. But what about the armies?

Ticket sales had been going well so I was able to persuade Dan Reade that we really ought to hire some costumes and kit out the whole of the massed band. He was horrified, because there were over three hundred of them, but in the end, to my amazement, he agreed. I hired enough costumes to kit out a Russian army and a French army from the theatrical costumiers Bermans and Nathans.

That still left the question of the conductor. I took Brian out for a very good lunch indeed, and by about four o'clock he had decided that he would like to ride in leading the massed bands (the French army) as Napoleon. He did, and he looked splendid; the bands thought the whole thing was a hoot. The combination of bands, cannon, Cossacks and fireworks was pretty impressive, and the audience went wild. It was perhaps only slightly strange that 'Napoleon' took the salute at the end of his massive defeat, to thunderous applause.

*   *   *

The finances were looking up but were still not good enough. In those days the Tournament lasted three weeks and usually the takings of the first two weeks paid for the show with the third week producing the profit for service charities. When it was decided to reduce the run to two weeks things became very dodgy. Earls Court were very keen on the Royal Tournament because it filled their July slot which was normally rather thin. By this time, the Earls Court and Olympia exhibition halls had been bought by P&O; fortunately Dan Reade was able to negotiate a profit sharing deal with them which just about lasted us to the end.

When I started out it was relatively easy to arrange the supply of equipment and labour for little more than a few free seats. As time went on this became more and more difficult. On the last Royal Tournament the Civil Service even tried to make us pay for shoes and nails for the horses, and also for the boot polish the men used.

The Royal family were great supporters of the Tournament from its earliest days and virtually all of them came each year. When putting together images for the last Royal Tournament I came across a film clip of the Queen aged about three with King George V and Queen Mary at Olympia. I believe she has been to every Tournament since. Royal patronage was extremely important. Apart from the pride and excitement it gave to the participants, in the latter days when we were desperate to raise money from sponsors an invitation to the Royal Box was a great incentive.

In earlier days, Royal cars would pull up to the Royal entrance and the Guest of Honour was escorted up the red carpet before being ushered into 'Queen Mary's lift'. Apparently Queen Mary was terrified of lifts and required heavy chrome rails inside to which she clung determinedly while being wafted all of twelve feet up to the Royal Box. It must have been the slowest lift in the world; the journey took about two minutes. The Earls Court lift man, whose full-time exciting and taxing job it was to drive this contraption, probably had not noticed that it was actually an automatic lift and could have been worked by anyone.

There were two Royal 'loos' to the left of the Royal Ante-room, one pink and one blue. In my twenty-seven years I never knew a member of the Royal family (as opposed to any other guest) ever use one, but religiously they were smashed to pieces after the last performance every year so that no one could ever say that they had used 'the Queen's loo'. The only member of the family that I ever saw go into one was the Princess of Wales, who went in to separate her two sons and their friends who were having a massive punch-up. She simply threw the children out one by one.

Tea and cakes were served in the afternoon and drinks and canapés in the evening. The tea included what we called 'self-destruct raspberry tarts' because one bite saw them shatter and fall to the ground. Just after the Falklands War the Prime Minister, Mrs Thatcher, took the salute. In the interval she gave me a rocket for having the 1812 Overture as the Finale instead of a Salute to the Falklands. I said, 'I'm sorry, Prime Minister, but we have to choose the programme a year in advance; so you need to finish your wars earlier!' She was just picking up a raspberry tart, and I warned her immediately about the dangers involved in eating it. She carefully looked it over and then very neatly ate it without a single piece falling to the ground. Not satisfied with that achievement, she rapped the table with a teaspoon, caught everyone's attention and proceeded to teach them all a lesson in eating raspberry tarts. From such little things is greatness made.

After the show, representatives of each of the acts would be presented to a member of the Royal family. This normally went off without a hitch but on one occasion I was escorting Princess Michael of Kent, who had made a number of strange comments to those in the line-up. She turned to me and said, 'I'm going to faint,' put her arms round my shoulders and collapsed. She was not an inconsiderable burden. I tried to catch her equerry's eye but got the distinct impression that I was on my own. I told my orderly to get a chair and tried to put her head between her knees, something I had read about in a first aid book. Meanwhile Prince Michael continued along the line-up, apparently not having noticed. My orderly got the Royal car backed up the red carpet and we bundled her into it. All was explained when we learnt afterwards that she had had a riding accident and that her painkillers had worn off.

I always put my orderlies on the end of the line-up so that they got the little perk of meeting the VIPs. I well remember taking King Hussein down the line. He was an extremely polite man and had a slightly disconcerting habit of calling everybody 'Sir'. As I was to discover when I did a lot of shows and royal weddings for him in Jordan, the word 'Sidi' is used extensively as a polite form of address – you could use it to your driver as well as to your boss – and the only possible translation in English is 'Sir', which is much more deferential than the Arabic 'Sidi'. I duly presented my orderly. 'Your Majesty, this is Lance Bombardier Muirhead who is looking after me very well.'

The King, who was very small, looked up at him and said, 'Sir, I would like to thank you for looking after the Producer so well.'

I then escorted the King to his car, little realising that I would be seeing a lot of him in the very near future, and went back to the ante-room where I found Muirhead standing as though transfixed. 'Effin' 'ell,' he said. 'I've been called effin' Sir by an effin' king!'

On another occasion the Prince and Princess of Wales came with Princes William and Harry. Harry was still quite small, but William decided to follow his father down the line-up at the end. As the Prince of Wales chatted to everybody, Prince William asked each of them in turn if he could try on their hats. One of them, a very tall Dutch grenadier, gave the Prince his extremely large bearskin with a broad grin. Prince William almost disappeared inside it, much to the amusement of us all. Little did we know then that the next time he wore a bearskin it would be as the Colonel of the Irish Guards on the Queen's Birthday Parade.

Every Royal visitor was given a special copy of the programme in a beautifully embossed leather cover with their monogram in gold. Princess Alice, Countess of Athlone, a grand-daughter of Queen Victoria, had been coming to the Tournament since the beginning of the century; she told us she already had about seventy 'blotters', as she called them, and could we not save money by giving her the same one next year? We certainly could, and did.

Diana Princess of Wales used to come privately, after the divorce, to the Tournament and watch with the two boys from one of the hospitality boxes. Her very last visit, by chance, was on the same day as Queen Elizabeth the Queen Mother's. Clarence House decided that it would be more satisfactory if they were all in the Royal Box together. At the beginning of the show Queen

Elizabeth and the Princess had sat down, but the Major General's seat between them was momentarily empty as he moved to take it. A press photographer took a photograph at that instant, and the next day the newspapers were full of 'Royal Rift!' headlines. It must have been so annoying to be so misrepresented, but I imagine they must have got used to it.

In the interval I went to the Royal Box for tea with Queen Elizabeth, Princess Diana and a very small Prince Harry who was playing with what looked like a bit of the air conditioning system. Diana leant forward and said, 'Ma'am, we are so looking forward to your hundredth birthday.'

'No, no, you mustn't say that; it's unlucky. I might be run over by a big red bus!'

I said, 'Ma'am, of all people I know, you are the least likely to be run over by a big red bus!'

'But you never know what might happen,' Queen Elizabeth said. 'Wouldn't it be awful if you had never done what you really wanted to do, and then one day – as the wheels crunched over you – you thought: Oh my goodness, all those things I wanted to do – I could have done so much more! That's the way you must live your life, as if tomorrow you will be run over by a big red bus,' she said with a huge smile. Sadly, the 'big red bus' came for Diana far sooner than anybody could have dreamt.

A huge cross section of the great and good would come to take the salute, everyone from King Hussein to General 'Stormin' Norman' Schwarzkopf, who came just after the first Gulf War. As he was so popular we arranged for him to drive into the arena so that everybody could get a good look at him. He arrived behind the main entrance in a huge American limousine but was rather too early. I told the arena master, 'Uncle George', to hold him there.

'I can't do that,' he protested. 'He's a four-star General!'

'Well, I'm the Producer,' I told George, 'and the four-star General will just have to wait until he's cued in.' This he did very happily and eventually came in to huge cheers and a standing ovation. I talked to him in the interval and found him absolutely lovely, rather bemused but highly entertained by all the traditional bits of the show. It was his last day in uniform; on the morrow he would be a civilian.

* * *

It had been a tradition of the Royal Tournament since its earliest days in the 1890s to have guest acts from overseas. The Vice Chairman and I, or sometimes just I, would travel to see the possible acts, which normally involved a pleasant trip abroad where one would be very well looked after. However, on occasions it had not been quite so jolly.

In the early days it was suggested that the Sultan of Oman's pipes and drums would be a good idea. The Sultan, having been at Sandhurst, was very pro-British and his armed forces were modelled largely on our armed services. Dan Reade and I flew to Oman in some style. It is a very beautiful place and the Sultan has been responsible for very sensible development over the years since he displaced his father. We were taken to be presented to the Sultan. I had never met him before but had already had an invitation to go over and help produce the vast Police Tattoo which they used to do there every year. Unfortunately the dates always clashed with the Berlin Tattoo so I could not accept. As we sat in very comfortable armchairs in the Royal Box of the Sultan's personal stadium, a terrible screeching sound started in the middle distance.

'Ah,' said the Sultan, 'here they come.'

Through the dust the massed pipes and drums marched on. The Sultan had been commissioned into the Cameronians after Sandhurst and was very keen on anything Scottish. Unfortunately that keenness had not communicated itself to whoever was instructing the pipes and drums. They sounded terrible and although I was by no means an expert it sounded as if the drones were not working or had been blocked – a problem I was to come across again later in Jordan. I scanned down the smart gold-embossed programme, looking for a familiar tune. I saw 'Over the Sea to Skye' so I said to the Sultan, beside whom I was sitting, that I was looking forward to hearing that.

'We've just had that one,' he said throwing gold coins into the arena for the band.

Oh dear, I thought. After the display we went into the palace garden and met all the senior Omani officers. They were absolutely charming, as are all Omanis I have ever met. We took the senior seconded British officer aside and said that we had a problem. He was horrified. 'You can't possibly refuse to invite them to the Royal Tournament,' he insisted. We said we thought it would be disastrous if they appeared, as they would just be laughed out of the arena. They needed at least another couple of years' training and we offered to identify some good instructors who could come over and help. In a lull in the conversation with the Sultan, I volunteered a thought. 'Would it not be fun,' I said, 'to combine Omani tradition with Scottish tradition? Why not have a pipe band mounted on camels?' The senior British officer suggested that it would be a very good idea if we were to leave the country as soon as possible. Which we did.

However, the Omanis did indeed mount their pipe band on camels, and it is now a great success and would go down well anywhere. Since then they have added a mounted corps of drums on camels, which is equally wonderful.

Very often I would find myself reinventing acts we went to see. In Kenya we had to combine many different tribal dances to make something that would fit into a ten-minute slot. Unfortunately the girl dancers were no longer allowed to dance topless. Jomo Kenyatta had decreed that they must wear bras. That was fair enough, but did they really have to choose bright white Marks and Spencer's bras? We did at least persuade them to wear black ones.

Papua New Guinea was also quite a challenge, not least because Port Moresby's only hotel was full of small lizard-like things which ran all over me all night. The Governor was the first Papua New Guinean to hold the post. He was a splendid man and was very proud of his morning dress which he wore all day. We drove off in his large limousine and found ourselves in a jungle clearing. Two chairs had been put out in which we sat in some state, with all the staff officers behind us. The Governor General gave a signal and we heard a rather familiar roll of drums in the trees. Into the clearing, playing 'A Life on the Ocean Wave', marched a sort of Royal Marine band wearing skirts. It transpired that a number of ex-Royal Marine musicians and drum majors had come over and instructed them and over the years had turned the Papua New Guinea police band into a facsimile of the real thing. I was somewhat horrified – the last thing we wanted was a foreign Royal Marine Band!

Over the next few days I explained that what we really wanted was something uniquely Papua New Guinean, i.e. mud men, native dancers, local music. They were very enthusiastic. Out went the Royal Marine drill; in came a new dance marching step.

The cymbals player had a party piece of playing his cymbals between his legs. He wrote a marvellous letter in Pidgin English to the Queen, which roughly translated as: 'Dear Missy Qween, Don't you go worrying about me playing my cymbals between my legs. I got ten children already and I don't want no more!' I sent the letter to the palace on my return but clearly it did not pass muster. When I asked the Queen whether she had read it and thought it was funny, it was clear that she had not been given it.

Anxious to emphasis the ethnic content I suggested to the Papua New Guineans that they should consider changing the leopard skin that the base drummer wore over his head, as in British bands. As there were no leopards in Papua New Guinea why not have a crocodile skin and head instead?

So off we went to a crocodile farm in the middle of the jungle, run by an eccentric ex-pat who had built himself what looked like a cardboard castle. He had a room full of regalia, orders and medals from around the world, including King Farouk of Egypt's decorations. One lot looked suspiciously like the Order of the Garter which is very valuable and should have been returned to the Palace.

The crocodile farm was next to a pig breeding unit and I got the distinct impression that the pigs were fed to the crocodiles and the crocodiles, having been skinned, were then fed back to the pigs. I was asked to choose one, which I did, a very splendid dark brown one with white markings, and a blob of white paint was put on its head. We then went and had fried crocodile for lunch and rather good it was too.

Back in England I arranged for a china clay mine in Cornwall to give us a huge bath full of white clay, and cleared with the local authorities the use of my lasers for the beginning of the act. My idea was to have green laser beams simulating shafts of sunlight passing through the jungle canopy. The mud men having jumped into the bath of white clay would then don their mud masks and start the act atmospherically 'in the jungle'. The local authority man ('Ealth'n'Safety had yet to be invented) asked if the masks complied with the regulations for laser goggles. I put it to him that they were hundreds, possibly thousands, of years old, so it was unlikely. He gave in.

When they arrived for their first rehearsal to my disappointment there was no sign of my carefully chosen crocodile skin. 'Very sad story,' they told me. The medal-collecting ex-pat from the cardboard castle had killed the croc, put it in the back of his car and driven to Port Moresby, where he had gone on a bender. When he got back to his car three days later there was a seriously disgusting smell, and the dead crocodile in the boot had turned to soup!

The act was a huge success. We had a small problem with the Papua New Guineans wanting to cook their food on the floor of their prefabricated bedrooms, but I told Earls Court they were lucky they weren't eating each other. The PNG police told me that this was still a slight aberration practiced at home.

In the afternoon we always used to finish the first half of the show with audience participation, when all the children would be invited down into the arena to let their hair down. I decided that they would all do the hokey-cokey that year and that the mud men would be excellent people to lead the lines. This they did with great gusto and the children loved being smeared with white clay. I like to think that in a few hundred years' time some latter-day David Attenborough will discover natives of the jungles of Papua New Guinea doing this very strange dance and will conclude that we must have copied it from them in the first place.

Most of the overseas acts just meant a pleasant few days in Holland, Hungary, Denmark or Hong Kong, or any of the other twenty countries we asked during my time. Most of the acts were very good, but there were exceptions. In 1987 we had horsemen from Pakistan from two different sides of the community who had never ridden together before. Their skills at tent pegging were variable, to say the least, so we had to make the pegs larger and larger. As Princess Margaret said after the show, 'It seems an awful long way to have to come to miss the pegs when you get here.'

One year we had the Bersaglieri, Alpine troops from Italy in splendid cockerel-tailed hats, who double around playing miscellaneous brass instruments. However, their commanding officer complained about the soil on the arena floor.

'We cannot run in the sand,' he explained. Colonel Dan Reade, who had fought the Italians in North Africa during the war, replied, 'Well, you managed it very well in the desert!'

Our foray into America also met with mixed success. We netted one excellent drill display from Rutgers University and one very dodgy Civil War enactment from Arizona. We had a lovely time in Phoenix until we saw the 'enactors'. Their uniforms looked as though they had been made by their mothers in a dim light and their 'cavalry' had no horses. We lent them horses from the Household Cavalry and the King's Troop but after a few days most of those who said they could ride had injured themselves falling off, leaving one horseman in the saddle, which did not make for a very impressive cavalry charge.

In 1985 I flew over to Jordan, where everyone was very friendly. I went with the Commander in Chief, General Zaid bin Shaker, to see the pipes and drums perform. They made a very strange noise so I played for time, and suggested I should come back with a pipe expert who might be able to help them because we were very keen to have them as they were all so lovely. Pipe Major Gavin Stoddart, one of the best pipers in the army who was later on to run the Piping School at Edinburgh Castle, listened to them and said it would help if they hadn't blocked the drones with corks. Apparently they did this as they felt they didn't have enough blow to make the whole instrument work. Gavin removed the corks, and fitted new reeds which he just happened to have with him, and they started to sound much better. Their enthusiasm and the personality of the Director of Music, Major Jamal Zuricat, were infectious and the audience loved them. Their liaison officer was Patricia (Trisha) Salti, an Englishwoman who had married a Jordanian. Her husband, Lieutenant Muffawak Salti, had sadly been killed in the Six Day War and was honoured as a hero and a martyr. Trisha was working in the Royal Household at the time and was full of enthusiasm and very switched on. She was to be of huge support to me in all the other things that I was to do in Jordan over the years.

We went all the way to Moscow to see the Russian Navy Band and were told that we wouldn't be able to because their new uniforms hadn't arrived, so we came home again. The Foreign Office said that it would be a good idea to have them in any event, so we did. The Cossacks from Ukraine were amazing horsemen who would prove very useful later on when I took them to Saudi Arabia dressed up as Arabs for camel battles.

*   *   *

I always used to look forward to Navy year. Firstly it meant we had the Massed Bands of the Royal Marines who are superb, and secondly it meant that we normally had a company of Royal Marine commandos. They were all extremely high-grade soldiers and their various skills made for a very good 'battle' act with their cliff climbing, death sliding (though we are not allowed to use that term now; 'Ealth'n'Safety prefers 'rapid descent'), and abseiling and descending from the roof. I always found the roof terrifying. I'm not good at heights in any event but I felt that I really ought to have a bash at everything I was asking them to do. So I gingerly went up into the roof and was strapped into my 'descender' and told how to use it. I was pushed out into space, and slowly descended through the dust and heat which gathered under the roof. I was petrified but carried on. What I didn't know was that if someone pulled the rope from the ground I would instantly stop. This was a safety feature, but if you do stop suddenly it has a profound effect on your delicate parts.

It so happened that that year I had been particularly hard on the Gurkha Band and Pipes and Drums who, though excellent, always over-ran their timed slot. Time-keeping was always a major problem; in fact, I think I expended more effort trying to keep everything on time than I did in producing it in the first place. Halfway down my very shaky abseil I suddenly jolted to a very painful halt. From below came the voice of the Gurkha Commander, a splendid old-school officer. 'Now, Michael,' he said, as I swung around in some pain. 'How many more minutes are you going to give me today for our display?'

Eventually he relented and allowed me to continue to the ground. At the daily meeting the following morning, for the first time ever I did not castigate the Gurkhas for their timings. But I did the next day.

* * *

A lot of what we were doing was potentially very risky. Accidents were common, and something that we were always anticipating. Only the expertise and training of those involved made accidents much rarer than they might have been.

Before the new synthetic climbing ropes were issued the Royal Marines had used sisal ones. These had a limited life span and had to be changed after a certain number of descents. On about day ten of one Tournament I was told that the Mass Abseil ropes near the main entrance were going to be changed for new ones for the next performance. About twelve men made a mass descent to start the attack, which looked very impressive. Then suddenly they were all lying on the floor, not moving. The medics came rushing on and it transpired that the ropes had been cut twenty feet too short. The men were badly hurt but fortunately all made a full recovery. The Commandant General, the Royal Marines, later told me that I was 'bad for recruiting'.

The motorcycle display teams were always very good value. The speed, skill and courage they displayed were hugely impressive. It always used to amuse me that most of the young men in the teams had not passed their driving tests and were therefore not allowed onto the roads. But they were allowed to do fast triple cross-overs at closing speeds of 50mph in the arena!

One year the White Helmets, the Royal Signals Display Team, had a series of accidents. You could always tell which acts the other participants liked because every nook and cranny would be filled with faces watching from the roof, the lighting gallery or the emergency exits. When the White Helmets came on there was not a space to be seen anywhere. The motorcycle teams were supposed to enter the arena at high speed, jumping over two ramps to do a cross-over in mid-air. On this occasion the first two bikes mistimed it, and hit each other with some force. Onto the ground they fell, and all the other bikes following closely behind piled up on top of them. The scene looked horrific, a twisted mangled mess of bikes, wheels spinning and men lying everywhere. I lit another cigarette. It looked much worse than it really was and one by one the men got up, dusted themselves down and wheeled their bikes off, until there was just one man left lying there. The stretcher bearers came on and carried him off. Fearing the worst, I asked the Arena Master if the man was badly injured.

'Not at all,' he said. 'He just split his trousers right up the middle and didn't want to show everything walking off!'

Whilst the White Helmets had very heavy Triumph bikes, the Royal Artillery team had much lighter ones and could jump very large distances. One year I thought it would be rather fun if they were to jump a very expensive Rolls-Royce. By chance Kit Aston, with whom I had done the Silver Jubilee, was now a Director of Rolls-Royce and he loaned three of them! One was an 'ordinary' saloon, the next a Corniche convertible and the last a Camargue, then the most expensive car they made. My driver was in seventh heaven with these three gleaming treasures to look after. We used a different one each day. One day, when I was being driven to Hounslow to watch the massed bands rehearse, I chose the Corniche. We pulled up at a traffic light beside a large lorry. We were obviously both in uniform and as I sank back into the luxurious leather in my 'shirt-sleeve order' and forage hat, a loud voice from above me said, 'I always thought you buggers were paid too much!' As we sped off at maximum acceleration I gave him a salute – or was it two fingers?

In the show the Rolls would enter at speed and do the closest a Rolls could to a hand-brake turn. The roof would open whilst the commentator was explaining how very expensive the car was. Then the bike would rev up, enter at speed, and jump the car to thunderous applause. One day the inevitable happened – the bike clipped the top of the windscreen and cartwheeled off across the arena. The bike was a write-off. Fortunately the rider was completely uninjured. But now the Rolls's roof wouldn't close as the frame was bent. I telephoned Rolls-Royce and told them what had happened. To my astonishment, the young man apologised profusely and said they would send another one immediately, which they did.

A few weeks later he telephoned and asked, 'By the way, were we insured?'

I said, 'Of course we weren't – who would insure such an expensive car to be jumped over by a motorcycle?'

'Of course not, Sir.' And that was the last we ever heard about it.

Some accidents did not have such a happy ending. I always felt personally responsible for anyone being hurt whilst doing what I had asked them to do, and it used to upset me a great deal, particularly if it was a horse that was injured, which from time to time they were. They were only obediently doing what they had been told to do when they came to grief through no fault of their own, and it always greatly upset everybody.

Quite the worst accident in my twenty-seven years happened on the afternoon of the wedding of the Prince of Wales to Lady Diana Spencer. The Musical Drive of the King's Troop, Royal Horse Artillery, is easily the most difficult, skillful and dangerous display in the world. The courage, concentration and skill that it demands speak volumes for the quality of the men, and now the women, who do it. In the fast cross-over, two teams of six horses, each with one and a half tons of gun and limber, without any brakes, canter very fast diagonally across the arena, missing each other by what looks like inches. It always used to have me gripping my seat with anxiety; now I cannot even bear to watch it. On this occasion the two teams collided. One gun catapulted over its team of horses and landed upside down. Twelve horses, apparently dead, lay tangled in their harnesses. Six men were also scattered around, lying prone and still. Dust rose in the heat and the wheels of the up-turned guns spun in the spotlights. There was a deathly silence from the ten thousand people in the audience.

The Troop had rehearsed for such an eventuality, never dreaming it might actually happen. During all Troop mishaps the house band plays the Eton Boating Song, for reasons which I have never been able to discover. The support teams and 'leg-over parties' then come on and do their tasks. Amazingly, on this occasion none of the horses was badly injured, mainly just winded or shocked, and once released from the entangling harness could be led off. The men were taken straight to the medical centre and I waited with trepidation for the report.

Then there was a bizarre interlude. I was told that one of the men had lost a hand. All the officers and leg-over parties inspected the arena carefully but couldn't find anything. We couldn't leave a human hand lying in the arena so I asked them to look again – they still found nothing. I telephoned the medical centre, told them we could not find the hand. The doctor sounded surprised. 'Hang on a minute,' he said, and went to look at the men.

'I can't think what the problem is,' he said. 'We have three men and six hands!' Presumably one the men's hands had been pulled up his sleeve, sparking panic.

I have happier memories of other animals taking part. In the early 80s I had used elephants in the Berlin Tattoo and I thought it might be rather fun to bring them to the Royal Tournament. Bobby Roberts' six elephants had taken part in the Silver Jubilee show at Windsor and the Great Children's Party in Hyde Park. In Berlin, we had his elephants drawing guns which had been specially made for them. These two huge pieces of armament were flown over to RAF Lyneham, arriving late in the evening. Only one man had been instructed to offload the two huge hunks of metal.

'I was told they were elephant guns,' he protested.

'They are,' said the pilot.

'I thought they meant guns for killing elephants!'

The guns were taken off the next morning by ten men and brought to London.

On the Sunday before the Tournament opened, we would always do a publicity parade, from Horse Guards Parade, along Birdcage Walk, past the Palace, down the Mall and back into Horse Guards. I decided to ride my elephant, Maureen, down the Mall in my Number One Dress – my Blues – much as I had done down the Kurfürstendamm in Berlin. My orderly was less enthusiastic when I informed him that he would have to hold on to my spur to keep me on. Off we set, bringing up the rear of the parade, and all was going well. When we turned down the Mall to march past the Major General, he asked whether he should salute, and if so how? 'Just keep holding the spur with your left hand and salute with your right,' I told him.

As we approached the Major General, I heard a distant sound. I suddenly remembered that I had arranged for the Red Arrows, the RAF aero-acrobatic team, to fly over as the parade finished. My orderly had just gone up into the salute as they thundered over. Maureen took great exception to this and reared up, taking the guardsman off the ground in mid-salute. I hung on for dear life. The Major General roared with laughter.

When we got home my orderly said, 'Sir, I didn't join the effin' army to hold an effin' officer onto an effin' helephant!' I took him away and bought him a large drink.

For another show I thought it might be amusing to have on parade all the mascots of the various regiments. These ranged from drum horses, ponies, elks, rams and wolf hounds to snakes, spiders and scorpions. We had a huge

Noah's Ark built that came down out of the roof and they all paraded through it to suitable music. Most of the animals came more or less ready for parade. I am afraid the tarantula was less ready. A young airman came into my office during one of the build-up days with a perspex box inside which was the spider.

'Where shall I put it, Sir?'

'Nowhere,' I said. 'You're on parade with it.'

'I can't march, Sir, I'm in the RAF.'

'Well, you've two days to learn!'

The first time he appeared in front of a ten thousand-strong audience he was pink with embarrassment as he marched in the procession holding his perspex box and its occupant gingerly in front of him. I swear I could hear him muttering, 'I didn't join the effin' RAF to walk around in effin' circles carrying an effin' spider.'

However, after a couple of performances he started to ham it up, pointing at his large black furry charge, and making funny faces. The applause became even more enthusiastic. I was forced to tell him, in effect, 'You didn't join the effin' RAF to play the effin' clown. March properly!'

Inevitably, the spider escaped. I was not told at the time. The RAF failed to find it, so the commandant sent an officer out to buy a replacement, hoping that no one would notice the difference. This young man started off at Harrods, having heard that they sold everything. Not in this case, however. He eventually found one in Kennington, and it was on parade later that day.

None of us would have known about this had not, a few days later, a very irate technical manager from Earls Court stormed into my office demanding to know why one of his workmen had taken a hammer out of his toolbox only to find a huge tarantula on it!

* * *

In 1980 Dan Reade told me he was going to retire. This was very sad for me as he had always been a great support against 'them'. He had a lot of which to be proud, having transformed the show and turned it back into a success. It was not until the very last night that I discovered that he had had a secret ambition during all that time. It was that Basil Reitz, the commentator, would lose his voice one night and that he, Dan, would have to step in and do the commentary. Each year he would meticulously prepare his script but, sadly, never ever got to use it. Had I realised I would have told Basil to feign a sore throat.

Colonel Iain Ferguson, late of the Scots Guards, was chosen as Dan's successor. I had met him and his wife Margaret briefly when he was commanding the Guards Depot and I don't think either of us imagined that we would be working together for eighteen years. I was rather nervous about a Guardsman taking over but, rather like the recent amalgamation of the Guards Club and the Cavalry Club, we got on very well. At least, I thought we did. However, it was not long before he presented me with a little wall plaque which he said reminded him of me. It had a picture of Napoleon with the words: 'Let's compromise – we'll do it my way!'

Iain and Margaret were both brilliant. Margaret was great at charming and chatting up everybody from a cleaner to the Queen; she was also a wonderful flower arranger, which meant the Royal Box always looked immaculate. He was great at spiriting money out of reluctant sponsors, which was lucky because the Civil Service were thinking of more and more ways of charging us for things that had previously been provided. In the 1970s sponsorship was still quite novel, and you had to explain to companies what it meant.

*   *   *

Security was always a major concern particularly when the 'troubles' in Northern Ireland were at their height. It was a major task to make Earls Court secure. But on at least one occasion it worked well; we discovered, sometime after the event, that the bomb that later went off at the Tower of London killing a number of innocent people had actually been brought to Earls Court but could not be got through our cordon and was taken to the Tower instead. It happened to be the day the Queen was coming, which the would-be bombers clearly knew. We were an obvious high-profile target but at least we were able to protect ourselves up to a point. Not so for softer and easier targets. One day during my daily 12 o'clock conference a terrible message came through that the Queen's Life Guard had been blown up in Hyde Park, and later a military band in Regents Park.

The Household Cavalry Musical Ride was in the show, as were a number of musicians who had friends that were victims. That afternoon there were not many dry eyes around.

Since before the War all the acts in the show were allocated their own pub. This was in the vain hope of avoiding inter-service punch-ups. We had tried for years to be allowed a drinks licence to open our own bars, but this had always been turned down by the local authority. Then one morning a knapsack containing a large amount of explosive was found in one of 'our' pubs. Its firing mechanism was faulty, which saved hundreds of lives. After that we had no difficulty getting our licences and the three Field Gun teams opened bars for all the participants. They were a great way of letting the boys relax in safe surroundings. It used to take me quite a long time to unwind after the show and I would quite frequently still be there at two o'clock in the morning. I would then walk home which was about ten minutes away. Very often I would discover my orderly following me to make certain I made it safely.

We used to have what I called 'wise virgins' meetings before shows when we would try to anticipate all the disasters that could befall us and how we would sort them out. Of course, it was usually something we had not anticipated that caught us out. But going through the options beforehand helped the team to cope when disaster struck. Disasters came in many forms, from funny to very serious. With so little time for rehearsal we very often got to the first performance without my having seen some of the acts. So it made everything 'fresh' when we and ten thousand other people saw it for the first time.

Sometimes mishaps were very complicated. In one RAF year, to make full use of their excellent musicians I decided that we would have Gershwin's 'Rhapsody in Blue' played on a grand piano that would be lowered eighty feet on a revolve into the massed bands. The pianist, Flight Lieutenant Stuart Sterling, later to become Principal Director of Music, was hoisted up an hour beforehand as the audience started to come in. He just sat there strapped to his stool reading a book with a torch until his moment came.

On the Queen's Day, there was a torrential downpour and water came through the roof and poured down to the cellar causing an electricity sub-station to blow up. Instantly half the lights in the arena went out and all the production power went. The massed bands of the Royal Air Force halted in a large circle, waiting for the grand piano to be lowered. They started the introduction to 'Rhapsody in Blue', and paused for the first chords from the piano. There were none. The band paused and looked up expectantly.

The pianist was peering down over the edge of the revolve, making 'It's not working' gestures. We bloody well knew that. The band decided of its own volition to strike up and march off; the audience was mystified and Stuart's mother, who had come specially to see her son play for the Queen, was very upset. Afterwards on the line-up I presented him as 'the phantom pianist'.

For the centenary of the Tournament we decided to have a Tri-Service Massed Band for the first time. In the Finale they were to march on in the order in which they had joined the Tournament – i.e. Army, Navy, Royal Air Force – and then play the well-known march 'The Army, the Navy and the Air Force'. As each band marched on a huge service flag was unfurled from the roof.

One day the RAF had cut it a little fine, and were not at the entry gates when their cue was given. 'Ladies and Gentlemen – the Royal Air Force!' Cheers! Then silence … large flag unfurls … further cheers … silence... Without any external prompting the bands struck up 'The Army, the Navy and the –' leaving the RAF out each time, to the amusement of the crowd. By now the RAF bands had arrived breathless behind the main gates and begged to be allowed on. After a bit we relented, and the audience cheered when they eventually appeared. The Director of Music had a very large bar bill afterwards.

Sometimes whole acts failed to materialise at all, but people seldom noticed. Unless it was going to be very obvious we never mentioned what was being left out. Another of my Rules was: 'Never tell people what is supposed to happen. Then they won't know when it hasn't.'

But it was impossible, in the RAF Mountain Rescue Display, for which we had constructed a seventy-foot overhanging cliff face, to hide the fact that the 'rescuer' cut the wrong rope so he and his 'casualty' crashed to the ground. Amazingly they were not hurt, as some of the other ropes broke their fall. But their salute at the end was rather rueful.

Nor could anybody could hide the fact that the Battle of Zeebrugge was all going very wrong. We had built a hundred and twenty-foot 'frigate' on a large articulated low-loader, known as a Queen Mary, and a Land Rover. It had to reverse into the arena through doors built twice the normal height, a very tricky operation. One day it failed to make the doors and came through the backcloth instead. There was much grinding and ripping as it burst through, bringing with it most of the scaffolding that held up the doors. We had no option but to stop the show and bring on the clowns from the motorcycle act whilst the 'ship' was cut out with acetylene torches. It made the newspapers, and next day when the Queen and the Duke of Edinburgh came the Duke said that he was rather disappointed that the ship had made it safely through the doors.

In another year I brought a huge mechanical dragon over from Berlin where I had used it in the Tattoo there. It was mounted on a long-wheelbase Land Rover and had five men inside. One drove, another worked the head, neck and fire-bursts from the dragon's nostrils, one was on each wing and

Dulwich Prep School innocent – if the cap fits.

Detmold 1812 – setting fire to the Colonel's House.

Sandhurst 1960- the six most likely to succeed?

Me, my Tank and L/ Cpl Bettam – "I didn't join the effing Army to...."

Praying that General Speidel does not shoot anyone.

At the 1977 Silver Jubilee Bonfire the Queen hands the torch to an Australian Scout.

What the world's largest Jelly might have looked like.

"I'm afraid, Ma'am, it's all going terribly wrong" – "Oh good – what fun!"

The Queen records her Christmas Broadcast at 'Joy to the World'.

Buckingham Palace 'explodes' for the G7 Summit.

The Palace at The Royal Fireworks in 1981 goes terribly wrong.

Queen Elizabeth making light of being called a Royal Highness at The Royal Albert Hall.

The skating Band at the last Berlin Tattoo…"We didn't join the effing Army to…"

The Queen of Greece asking Princess
Margaret if she could use the Royal
Retiring Room at 'Joy to the World'.

The Prime Minister failing to take
direction at the opening of the World
Chess Championships 1986.

The Original Tiller Girls at 'Great Event'
for the Queen's 40th.

The Finale of the last 'Joy to the World'.

Prince Andrew in the producer's box at the Royal Tournament having recorded part of the commentary.

About to ride Maureen the elephant down the Mall.

The final parade of the Massed Cavalry Bands at the Royal Tournament.

Prince William trying on the Dutch Grenadiers Bearskin at the Royal Tournament.

The young boys of the 'Imps' Motorcycle Display Team at Edinburgh.

The Edinburgh Tattoo 1992 – it never rains!

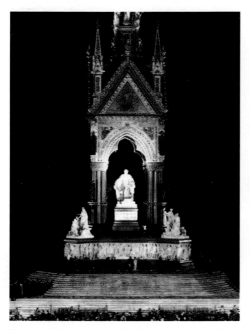

Prince Albert in his full Memorial glory for the first time since World War 1.

Rehearsals for the Queen Mother's 100th – The Major General about to be run over by a procession.

50th Anniversary of VJ Day – a Lancaster bomber and a million poppy petals.

The Massed Pipes and Drums kindly producing background music for one of my dinner parties in the Officers' Mess behind.

The Court of the Grocers Company about to be decanted from their camels at The Queen Mother's 100th.

The Finale of the last ever Royal Tournament 1999.

the last brandished the tail. The Tournament opened with the dragon being slain by Saint George, played by a young Household Cavalry officer called James Hewitt, later to become notorious as Princess Diana's 'love rat'. He was supposed to gallop in on his large grey charger with a long lance and 'kill' the dragon. This he did well enough on most days, but on the last night he galloped in, drew a pistol and shot it instead. The audience thought it hugely funny; I didn't, as he was supposed to be symbolising the triumph of Good over Evil. So I had the Arena Master arrest him as he rode out to deafening cheers.

I thought no more about it until I went to the Royal Box after the show to see an old friend, Field Marshal Sir John Stanier, the retiring Chief of the General Staff, who had taken the Salute. I apologised for the shooting and told him what I had done. 'Oh, for Heaven's sake,' he said, 'let the boy go. It was the best part of the whole show.'

At another performance the driver of the dragon, who couldn't see anything and had to be directed by radio, veered to one side and a whole rank of Guards musicians was mown down, with their bearskins rolling around in the dust. There was a collective 'sense of humour failure'.

Many of my strangest ideas were realised by 'Merv' Harridence, a lovely gnome-like figure who, apart from painting the backcloths from my originals each year, would produce anything from a two-thirds-scale Harrier jump-jet which could travel at thirty miles an hour mounted on a Morris Minor, to the black inflatable front end of a nuclear submarine, fifty feet in diameter with fins and one hundred feet long. The boys, not unnaturally, called it 'the biggest French letter in the world'. It came on as part of the Finale with the massed bands of the Royal Marines playing underneath, surrounded by Royal Marines in diving suits and flippers going up and down on 'Peter Pan' flying wires blowing bubbles. Inevitably there was a lot of: 'I didn't join the effin' Royal Marines to bounce around wearing an effin' rubber suit blowing effin' bubbles.'

Come the dress rehearsal, Merv still hadn't quite got right the huge fans that inflated the sub. As the music reached a crescendo the sub exploded with a loud bang and deflated rapidly. The bands stopped playing and burst into laughter. That night at about one o'clock I found Merv and his partner Diana forty feet up on a hoist with a small sewing machine, trying to sew the sub back together again. It worked fine after that.

Merv's mini-Harrier was used in 1984 when the theme was 'A day in the life of a young naval officer'; it was set on an aircraft carrier's flight deck.

Prince Andrew, then still serving, agreed to record the commentary links. These were written by Rosemary Anne Sisson, who has a wonderful knack of making dialogue sound natural and who was to write for many of my events. Prince Andrew sat in the Control box for one show and I suggested he might like to do the links live. His reply was in the best traditions of his father!

We all had great respect for the Duke of Edinburgh, whose sense of humour is just up my street. One year the theme was 'The Story of Flight', and the Finale featured an eighty-foot-wide RAF eagle cap badge (commonly known to other services as 'the shite hawk') which motored on tracks in the roof to the centre of the arena where it started to revolve with fireworks coming out from underneath. The Duke said afterwards that 'it was great to see the shite hawk shite-ing.'

Merv had made a full-scale working model of Leonardo da Vinci's wing-flapping contraption, which was to 'fly' down the arena on Peter Pan wires. As it would reach a height of sixty feet I decided it would have to be manned by a rigger. The chap chosen muttered something along the lines of: 'I didn't become an effin' rigger to pedal an effin' wooden bird in front of twelve thousand effin' people.' But he did, and in a very skimpy loincloth at that. When he got to the end of the arena there was supposed to be a black-out so he could be lowered to the ground and get out of his harness. But, inevitably, on one occasion he couldn't be got out of his harness so he had to be hoisted fifty feet up again, where he stayed until the interval an hour later, with a marvellous and unique view of all the acts, including the King's Troop galloping around just underneath him. When he was eventually lowered and released to great cheers from the audience, he had to rush very quickly to the loo so didn't have time to come up and thump me!

*   *   *

In 1993 I started having trouble with my heart. In 1994 it got worse and I was told that I would have to have a new heart valve. 'Sorry,' I told them. 'I've got the fiftieth anniversary of VE and VJ next year, so it'll just have to wait.'

Unfortunately, on the Queen's Day (naturally!) I had violent palpitations during the first half of the show. At the interval I told my orderly to get the doctor to meet me outside the Royal Box. I was talking with the Queen, feeling pretty rotten, when suddenly the doctor rushed in asking who needed him.

'Well, not me,' smiled the Queen. 'I'm fine!'

Once I got out of the Royal Box I suppose the adrenaline stopped pumping, and I collapsed. I can remember them trying to get me into a small Army ambulance, but they couldn't get the doors closed because of my spurs. I heard my orderly, a splendid chap called Corporal Gaskell, saying, 'You can't take his spurs off unless you take his boots off. And you can't take his boots off until you take his trousers off. And you are NOT taking his trousers off!'

So they tied up the doors with string and off I went to hospital. They managed to get me back to normal after a bit, but I was now worried that directly after the Tournament I had to go up to Scotland to do the Edinburgh Tattoo. But that is another story.

*   *   *

As time passed I became more and more aware that the Tournament was being overtaken by other entertainments. In the nineteenth century, and for most of the twentieth, it was the only live, exciting and dangerous show available to the public. Now that the young had computers, virtual reality games and films with stunning special effects it was more difficult to attract our key 13-17 year old age group. They seemed not fully to understand that all our stunts were real and potentially really dangerous. They expected the men, having abseiled into the arena, to turn into blobs of mercury and zoom off on motorbikes as they did in computer games. Injuries, unless there was lots of blood, were assumed to be as fake as those in the cinema and all human prowess and skill seemed to be subconsciously discounted as computer generated imagery.

Not only that, but manpower, which had always been a problem, was getting more and more difficult to obtain. It was clear that the Navy were not going to be able to continue to find men for the Field Guns, and both the other services were pushed as well.

Money was becoming tighter and tighter, and Civil Service charges were rising the whole time. The reduction of the show from three weeks to two was a big financial blow. We were also worried about safety, not our current pathetic 'Ealth'n'Safety regulations but real concerns about the reduction in training periods for displays like the Field Guns. During most of my time 'Ealth'n'Safety was still only an emerging black art but it did start to affect us. What the pious little bureaucrats with their rule books did not seem to understand was that we were far more concerned about the real safety and well-being of our performers than they would ever be. One year they insisted that we put handrails up in the roof, at huge expense, so that the men could get from the walkways to the holes in the ceiling tiles to abseil or parachute down.

'What then?' I asked.

'Oh, then they can jump through if they like.'

'Don't you think they should have a handrail on the way down?' I said.

'Oh no,' came the reply. 'That would be silly.

Quite.

*   *   *

Sadly, it looked as if our time was up. After much soul searching we decided that 1999 would be our last year. For me, this represented the end of twenty-seven years of my life, and I was to find it very strange to discover that other things actually happened in the world during July.

Because it was clear that we were not going to go on, it seemed unfair to fill the vacant post of Secretary of the Tournament just for one year. I decided that the best thing was to 'lend' my outstandingly competent PA Catie Bland who did a fantastic job, probably better than it had been done before. All the old Tournament hands lived in fear of her and her clipboard full of lists of things to be done.

I was very keen to end on a high note and not just fade away, and I set about trying to make the last Tournament the best ever. We decided it should involve all three services, and would tell the whole history of the show over its hundred and twenty years using the best of everything.

I designed a backcloth centred round the Royal Standard with the cyphers of all the monarchs with whose support it had existed. At the top a scroll said: 1880-1999 The Last Royal Tournament. We had to get permission from Buckingham Palace to use the Royal Standard. They asked us not to call it 'The Last' Royal Tournament so I changed it to The 109th Royal Tournament.

There was great public regret at our passing. For those of us who were so heavily involved it was traumatic. As I did the research for the final script, I realised how much the show had contributed, not only to service charities and the public perception of the services, but to the traditions which it strove to uphold, many of which it began in the first place. The Field Gunners in particular took it very badly, and petitions were raised for a rethink.

As usual most of the Royal Family attended. The Queen was originally asked to the final performance but the message came back that she would prefer to come on her normal day and send her daughter to the last show, as 'she is less emotional'.

The Opening of the last Tournament was the most complicated I had ever done. All the acts took part, with representatives of every country that had ever been in the show. Massed bands, mounted bands, pipes and drums, motorbikes, dogs and racing cars were accompanied by period music and archive film and images. Over seven hundred people opened the show, slightly more than the ten trumpeters who opened it the year before I took over!

Rowan Atkinson had always been a great supporter of the Tournament, bringing his children each year, so I asked if he would make a special appearance as Captain Blackadder during the very last performance, and he agreed. In fact, careful inspection of our records revealed that a Lance Corporal J.W. Blackadder of the Ist Lothians and Border Yeomanry had competed in the Royal Tournament in 1898, so he was only following in his 'ancestor's' footsteps.

Rowan organised his own costume, and asked Ben Elton to write his script. He told me his 'spot' would last about six minutes. I told him I was afraid that was too long; three minutes would be perfect. He said I was the only person ever to cut a Ben Elton script without even reading it. It was brave of him to agree to appear as he was not really used to performing in a huge arena with an audience of over twelve thousand. I got my orderly, Staff Sergeant Baynes, to look after him and cue him to go on. Staff was convinced that he wouldn't go on at all, as he appeared very nervous. All good performers were nervous, I told him, and if absolutely necessary he should push him on when I gave the cue. Rowan did go on, and was exceptional. We had promised that there would be no television coverage or any recording so he could be quite outspoken, and he was. He finished by exhorting the whole audience to go with him to Waterloo (of course!) Station, board Eurostar and invade France! The audience went wild and we had difficulty getting on with the show.

There had been a lot of talk in the press of the Field Gunners wearing black arm-bands in mourning for the demise of the show and their competition. For many it was their whole life, and their only ambition was to run to win, and to run again. An order came through from the Admiralty that on no account were black arm-bands to be worn. The Field Gun officers were rather dubious about their being able to enforce this, rightly as it turned out. In spite of inspections, confiscations and senior ranks searching the sailors just before they marched on, most of them were somehow sporting the illicit arm-bands before they reached the centre of the arena. This caused an acute sense of humour failure on the part of a number of admirals, but the point had been made. The Finale on the last night had almost twelve hundred people and over two hundred horses. The entire Kings Troop, with all officers and detachments, together with over one hundred Household Cavalry horses that came from Knightsbridge specially, slow-marched through smoke along with the entire cast to 'Conquest of Paradise'. It was an extraordinary sight.

As the years had gone by, and the sets and backcloths had grown more and more ambitious, I got sadder and sadder every year as they were broken up and taken away. On the very last show of all, we all sat up there – the whole of the technical team – crying for the last time. I still have, on the walls in my study, the original paintings for all the twenty-six shows I did.

Afterwards all the streets around Earls Court had to be closed to allow the horses and vehicles to disperse. Hundreds of local residents came out to say good-bye, not caring for once about the disruption, as a little piece of history disappeared into the darkness.

CHAPTER SEVEN

❧

Everything That Could Go Wrong …
– The Silver Jubilee

During my twenty-seven years of producing the Royal Tournament, I also – as I mentioned earlier – did a great many other things in the other eight months of the year. By 1976 I had been running the antiques business with my aunt for some time, but never really saw myself as a shopkeeper, so I was looking for something else to do.

Then one day a telephone call started my first involvement with a major national event. It was *The* Major General – Philip Ward – asking if I would like to have lunch with the Mayor of Windsor and Maidenhead. With visions of a boring municipal lunch, I said there was nothing that I would like to do less. 'I really think you ought to come,' was the reply. 'The Mayor is rather special.' And so he proved.

Kit Aston was a director of Ready Mixed Concrete and had a very elegant office in Chesham Place, full of fabulous antique furniture; the walls were covered with wonderful murals by Graham Rust. I realised at once that it was indeed going to be a rather special lunch. Also there was Philip Ward's brigade major Charles Guthrie, later to become Field Marshal Lord Guthrie, Chief of the Defence Staff. Kit was to become a dear friend, with whom I shared one particular joke over the years. My friend Sarah Norrie's Aunt Peg once commented that somebody was suffering 'night starvation'. Advertisements for Horlicks used to claim that it 'guarded against night starvation'. It took me a moment to realise that she meant 'knight' starvation. From then on Kit and I referred to those hopeful of a knighthood as 'needing Horlicks'. Years later, when Kit was knighted, he telephoned excitedly to say he had 'got his Horlicks'. Sadly, it came at about the same time as he heard that he had cancer.

Kit had a number of plans for the Silver Jubilee celebrations in Windsor, and needed someone to help him pull them together. I took to him immediately; he was enthusiastic and had excellent ideas and, almost as important, he had an extremely large and excellent wine cellar. I was to spend the next year or so doing my best to empty it.

That afternoon, after many bottles of Château Beycheval, Latour and Montrachet, we made good progress. I was given responsibility for the Queen's Bonfire, and a nationwide chain of beacons. The Royal Institute of Chartered Surveyors had chosen over a hundred and fifty sites that covered the whole country. Each beacon site was 'inter-visible', which meant that it could see the site before it and be seen by the site after it. This, of course, was how simple signals had been sent at the time of the Spanish Armada and even before.

All the bonfires were very carefully planned. Instructions for building them had been sent out with tips for celebrations to be held around them. This was all right for most sites, but not for Ely Cathedral, the roof of which was the only raised place in that part of the country. The Ely Beacon had to be very controlled!

Other events we organised at the same time included a Rolls-Royce Parade past the Queen in Windsor Castle, the Royal Command Variety and Circus Performance in the Home Park, the Air Tattoo at White Waltham, and the River Pageant on the Thames between Windsor and Maidenhead. Kit had also set up The Queen's Trees, a programme to plant thousands of trees in the Queen's name. Each donor got a beautiful engraving by Graham Rust of the tree they had chosen to plant.

However, I concentrated on the Queen's Beacon, which was to be built just by the 'Copper Horse' statue of George III at the end of the Long Walk from Windsor Castle, and set to work with the BBC to make what was at that stage a pretty simple event into something that would justify an hour-long television programme. Again, many alcoholic lunches at Shepherds Bush helped with our creativity.

At the start of 1977, the experts were saying that the public would not be the least bit interested in the Silver Jubilee and that no one would come to any of the events. Yet there was to be nationwide television coverage from each part of the United Kingdom, as well as international television links. So I decided to do what I was frequently to do in the future – involve as many participants as possible. I worked on the principle that everyone performing in some way would bring with them 'a Mum, a Dad and an Aunty Glad', thus increasing the audience considerably. We also needed to make money out of the event because, although it was all going to be paid for by private sponsorship, we hoped to make enough money to set up a Windsor Jubilee

Trust for the benefit of the people of Windsor. We were in fact to achieve this, and I am happy to say that the Trust is still supporting good causes in Windsor and Maidenhead.

The simple bonfire/beacon idea soon turned into a full-blown extravaganza with a large military band and fireworks, and I asked the Lewes Bonfire Society and the Sealed Knot Society to take part. The Lewes Bonfire Society was – indeed, still is – a marvellous bunch of pyromaniacs who parade each year in costume, carrying scores of flaming torches. I asked for a thousand of them. The Sealed Knot is a group of 'enactors' who relive and refight the Civil War. They were led by the gallant Brigadier Peter Young who had been a military history lecturer at Sandhurst when I was there. They were all slightly barmy but very enthusiastic, and loved dressing up in wigs and copious layers of lace. I asked for three thousand of them.

Kit and I met frequently with Lieutenant Colonel Sir Martin Charteris, the Queen's Private Secretary, to go through the details of the three events – the Bonfire, the Rolls-Royce Parade and the Royal Variety Performance – to which the Queen would be coming. As the weeks went by, more and more people piled in with offers of help. The Army Catering Corps offered to roast an ox which the Queen kindly gave from the Great Park herd. The fireworks were donated by Pains Wessex. Guinness would put up a very welcome Black Velvet (champagne and Guinness) tent at the back of the Royal enclosure, and we sold tickets for the best viewing points. The Royal Box was built in front of the Copper Horse, facing the castle with, to the left, a stand for the Massed Bands of the Household Cavalry.

For the bonfire, Roland Wiseman, the Deputy Ranger who ran the whole of the Great Park, had designed an impressive edifice some forty feet high, which the Great Park staff had built on top of the hill. It was so large that you could climb up ladders inside it. One day a lady rode past and remarked that the bonfire was in the wrong place. This might not have mattered much, except that the lady in question was the Queen. The bonfire for King George V's Jubilee had been down the hill, Her Majesty told us. I explained that it had to be on the top of the hill so it could be seen by the next ring of beacons, which would pass the signal on to all other parts of the country. The Royal Household were obviously not convinced, and the Great Park team was quite depressed by the prospect of dismantling something that had taken many weeks to make and rebuilding it somewhere else. These were the days before mobile telephones, so telephone lines had been laid at considerable expense. Our telephone was nailed to a tree. Martin Charteris had promised to let us have an answer that morning, so we stood around waiting for the tree to ring. When it did, with the news that the bonfire would be allowed to stay where it was, there was great relief all round.

The Sealed Knot crowd arrived and set up camp in the Home Park. They had brought their wives and girlfriends with them, and judging by the noises in the woods at night they seemed to be less interested in fighting a battle for us than in ensuring that there would be a new generation to take over from them. One morning I was surprised to see a chap in civilian clothes carrying a suitcase being frog-marched to the station with an escort of pike-men in full kit. He had apparently been 'court-martialled' and was being sent home in disgrace. Later we heard that their horsemen had been galloping around in the private part of the Park. When apprehended they insisted that as 'the King's Cavalry' they were entitled to do so. It was forcefully pointed out to them that we now had a Queen, and that they were not entitled at all.

Because of the Coronation Day link we had asked Lord Hunt, who led the successful conquest of Everest in 1953, to be in the Royal Box, and Sir Edmund Hillary was going to join in by satellite link from New Zealand. We had even tracked down Sherpa Tensing and sent money for his airfare, but sadly he never turned up.

Apart from the Royal Family, a large number of VIPs were coming and all the ladies were asking what they should wear. We asked Martin Charteris, and back came the answer: 'The Queen will be wearing night-time point-to-point kit', with no hint of what that actually meant!

*   *   *

The evening arrived at last, and it was a fine one. I was standing by the Copper Horse, and in the distance I could see people surging up the hill Eventually, the waves and waves of 'people that would not turn up' had reached about forty thousand and began to resemble an incoming tide in the gathering dusk. We were clearly going to have a major Loo problem – we didn't have any. Unforgivably I sent my friend Francis Gradidge off to try to purloin a block of Ladies Loos from the 'Sealed Knot' in the Home Park. History does not relate how many he got or whether or not they were occupied at the time.

We were clearly running very late. I was really frightened now and feeling rather sick because, although I had been working on this day for over a year, it had only just occurred to me that I was going to be held totally to blame for whatever happened that evening. The live television cameras would ensure that, if there was a cock-up, every last detail would be sent around the Commonwealth and the World.

Somewhere in the distance, I hoped, the Queen and the Royal Family were making their way towards us to light the first beacon of the nationwide chain. But the massive crowds had delayed the thousands of the Sealed Knot Society who were marching from their campsite in Home Park, and the members of the Lewes Bonfire Society with their flaming torches. Poor Raymond Baxter, the BBC commentator, was well into his second book of background detail but still there was no sign of the Royal party.

My glum thoughts were diverted for a while by having to arrange for the BBC to borrow one of our generators – theirs had blown up – and getting the TA boys to illuminate the resulting darkness with their World War II searchlights.

In the distance I suddenly caught sight of the Queen standing up in the State Land Rover waving happily to the hugely enthusiastic crowd – ah, this was better. She was wearing a green headscarf and matching coat – so that was what was meant by 'night-time point-to-point kit'! A note of optimism crept into Raymond's running commentary.

At last, having had an interminable line-up of the great and the good presented to her, the Queen was ready to take the torch to light the bonfire. But the torch wasn't ready for her. In fact, it had gone out. Then, once it had been frantically re-lit, the little boy who was to present it to her dissolved in tears – I knew just how he felt. Finally, the Queen went forward and lit the fuse.

I had been worried that the bonfire might not burn quickly enough to make an impressive show for the television cameras, so the Pains Wessex men had stuffed the inside with electrically-ignited incendiaries. I had asked a Major in the Royal Signals to be on the firing button, assuming he was a sensible sort. It would turn out my assumption was quite wrong. The Queen's fuse was burning nicely along the ground when suddenly, quite some yards away and well before time, the bonfire very obviously caught light. Having seen the fuse flare up, the 'sensible' major had pressed the firing button.

However, at last the two sources of fire were conjoined and our forty-foot high bonfire burst into impressive flames.

When a maroon exploded deafeningly in mid-air instead of the visibility flare that was supposed to go up, I gave a deep sigh and decided that I would have to come clean and admit what was happening. So I said, 'Your Majesty,

I'm afraid it's all going terribly wrong...'

And my already very high regard for Her Majesty rocketed even higher as she beamed up at me, and said, 'Oh, *good*. What fun!'... . I heaved a great sigh of relief.

Unfortunately things were about to get much, much worse.

We walked up the steps to the Royal Box where three chairs had been set out, one for the Queen, one for Queen Elizabeth the Queen Mother and one for the Duke of Edinburgh. I had been surprised that so few were requested and I was right, as the Duke of Edinburgh had to give his up immediately to Princess Anne who was expecting her first child. Lord Hunt was presented and we settled down for the 'Spectacular'.

In the dark somewhere, the band was playing determinedly. I explained the generator problem. The fireworks went off in lines down the Long Walk – impressive, but actually right in the middle of the forty thousand people who were 'not going to come'. It was a miracle that we didn't incinerate anybody. The final part of the display was a forty-feet-square 'set piece' firework of the Silver Jubilee logo. It went off on cue and for one brief second it looked fantastic. Then the wind changed and the smoke billowed towards us so we couldn't see anything at all.

The next part of the programme consisted of a series of live satellite television links around the world. These were supposed to be self-explanatory so I thought I could relax for a bit. We all looked hopefully at a large video screen to the right of the Royal Box. On it we saw Sir Edmund Hillary, mouthing what I felt certain were complimentary words about the Queen and the Commonwealth, but the sound had failed. Then Sir Edmund picked up a guitar; he and his companions were obviously strumming and singing to us. The Queen asked what was going to happen, and I explained that at the end, which couldn't come too soon for me, he would raise a glass of champagne and toast her. At that moment the television would come back on to the Queen so that she could acknowledge the toast. Eventually, the glass of champagne appeared and the Queen smiled and nodded.

Viewers at home apparently had no idea that we were having all these problems, as they were getting the sound perfectly.

We went then to Cardiff where a Welsh male voice choir was singing to us – in total silence. The whole Royal Family was transfixed by the silent mime show. We had put a television monitor in front of the box just in case we could not see the screens well enough. Through our legs crawled a BBC floor manager (Simon Betts, later to become a very accomplished producer), pushing everyone aside until he got to the monitor which he then thumped hard and frequently. The Duke of Edinburgh said to the Queen, 'There you are, even the BBC do it!'

The glass of champagne appeared soundlessly and was acknowledged, then we went up to Edinburgh Castle, where silent pipes and drums were playing with obvious gusto. I had resigned myself to complete failure when suddenly Simon Betts' thumping paid off and at a deafening volume the sound resumed. Again the Toast was offered and graciously acknowledged with no problem. It is interesting to note that it had taken only twenty-three minutes for the Beacon chain to reach Edinburgh.

Then to Northern Ireland, where a very young Gloria Hunniford – who was later to become a friend – did her bit impeccably. The glass of champagne went up and we were all fine.

Then it was time to walk down to where the Army Catering Corps was in charge of the ox roast. The huge beast had been slowly turning beside its raised fire for almost twenty-four hours, and the soldier turning the spit had that look on his face which clearly said: 'I didn't join the effin' Army to wind an effin' crank handle and turn an effin' cow ...'

Afterwards, as the Royal Family drove away, I thought ruefully that this was probably the last national event that I would ever be entrusted with. I went home exhausted and watched the next day's celebrations in bed. Much to my surprise, I was bombarded with messages of congratulation. Apparently, to everybody who was not actually there, it had been a huge success. To me, that just proved the old saying: 'You can fool most of the people most of the time.'

* * *

I started work on the next event, the Rolls-Royce Parade, immediately.

The Parade was made up of over two hundred vintage vehicles from all over the world, many from the United States. Most had been bought as an 'engine and chassis', and local coachbuilders had completed them, so no two were alike; the owners were pretty colourful too. We had arranged that we would form up on the Home Park in Windsor, drive in convoy up into the Castle, past the Queen in the quadrangle, and then down the Long Walk past the Copper Horse to Ascot Racecourse, where the cars would stay on public view for two days. It was all pretty simple really. What could possibly go wrong?

The Queen was surrounded by the great and good of the motor trade, who were about to present her with a magnificent new Bentley to celebrate her Jubilee. The Castle had provided a small dais for her to stand on but, probably in order to get a better view of the cars as they drove past, the Queen decided to stand not on the dais but on the edge of the path. This meant that a number of drivers, particularly those wearing large Stetson hats, did not notice her. So instead of turning to go down the Long Walk they tried to go round the quadrangle again to try to spot her, causing complete chaos as they fought their way back into the procession. Sir Martin Charteris and I rushed down to the gates and stood in the middle of the road blocking their path, and refused to budge. We learnt a lot of new American swearwords that day.

To finish the television coverage with a good shot I got a Spitfire, with its Rolls-Royce engine, to swoop down and do a low pass to salute the wonderful veteran cars which filled the whole of the Long Walk. It looked and sounded marvellous.

＊　　＊　　＊

The next event was a Royal Command Performance in a very large circus tent in the Home Park, at which the best of variety and circus artists came together in a strange but effective mix. Bruce Forsyth compered, it and when I spoke to him about it recently he remembered every detail vividly even though it was some thirty-five years ago. Mike Yarwood was going to do his 'Prince Charles' impression for the first time, Dame Edna Everage was making one of her earlier appearances in this country, and Olivia Newton-John was singing. Leo Sayer was the headline singer, and a small chap I had not met before came a little lower down the list. His name was Elton John.

The rehearsals were very fractious because of the continual streams of aircraft heading to Heathrow. A friend in Air Traffic Control had unofficially agreed to reduce air traffic for the actual performance, but not for the rehearsals. There were a lot of hissy fits going on, so I telephoned to plead with him and he said he would see what he could do. We could see lots of aircraft backed up far into the distance, when suddenly the first one turned and went off in another direction and all the others followed. My street cred with the stars soared.

The show went well, though at the presentations afterwards Dame Edna could not decide whether to curtsey or bow.

＊　　＊　　＊

The Air Tattoo at White Waltham, to which the Prince of Wales came, was itself incident-free but had a tragic aftermath. Hugh Lovett, a friend of mine from the Regiment who had left the Army and was now flying helicopters, asked if he could come and do joy-rides for us at White Waltham. But my team thought it too unsafe to have a helicopter flying around with so many vintage aircraft with no radios. So he went instead to the Biggin Hill Air Display where later that afternoon his helicopter hit a light plane and he and all his passengers were killed.

A few days later I was asked to go to the top of Shell Mex House on the south bank of the Thames in London to watch the River Pageant and firework display to which the Queen was coming. It was lovely for me, to watch an event that I did not have to worry about. I didn't think the River Pageant was very impressive – in fact we didn't even notice it – but the fireworks, which exploded either level with us or just below, were absolutely magnificent.

For me, the working year continued with the Royal Tournament and the Berlin Tattoo and other smaller events. A few days after that year's Royal Tournament finished, I received an important-looking package stamped with the Queen's Cypher with a note from her Private Secretary and a Silver Jubilee medal. Sir Martin had obviously asked if the narrow group of those who received this medal could be widened slightly to include me. I was thrilled; it was a marvellous souvenir of an extraordinary year.

CHAPTER EIGHT

Miles of Sausage and Lost Children – The Biggest Children's Party Ever

Once things had settled down after the Silver Jubilee I decided that I could afford to organise a large event without being paid every two years. I had the Royal Tournament and the Berlin Tattoo permanently on the books, and I was forever being asked to organise smaller events as well.

One day in 1978 a customer, Neville Labovich, rang me in the antique shop. He lived round the corner and had been involved with the Silver Jubilee Exhibition in Hyde Park for which he had received an MBE. He told me that the Queen had asked him personally to put on the largest children's party in the world in Hyde Park in 1979. Would I help? I said of course I'd be delighted, and immediately set about sorting out some military participants.

At the first committee meeting, which was full of many of those in search of 'Horlicks', I was able to announce that we already had acceptances from the King's Troop, Royal Horse Artillery, the Household Cavalry and the Massed Bands of the Household Division. We also had the Royal Artillery Motorcycles and the Red Devils Free-Fall Parachute Team. The committee seemed rather surprised. It then transpired that the Queen hadn't asked Labovich to put on the party at all, though she would be coming to it. It was actually the International Year of the Child, of which Lady Mary Soames, Churchill's youngest daughter, was the Chairman, that wanted to organise it. By then, though, everybody had agreed to join in so I didn't think I would mention the slight and subtle difference.

I was to be greatly helped by David Barnes who was, in his spare time, a professional clown called Barney. He also worked for Westminster City Council in a senior position (in our dealings with them it was sometimes hard not to conclude that the rest of the council officials were clowns as well). David was a great chap, very good at organising things and hugely enthusiastic.

It was in the run up to this party that I met the wonderful Gary Withers for the first time. Gary had started and was running 'Imagination', which was to become the most inventive and creative production company in Britain, if not the world. He was fitting up a television studio for DER for which I acquired a huge inflatable Harrier hide from the RAF, and was also building the world's largest Scalextric set. Years later we were to do 'Joy to the World' together in the Royal Albert Hall.

Over the months, I gathered together almost six thousand performers. Every performing group you could think of was happy to come and take part. A whole circus, hot air balloons, massed Punch and Judy shows, massed story-tellers, theatre groups, play groups – the list stretched on and on. The party would run for two days, with about fifty thousand underprivileged (today they would be described as 'disadvantaged') children being invited each day. The Commissioner of the Metropolitan Police observed, 'You do realise, don't you, that you've invited every single street gang in the country!'

We asked ninety charities involved with children to take part, giving them free tentage and power, and the committee set about raising the considerable amount of money needed to make everything free for those who were invited. Everybody gave their services for free and received no expenses at all. Food was a major problem, but we managed to get together enough to feed, not five thousand, but fifty thousand – twice! Here the plans for this party merged slightly with one I did for St John Ambulance in 1985, six years later, as many of the same people were involved. After the first Great Party I held a thank-you party for everyone who had helped, which was when I discovered how very much St John Ambulance had contributed, which is why the second party came to happen at all.

I thought it would be rather fun to have the longest sausage in the world. Sam Vestey (Lord Vestey, past Lord Prior of St John and now Master of the Horse), Chairman of Dewhurst Master Butchers, very generously donated a Cumberland sausage. I had arranged for a hundred Scouts to cook it, and British Steel donated four hundred-foot-long frying pans. At that time the longest one had been made in Canada, but it was a mere eight miles long. On the evening before the party the sausage factory telephoned.

'We've reached nine miles,' they announced proudly. 'And we've got enough skin for thirteen. Do you want us to carry on?' They had a chap from the Guinness Book of Records measuring it off as it came out.

I immediately rang the leading Scout, Peter Ingram. 'Thirteen! We won't even be able to cope with nine!' So I telephoned the factory and told them to stop at nine miles. But it took them a while to stop the machines, which is why the longest sausage in the world ended up being 9.98 miles long.

We couldn't have a children's party without a jelly so I designed a huge one twenty feet square and six feet high in the shape of Buckingham Palace. The jelly, donated by the manufacturers, would come down from 'up north' by tanker. A refrigerated base and a removable Perspex mould had been made. The idea was that just as the Queen arrived the mould and cover would be removed and a Royal Standard put on top, and she would be offered the first spoonful. But about five days before the event a man from the jelly company came to see me. He was a 'jelly technician', he told me. 'You need to be aware that if the ambient temperature were to rise by more than three degrees, the jelly would melt and probably drown the Queen.'

I said, 'Well, you'd be the most famous jelly company in the world – very few British sovereigns have been drowned by jelly!'

The august gentleman drew himself up in his chair and said gravely, 'We Take Jelly Very Seriously.' So that was the end of that.

The Queen had again donated a beast from the Windsor herd for the ox roast and we were given half a million slices of bread. In the end we were offered so much food and confectionery that David Barnes set up a bartering station near Speakers Corner where we swapped things we had too much of for things we still wanted. So five thousand Mars bars might be swapped for five thousand packets of crisps, with the various wholesalers also getting what they wanted.

Hugo Vickers, later to become a well-known royal biographer, ran the International Village, a wonderful mix of entertainment from all over the Commonwealth.

Some of the charities were very annoying, complaining about absolutely everything – it was an eye-opener to me just how uncharitable some people who work in charities can be. I told them that they were getting everything for free, so they could just get on with it and stop moaning. The final straw came when, just before the Queen was due to arrive, a lady from a children's play charity demanded that the whole site be closed down immediately. I looked round at the tens of thousands of children already gathered and said I thought it was a bit late to do that.

'But the site is unsafe!' she insisted. 'I've just found a splinter on one of the see-saws!'

So I handed her over to Mary Soames, who took her a few paces away. I never knew exactly what she said, but the lady concerned looked as though she was being punched by Muhammad Ali. The site stayed open.

The opening ceremony for the first party featured bands, and thousands of London children dancing. I had suggested to the schools authorities that they could have a competition to choose who would perform for the Queen. 'Oh no,' they said. 'We don't have competitions – someone might lose.' So they chose them instead.

The Queen and the Duke of Edinburgh arrived. The children had asked if the Queen could come in a coach, wearing a crown. Buckingham Palace said that the coach would be all right, but no crown!

As the Queen got out of the coach she asked, 'What's going to go wrong today?' I replied.

'I'm afraid everything, Ma'am.' She smiled broadly. But it was not far from the truth.

The Queen and the Duke got into the State Land Rover and toured the site, with me walking behind. I had chosen a route that kept to tarmac paths rather than going across grass, in case the weather was bad. As we went up to the top of the site before turning towards the circus tent, and the crowds started to thin out a bit, I realised to my horror that there – in splendid isolation at the end of the path – was one of the ladies' loos. As always, it was a very popular attraction and had a long queue outside. The Duke gave the ladies a cheerful wave as the State Land Rover drove by, and they looked horrified! For the next day, I remembered to move the loos.

We had organised a competition for children to paint a picture of the Queen. I hadn't seen the results until we came to the tent where the short-listed artists were waiting to meet her. The winning picture showed the Queen in a crown and robe, with lots of jewellery and carrying a handbag. That was all fine, except that the Queen was black. We all roared with laughter and Prince Philip said, 'Darling, you're going to have to check your make-up!'

Wherever they went the Queen and Prince Philip were surrounded by masses of very excited children. At one stage, when they had almost disappeared from sight, one of the protection officers remarked, 'It's lucky we live in a friendly country, isn't it!'

The format of the St John party, which was to celebrate the hundredth anniversary of St John Ambulance in 1985, was very similar to the Great Children's Party, but we were a little better organised the second time around. The party opened with thousands of St John volunteers formed up in a large St John's Cross. I had been working for months on this with Lady Ursula Westbury and my big ally in St John Gina Phillips, later Lady Kennard. A sausage even longer than the 9.98-mile one was delivered to Kensington Palace where it was 'met' by the Duke of Gloucester, who was Grand Prior of St John. It weighed just over four and a half tons and came in a huge refrigerated truck, laid out on special shelves so it could be pulled out a hundred feet at a time by the Scouts. I had devised a little ceremony; the Duke's cook came out with a large frying pan and we cut off a yard of the sausage and cooked it – it was delicious.

*   *   *

At the 1979 party, one of the biggest problems turned out to be lost children. For the first party I had put up a large tent which the military charity SSAFA agreed to man. Before the gates opened I went in and found a lovely old lady sitting knitting in a corner. I wondered if she was going to be quite enough. 'Don't worry,' she said. 'My friend's coming to help me at mid-day.'

I checked in a little later to find she had over seven hundred lost children and was in tears. So I got the circus to send in the clowns to keep the children smiling, and arranged for one of the bands to lead a procession around the site in the hope that parents would spot their children. It didn't help that I had sited the face-painting tent, run by the American Embassy, next to the lost children's enclosure, so the procession consisted of scores of unrecognisable painted lions, tigers and clowns.

By the end of that first day we had reunited all but twelve of the children with their families. The remaining twelve were taken by the police to their own homes for the night and returned the next day in the hope that they would be claimed. At the end of the second day there were still nine left over, and the poor little things had to be taken into care. 'It's not that unusual,' the police told me. 'Some people come to these sorts of events just in order to 'lose' their children for good.' I found that sad beyond words.

But the St John party lasted only one day, and fortunately no one was 'left over.'

CHAPTER NINE

❧

Of Loos and Ships and Ceiling Lights, And Cabbages and Kings

For me, the best thing about that year was getting to know Mary Soames, who is the most remarkable lady. She took me out to lunch after the children's party and I told her how I had completely failed to teach her son Nicholas gunnery at Lulworth, which didn't seem to surprise her at all!

She asked whether I could think of a suitable way of bringing the International Year of the Child to an end. I was about to rush off to Berlin for another Tattoo, so I thought quickly and said, 'Why don't we take twenty-five thousand children to Buckingham Palace to sing carols to the Queen? She could come out on to the balcony to listen to them.' Twenty-five thousand just seemed a good round figure; I had no idea where we would get that many children, but then I didn't really expect the idea to be accepted. I had only been in Berlin for a few days when I received an excited telephone call from Mary – the Palace thought it was an excellent idea. So I was hoist with my own petard. How the hell was I going to achieve it?

Once the Tattoo was safely under way I spent a lot of time on the telephone to London and sucked all my contacts dry. I soon had promises of a Household Division band and about ten thousand children. But when I got back to London in mid-November I hit my first major problem – the groups producing most of the children were adamant that I could not use a military band. They said the musicians were 'professional killers'! I told everyone not to be so ridiculous – the worst they might have done was to deafen somebody. I would have liked to ask what sort of life they thought their children would now be leading if their grandparents and great-grandparents hadn't bothered to fight Hitler! So I was introduced to a Salvation Army band who, I was assured, had played at Wembley (and probably lost...).

Then I heard that Cliff Richard might be willing to sing. This was very good news and I went immediately to the Hammersmith Apollo to meet him.

The place was surrounded by hordes of screaming women, the like of which I had never encountered before. But once inside, all was peace and quiet; Cliff was charming and could not have been more helpful. This was to be the first of many times that he was to generously support events I was organising. We agreed the carols we would sing and I put him in touch with the band and wished him the best of luck.

Because it was going to be dark I had asked for two thousand members of the Lewes Bonfire Society with their blazing torches to take part. I had not appreciated that they would have to carry a number of torches because each one did not last for very long. So we would have to put three pairs of water-filled skips down the side of the Mall and one pair just inside the gates of the Palace for them to deposit their used torches. We had also got permission to use the World War II searchlights that we had used at Windsor. These were to be manned by young cadets from a TA unit at Hounslow, who insisted that the proper words of command should always be used. So we were not allowed to turn the lights 'on' or 'off'; they had to be 'exposed' or 'doused'. The searchlights would be in the forecourt, with their generators hidden out of sight and hopefully out of sound. The Palace had agreed a dressing room for Cliff, and the band would use the guardroom.

All the participants would form up on Horse Guards Parade and be controlled by London District Head Quarters. BBC Television suddenly decided to cover the event live, which meant a mass of cameras and cables and, from my point of view, the prospect of not being able to hide what was going wrong. I just had to hope that nobody would notice.

The evening came and it was fortunately dry. On the cue from the BBC, I set the procession off. It looked marvellous as it came down the Mall, with the torches burning and the children singing. The Queen remarked afterwards that it looked much like the march on the Tuilleries during the French Revolution!

As the children came into the forecourt, the torchbearers threw their last torches into the skips just inside the gates. The Queen came out onto the balcony to listen to Cliff and the children, and was picked out by the searchlights, and the whole setting looked wonderful. But unfortunately, the skips had leaked and there was no longer any water in them, and after a while they turned into raging infernos – impressive, but not what had been planned. As the carols continued the Fire Brigade came in from the sides and put the fires out. The television coverage cleverly managed not to show most of this.

Afterwards, the key people went into the Palace and up to the Chinese Dining Room to be presented to the Queen. We made a strange sight – me rather boring in a suit, Cliff rather smarter in his 'show jacket' and the bandmaster in uniform. There was also a gaggle from the Bonfire Society, led by a splendid fellow called Les Ower who had come dressed as a Zulu in a home-made costume consisting largely of loo brushes. There was also a very strong smell of kerosene which filled the room. The door opened and a couple of corgis bounded in, took one sniff and bounded out again. The Queen came and met everybody, but kept her distance from Les and his associates.

*   *   *

I was constantly looking for different things to do, for bigger challenges in different fields. For some time I had thought of using Horse Guards Parade for an event, but I wanted to turn it around so that the audience was looking at the beautiful buildings and not at St James's Park, which is the way that most events are done there. Every so often I would try out my ideas for turning around the Queen's Birthday Parade with the new Major General. They never agreed.

I really wanted to do something for the service charity SSAFA (Soldiers, Sailors, Airmen and Families Association). By chance, in 1982 I met their boss, General Sir Napier Crookenden, a tiny, bubbly, very enthusiastic chap, who asked if I would think of an event to do for them. He suggested a Son et Lumière. I had never been completely convinced about Son et Lumières and had never seen one that captured my imagination, but he was a great fan of them and had just seen one in France which he had enjoyed very much. I said I was willing to have a go, and he suggested that we ask Rosemary Anne Sisson – who had recently written one for Pembroke Castle – to help. Her track record at that stage included episodes of *Upstairs Downstairs*, *Elizabeth R*, *Henry VIII and his Six Wives* and many other well respected works.

However, I was deeply suspicious of anybody 'arty-farty' coming in on the act, and Rosemary was, in turn, pretty unimpressed with having to work with 'a thick army officer'. But by the end of our first meeting we had both changed our views of each other; we became firm friends and later collaborated on many major events.

She and I had many happy meetings discussing the range of buildings overlooking Horse Guards which encapsulate so much of our history. As you face them, first on the left is the Citadel with its grass roof – the wartime communications hub. Next to it is the Admiralty, with the aerials from which signals were sent to the fleet during both World Wars. To the right of the Admiralty is the Admiralty House where many famous politicians lived, not least Churchill who walked across from there to Downing Street on becoming Prime Minister. The next is Wellington's office in the Horse Guards building itself, then Dover House (now the Scottish Office) in the lower ground floor of which Lady Caroline Lamb carried on her affair with Lord Byron. Then come the Treasury, the Cabinet Office, Numbers 10 and 11 Downing Street, and finally the Foreign Office – an amazing line up of famous buildings.

Rosemary decided to call the show 'Heart of the Nation' and wrote a brilliant script full of humour and historical interest. She wrote it from the point of view of a young Guards officer who was going to be carrying the Colour at Trooping the Colour the day afterwards. I found it fascinating working with a professional, having tried so often to write 'the words' myself – it's much more difficult than one thinks. Script writers seldom get the praise they deserve; it's always the star who takes the glory, but without the writer there would be nothing for the star to say or do.

We managed to get the services of Christopher Venning, a brilliant BBC radio director who taught me how to *listen to* voices rather than just hear them. Robert Ornbo, the lighting designer of the Royal Tournament, took on the task of covering a huge area on a very small budget. The BBC lent us a sound engineer, a mixed blessing as he worked in a very strange way, but at least we got the free use of his studios.

Using all our contacts, we gathered a truly amazing cast together to record the show. Anthony Andrews was the perfect person to play the young Guards officer. Keith Michell played his Henry VIII. Timothy West, Prunella Scales, Hannah Gordon and Robert Hardy all very generously agreed to take part, as did Edward 'Teddy' Woodward (a particular favourite of Rosemary's), Gordon Jackson, Maurice Denham – the list went on and on. I telephoned Barbara Windsor and asked if she would like to play Nell Gwynn. She was thrilled; she'd always wanted to play Nell Gwynn, she said. I thought it would be unkind to tell her immediately that she would only have one line.

Paul Schofield played Charles I, which we recorded in Horse Guards Building overlooking the actual site of the king's execution. The sound man brought a whole lot of cabbages with him; apparently cleaving a cabbage with a machete is the closest one can get to the sound of a head being cut off. I am not quite certain how they discovered that! We spent an extraordinary hour recording take after take, and chopping away until we were knee-deep in shredded cabbage, and all had a fit of giggles. Charles I very nearly went to his death laughing.

Sir John Gielgud had agreed to play Wellington with Jeremy Irons playing Nelson. Unfortunately Jeremy was called away at the last moment to film, so Christopher Goode gamely agreed to step in. Sir John turned up a day early, which we only discovered from the BBC when we arrived on the proper day, and duly turned up again, charmingly vague as to why he had come before on the wrong day. I introduced him to Christopher Goode. He looked him up and down and said, 'Oh dear, you're not Jeremy Irons, are you? How very disappointing.' Poor Christopher looked crestfallen but carried on and recorded excellently. Unfortunately, we had given Wellington the wrong lines to say, and did not realise until afterwards. 'You will never have confidence in yourself until others have confidence in you' should have been 'Others will never have confidence in you until you have confidence in yourself', but I didn't feel I could ask Sir John to come and record it again, and nobody ever noticed.

We got permission to put lights inside all the buildings but I was the only one with clearance to go into 10 Downing Street each evening to check that their lights were working. The Prime Minister, Margaret Thatcher, nearly caused a nasty accident when she threw open a window one day to ask one of our electricians if he would like a cup of tea and almost knocked him off his ladder. I would often meet Denis in the evenings, padding around in his slippers. 'Ah, dear boy, how about a small drink?' he would enquire. Sadly, I had to refuse every time as I had too much to do.

We managed to get quite a lot of publicity. Much to our amusement, on the opening night the BBC News outside broadcast van turned up to show it 'live' on the news.

'Where,' they asked, 'will Henry VIII and his entourage enter?'

I pointed out that a Son et Lumière took place entirely in the imagination. The reporter didn't seem to understand, and persisted. Quite what they showed on the news we never did discover, but the event was completely sold out and we made a very good sum of money for SSAFA. It was the first time that anybody could recall that the Parade Ground had been used that way round, and I hoped it boded well for future events there.

* * *

In the same year, 1983, I became involved with the America's Cup in

Newport, Rhode Island. Through a friend, Phyllida Stanley, I had met Peter de Savary and had organised the Naming Ceremony of our main yacht *Victory '83* on the Hamble. Prince and Princess Michael came and it was judged a great success. Peter asked me to go out to Newport and help him run a Royal Ball just before the racing started.

I went over and had a good look at all the possible venues. It obviously had to be one of those ultra-grand mansions overlooking the ocean, of which Breakers is the most famous. I rather fancied Rose Cliff, a pale pink copy of the Petit Trianon at Versailles, which could hold six hundred people for dinner and dancing. It was only by chance that I discovered that there were only two loos for the whole of the ground floor, and that they were unwilling to allow us to put in temporary ones, so we used the not-nearly-so-grand house next door, where everyone was much more co-operative and understood that people do need to relieve themselves from time to time.

Prince Andrew was coming out for the occasion, and the Americans were getting very excited. The bands of the Irish Guards were going out as well and the whole of Newport society paid through the nose to be there. The actual Ball itself took place during the run of the Tournament so I had to leave, having drawn up detailed instructions for someone else to put into effect. Sadly, *Victory '83* did not live up to her name and the America's Cup was won by the Australian Alan Bond.

* * *

In 1986, in my quest for different things to do, I found myself organising the opening ceremony of the World Chess Championships in London. Anatoly Karpov and Garry Kasparov were the two protagonists, and there had been much press speculation about whether either of them would turn up. I just got on and designed the thing. It was going to be in the Park Lane Hotel (which is, confusingly, in Piccadilly). I covered the whole of the ballroom floor with a huge chess board, and got Mervyn Harridence to make some eight-foot high chess pieces on which to put the vodka and caviar for the guests. He also made two even larger chess pieces – Knights designed by me – for the actual draw for who was going to play White and therefore have the first move. Levers opened the horses' mouths, and a mechanical hand would bring out a card. But the mechanism was slightly temperamental. Although I had learned from the raspberry tart episode that Margaret Thatcher, who was going to do the opening, didn't like to take direction, I still warned her to pull the lever firmly but not to jerk it. She immediately jerked the lever. The mouth opened, the hand came out then immediately went back in again, and the mouth closed. She looked at me quizzically, I mimed 'Pull it *firmly!*', and she tried again. This time all was well, and I went back to the serious business of eating as many different types of caviar as possible.

Incidentally, that wasn't the only time a recalcitrant mechanism nearly spoiled everything. In 1998, after many years' work by English Heritage, the Queen unveiled the newly-restored Albert Memorial. Albert's gilding had all been chipped off during the First World War as people thought Zeppelins were using the sun glinting off it to aim for London (this was rubbish, but the gold went anyway). Dame Judi Dench played Queen Victoria, Peter Bowles Prince Albert and Judi's husband, Michael Williams, the designer Gilbert Scott.

Just as the Queen walked up to us one of the riggers tapped me on the shoulder and said, 'I forgot to tell you – the button for the unveiling only works when you let it go, not when you press it. If she goes on pressing it, it won't work.' I could have thumped him. I quickly told Sir Jocelyn Stevens, the organiser, to tell the Queen. He said, 'I wouldn't dare tell the Queen what to do – *you* tell her!' So I did. It all worked rather well and only a few trees were burnt.

*   *   *

Planning for the fortieth anniversary of the Queen's accession began in 1991. I was always interested in doing any event that paid tribute to the Queen although I did not think that forty really counted much as a 'red letter' anniversary, but it seemed a good opportunity to try something different, and I had a number of ideas floating around in my mind. 'Floating' is the right word, as I get most of my ideas in the bath – there's something about hot water, steam and gin and tonic that makes my imagination work well.

A Royal Anniversary Trust (more 'Horlicks' seekers!) was set up to raise money for a number of good causes, mainly involved with young people. The Trust had been given the use of Earls Court 2, the new extension to the old Earls Court building which we used during the Tournament as sleeping accommodation for a cast of nearly a thousand. It was now to be the stage/arena and audience seating area. It was a long, high tunnel of a building with definite possibilities, having a very large floor space, a strong roof and good entrances and exits.

So when I was asked by the Chairman of the Trust, Robin Gill, to do a 'great event' there I was delighted. In fact, it ended up actually being called The Great Event, but I gave it a subtitle – Forty Glorious Years.

Guided by one of my Rules – 'If it's easy to do it's not worth doing' – I devised the most ambitious event I could think of. I came up with the idea of recreating the Royal Opera House Covent Garden inside Earls Court 2, but with a proscenium arch that opened up to reveal a large performance area behind. We would paint a three hundred-foot square map of the world on the floor of the hall, and there would be three motorised stages, each the size of the Royal Opera House stage, which could move around over the map. At the back, initially hidden by a Royal Standard gauze, would be a seated choir of a thousand, which seemed to be a good round figure.

Between the front of the proscenium arch and the seating stands would be a track which could be used by horses, vehicles and people. I did a sketch of what I had in mind and showed it to the Trust. There were a number of raised eyebrows but Robin backed me and we went off to talk to the BBC. Sir Paul Fox, who had recently retired as Controller of BBC One, ensured that the BBC gave it their full support. They were to prove tremendously professional and resourceful in turning my somewhat scrappy plans into something really special. For me, it was wonderful to have a professional designer, the BBC's Carol Golder, and a professional director and choreographer in Dougie Squires and Ken Caswell. Dougie was to become a great friend and was to direct all my shows from then on. The BBC producer was Michael Begg who had done the Queen's Silver Jubilee bonfire at Windsor so well. Altogether it was a very senior team.

For the first time I realised that I needed to set up a 'proper office'. Until now I had worked on the principle of not sending letters as it would only encourage people to reply. There is virtually no paperwork for any of my earlier shows. Alan Jacobi persuaded me to take on a PA. This I did, with some initial reluctance, and chose Catie Bland, the daughter of my friend Simon Bland who was private secretary to the Duke of Gloucester. Previously Catie had been PA to Julie Andrews and then to Queen Noor of Jordan, where I first met her. After looking after me immaculately for so many years she now works for the Prince of Wales. I have undoubtedly been the low point of her career!

With Catie's help many of my fanciful ideas began to become reality and we started recruiting stars and performers by the hundred. The finance was to come from sponsors, mainly the Royal Bank of Scotland, RTZ and Glaxo.

The show would feature the Massed Bands of the Household Division, the King's Troop, Royal Horse Artillery, the Pipes and Drums of the Scots Dragoon Guards, a large escort from the Household Cavalry Mounted Regiment, and from the Royal Mews the Gold State Coach and an Ascot landau. The BBC Concert Orchestra was joined by the National Youth Orchestra of Great Britain, and a choir of one thousand would include the Bach Choir under Sir David Willcocks and also a choir of boys from the Chapel Royal, St George's Chapel Windsor, and St Paul's Cathedral. On top of all this we had children from thirty-three Commonwealth countries – so nothing complicated then.

The list of participants kept growing by the day. One normally expects at least half of those approached to not be able to do it. But everybody I approached agreed to take part, and it was becoming a bit of an embarrassment as we already had so many. The construction was done by Alan Jacobi of Unusual Rigging. Worryingly, the whole show would have to be run by computer, since nothing as ambitious or complicated had ever been attempted before and normal methods could not be used.

Rehearsals were a complete disaster. Many of the stages and props were hugely complicated and the whole event depended on one very young-looking computer operator. The mechanics became more and more complex, and his brain and mine were going into overload. I was only saved by my excellent team. A continuous procession of stars and personalities – everybody from Sir Roger Bannister to Cliff Richard and Bobby Moore – came to my home for briefing before we started. Tommy Steele came one day in an open sports car which he just left outside and never got a parking ticket.

On the opening night, as I saw the heaving masses before me, I could scarcely believe that I had dreamt up all this in my bath. The Royal Opera House set looked fantastic as the Royal cars drove in, in front of the Royal Box. The audience were completely taken by surprise as they had not noticed the pathway. The curtain opened to reveal the full orchestra and Sir Ian McKellen. As he finished the introduction the orchestra and its stage moved backwards into the choir with Sir Ian clutching on to a lectern.

At the same time the King's Troop, Royal Horse Artillery galloped through the audience, and the wings above and at the sides of the stage flew out to reveal the vast map of the world. As the orchestra stage motored backward people behind it were picking up the cables. Alan and I sat clutching each other in total fear. The stage had almost gone back into the choir when suddenly it stopped. We prayed that it had not run over a cable as that would have been the end of the show.

Because the orchestra was still too far forward the guns of the King's Troop had to go into action further down the arena. This meant that Peter Hannam, the conductor of the hundred fanfare trumpeters, had to stand right in front of the guns. I looked through my binoculars at the back of his bearskin and tried to imagine how he felt staring down the barrel of the gun in front of him. After the crowning fanfare the guns fired a salvo. When the smoke cleared I fully expected to see the Director of Music lying on the ground. But Directors of Music are made of sterner stuff and he marched off gingerly, deafened but all in one piece.

Lord Hunt and Sir Edmund Hillary, this time in person, then told us about climbing Everest, and the composer Julian Slade played the piano to accompany a group of actors and dancers in a selection of his own music from *Salad Days*.

A full recording studio had been built, and we had The Archers in the flesh; it was quite strange to see what the people whose voices we knew so well looked like. Peter Dimmock and Brian Johnson introduced the dozens of sporting stars who were there, including eight members of the winning 1966 World Cup team in an open-top double decker bus.

Darcy Bussell danced beautifully, and Lonnie Donegan led us into a tribute to London that included Dame Vera Lynn and songs from *Oliver*! Wendy Craig came on with 'Christopher Robin' to sing 'They're Changing Guard at Buckingham Palace', and suddenly out of the wings the Massed Bands of the Household Division marched on in front of them. It was all totally splendid, particularly as it had not worked at all at rehearsal.

I had managed to round up a troupe of former Tiller Girls (more of them later), who were followed by Petula Clark, and Dame Gwyneth Jones with a touch of Wagner.

Throughout, a crown-shaped screen above the stage showed archive footage, and our one sad and reflective piece of the evening showed the children of Aberfan whilst a Welsh male voice choir dressed in miners' helmets and lamps sang 'David of the White Rock'. It was all very moving.

Raymond Baxter and Larry Adler introduced forty cars of the Queen's reign. I put Cliff Richard into a Mini, and when he asked why, I told him that his career and the Mini's had started at the same time (that's what researchers can do for you).

Judi Dench represented the National Theatre in her usual inimitable way; it was the first time I had met her, and she was to be very generous with her time and talent in the future. Then there was a My Fair Lady scene featuring Evelyn Laye in the Ascot Landau. She was getting on a bit and very doddery, but refused to take any direction about which way she should wave. 'It's quite all right, darling; I know all about these things,' she declared, and then proceeded to wave graciously to the orchestra, completely ignoring the Queen and the Royal family on the other side as she drove through. The legendary racehorse Desert Orchid was part of that scene as well. After that, Felicity Lott, Cilla Black and Michael Ball led into the Pipes and Drums and Irish dancers.

At last it was time for the Finale. I was by then a nervous wreck, and kept thinking of the poor young computer operator, who had not slept for two days and who held my entire future in his hands.

I had asked Derek Bourgeois, a friend from prep school and now conductor of the National Youth Orchestra of Great Britain, to write a drum symphony 'for all the Commonwealth children'. There were about two hundred of them and we had great trouble with them at the rehearsals that afternoon. They had all brought their national drums, and were supposed to sit on their own country on the great map of the world. But they wandered around in all the wrong places until I was moved to shout, 'Why don't you all go back to where you bloody came from!' There was a pregnant pause – a number of the escorts were clearly offended. What I had meant to say, of course, was: 'Go back to the place on the map where you started'. When the real finale arrived the children came on but, unbelievably, forgot to bring their drums so in the middle of the music they all went off again to collect them.

In the meantime, the newly commissioned Commonwealth Mace was to be presented to the Queen. Four young children from England, Scotland, Ireland and Wales went up and stood in front of the Queen in the Royal box. The Queen stood up and so, obviously, did everybody else in the box. The children, though, did not present the Mace, so after a while the Queen asked them for it. 'No,' the leading boy firmly told the Queen, following my instructions rather too exactly. 'Only after the music stops.' The Queen smiled broadly.

Anna Massey, as Queen Elizabeth I, was making a stately progress across the map towards the Royal Box to deliver the final speech when suddenly the drums started up again. Bourgeois had decided to play his Drum Symphony once more. Elizabeth I came to a halt somewhere in the middle of central Africa, and hovered uncertainly.

At last the music finished, the Mace was presented beautifully, and Anna then spoke part of the famous Golden Speech of Queen Elizabeth I, which includes the words, '...though God hath raised me high, yet this I count the glory of my Crown, that I have reigned with your loves.' She then performed an immaculate and very deep curtsey in her jewel-encrusted dress. Bizarrely, the only decent Elizabeth I costume we could find was one that had been used in 'Blackadder'.

At last came the National Anthem. Afterwards, the whole Royal Family joined the cast and audience on the map of the world, and Paul Fox and I presented the stars to the Queen and Duke of Edinburgh. Halfway down the line I noticed that Paul, with the Queen, had a slight hiatus but thought no more about it. Shortly we came to Evelyn Laye, who I presented to the Duke of Edinburgh. She looked blankly at him, and asked me, 'Who is he, darling?' I realised that she had probably asked the same of the Queen.

Some idea of the size of the stage could be realised from the fact that we had a milling crowd of two thousand people drinking on it, and there was still plenty of room to spare. As I was standing talking to Vera Lynn, I felt someone take my hand. It was young Oliver Sammons, Choir Boy of the Year, who had sung the role of Oliver Twist so bravely earlier in the evening, but now needed a little reassurance in the large crowd.

At the rehearsal that afternoon I had told Prince Edward, who spoke briefly about the Duke of Edinburgh's Award, that they had all better bring pyjamas because the show was going to go on forever. I was not far wrong. It was supposed to last for one and a half hours – we finally made it in just over three!

We saw the Queen into her car and I apologised again for the long over-run, but she said she had enjoyed it very much and congratulated me. We all then went up to the Gala Dinner, which by then had been cooking for two hours longer than planned.

A few days later a lovely signed photograph of the Queen and the Duke of Edinburgh arrived. Later still a certificate came from Robin Gill 'in recognition of practical and substantial support'. I suppose that was one way of putting it. He later congratulated me for realising 'his' concept. So all my musings in the bath had obviously been quite superfluous.

*   *   *

I love Christmas and have always thought it strange that the most popular festival of our year should be marked only by carol concerts and pantomimes. There was no big spectacular treat that I felt the occasion warranted. In 1981 Philip Gay, a friend from the Regiment, asked if I would like to be involved in 'The Story of Christmas' at St George's, Hanover Square. They had a small military band and lots of stars to do readings. Every year, the evening raised considerable sums of money for charities, particularly those for homeless young people.

I was delighted to be included and over a period of six years, with my friend Gary Withers of 'Imagination', I helped raise the production values. We made the relatively small church into a large theatre full of lights, with projections of stars on the ceiling and lights outside shining in through the stained-glass windows. Fanfare trumpeters from the Household Cavalry, in heavy Gold State Dress, played squeezed tightly together at the altar rail, only a few feet from the front row which normally included a member of the Royal family. We managed to deafen quite a lot of very important people.

But at the same time Gary and I became slightly frustrated as there seemed to be little more we could do with the show in its current setting. The whole thing had settled into a fixed format. I still felt that there was an opening for a large Christmas Spectacular but not, unfortunately, in St George's. By chance another friend, Maggie Heath, whom I had known for years, was Chairman of Save the Children's carol concert at the Royal Albert Hall. She felt there was scope for improvement and asked if I could do any better. I replied that I certainly could, but not with only a one-day hire of the Hall. We needed it for two days, one to build, the other to rehearse and perform. The day after Save the Children's concert was usually booked every year by the Oriana Choir but we persuaded them and their conductor, Leon Lovett, to join with us so now we had two days in which to do our special show. We decided to call it 'Joy to the World', in my experience the only time a committee has come up with a good title.

Gary Withers threw himself into the challenge with gusto. He produced a wonderful design, the highlight of which was a huge choir of fifty thirty-foot golden cherubs up in the roof. An extremely large chandelier would be lowered with Father Christmas on top, and for the Finale a Christmas tree sixty feet tall would rise out of the central stage. Even with two days this was extremely ambitious.

We gathered a wonderful cast. I telephoned Cliff Richard who immediately agreed to take part. In fact, he was to do nine of the ten 'Joy to the World' shows that we did. As a guest star Cliff is totally perfect. Apart from his obvious singing talent and great charm, he has no airs and graces, no vast ego that needs feeding and no tantrums. Just a thoroughly nice and co-operative chap.

I was determined to do the Twelve Days of Christmas properly. We would have real drummers, real pipers and ten real Lords A-Leaping; we would use ballet dancers as swans, we would have pantomime geese, we would have cancan girls as French hens, and so on. I hit a snag with the Nine Ladies Dancing. The only dance troupe I had ever heard of was the Tiller Girls, and they had stopped performing some years previously. However, I heard that a retired Tiller Girl was running the duty free shop at Heathrow. I got in touch with her and she agreed to see if she could persuade some of her old colleagues to join her. She could and she did, and I used them for many charity shows over the years. They were wonderful.

The ten Lords were brought together by Lord Colwyn, a very successful band leader and dentist, and caused endless mirth. Some were far from young, and one had even forgotten his own name, probably because his title had recently changed. They brought their parliamentary robes, and managed some impressive leaps on cue. We gave each of them a Dancing Lady afterwards to console them.

The BBC had agreed to televise the show and the producer was unusually laid back which was a huge help in our first uncertain year. Never one for doing things by halves I decided that we should invite President Reagan to say a few words by satellite from Washington, and Mikhail Gorbachev to say a few words from Moscow. We then asked the Pope if he would provide a televised message too. Everything was going well until Save the Children had second thoughts about using the Pope, I believe because of his Church's stance on birth control. I must be one of the very few people ever to have stood a Pope down for an event!

Gary and his team, with his preferred director George May, did a great job of putting the various bits together. The audience had no idea what to expect, but even so our committee of Maggie Heath, Gerald Powell and Hugh Taylor, initially under the chairmanship of Sir Christopher Benson, managed to sell the Grand Tier seats for £1,000 each, which at the time was a considerable amount of money.

The rehearsals were impressive but patchy. Gary and I never saw the second half of the show at all until it appeared in front of us live. The Princess Royal arrived, and the evening started with twenty fanfare trumpets. Then Ben Kingsley, James Grout and Peter Bowles started the story with T.S. Eliot's The Journey of the Magi – 'A cold coming we had of it...' It was not until we got to the Twelve Days of Christmas and three very saucily-clad

French Hens doing the cancan that the audience realised what sort of show they were in for. They relaxed immediately and enjoyed it hugely from then on. The first half finished with Father Christmas atop a great chandelier, being lowered from the roof. He was Alan Jacobi, who was in charge of all the rigging, and he was dressed, correctly, in green. Alan had been working all night and was exhausted, and had fallen sound asleep. Gary and I shouted at him as he came down, and the applause woke him, so he sleepily stood up and waved.

Before that, Ronald Reagan in Washington, obviously reading from a cue card, said, 'Welcome to all of you there in the Royal Albert...' – long pause – '...Hall.' Mikhail Gorbachev unfortunately had been called away because there had been a terrible earthquake, but we did have the Harlem Boys Choir from New York and a boys' choir from Moscow; they sang together, then all walked out hand in hand which was really rather moving.

The second half was sheer joy; we had never seen it before, so we were in the same position as the audience. Although we sat on the side lines grumbling away like Statler and Waldorf in The Muppets, Gary and I were thoroughly impressed by how clever we had been as we watched our plans unfold in front of us for the very first time. By the end of the night we had made over £800,000, which was pretty amazing for a carol concert.

*   *   *

In the second year we invited the Queen to be the Guest of Honour with the Princess Royal, who was President of Save the Children. We were thrilled when she accepted, and I immediately included children from all the Commonwealth countries in the programme. Soon after the Queen had accepted I received a telephone call from her Private Secretary, Sir William Heseltine, who asked me to come over to the Palace with Nicholas Hinton from Save the Children. I was amazed when he asked if I thought it was practical for the Queen to record her Christmas broadcast at the show. There had recently been a lot of controversy about the broadcast because someone at the BBC had leaked its contents the year before. I said that I thought we could cope with any practical problems, but I was concerned about how we would stop the Queen's speech appearing in the newspaper the next day.

The answer was that we would only tell the minimum number of people what was happening. In 'Imagination', only Gary knew. Our committee of five knew, and obviously the BBC. But we made sure that none of the production crew knew anything about it, even though they would be involved in its stage management. The BBC was going to provide an extra camera and microphone. We would produce the lectern but tell anybody who asked that it was for the Princess Royal.

The Christmas broadcast in those days was produced by the brilliant David Attenborough and we had a couple of meetings beforehand to go through the details. I also went to the Palace two days before and we taped out, on the ballroom floor, the size and shape of the stage, the positions of the lectern and the steps down to it, and then I walked the Queen through the physical detail of what she would have to do.

During rehearsals on the day nobody took any notice of the grand lectern coming on and a small lady with a handbag standing behind it chatting. This was Ella Flack, who was exactly the same height as the Queen and was used frequently by the BBC as a stand-in for camera angles and lighting.

We were sold out as usual, and as the audience came flocking in I was still rehearsing the Commonwealth children up in the Elgar Room. They were all going to be carrying the flags of their nations and in the interval they were going to come up and meet the Queen. The television broadcast would actually show them meeting her after the speech but in reality it was before. The children asked if they could give a Christmas card to the Queen. They had drawn it themselves and all signed it. I chose a tiny little girl from Nigeria to present it. Unfortunately, David Attenborough did not want to film the card presentation so I said we would do it after all the cameras had been switched off.

The show, which was once again written by Rosemary Anne Sisson, started with fifty Fanfare trumpeters in Gold State Dress. Then came the Creation (a minor theatrical miracle) and a very amusing Noah's Ark with Molly Sugden and Stratford Johns as Mr and Mrs Noah. Noah's 'children' included Ned Sherrin who wrote to me asking if he could play Ham, as that summed up his style rather well. The costumes for the animals were breathtaking and very funny. Later the Duke of Edinburgh wanted to use them for his new charity Arts for Nature (of which more later).

In the interval the Queen met the children, who were all thrilled. When she came to the end of the line the cameraman asked if I could ask her to turn to the camera and say 'Happy Christmas' to everybody. I said I thought that might be difficult to make look natural as the Queen was not an actress. But he persisted, so I asked her and she did it splendidly. When the cameras had been switched off, and the little Nigerian girl presented the signed Christmas card, the Queen broke into a wonderful smile and held out her arms and wished all the children 'a very, very Happy Christmas'. The cameraman asked if I could get her to do it again with the cameras running. I said I thought not.

Earlier Bill Heseltine had surreptitiously handed me the Speech, which I put into the special leather folder that we had had made for it. I later handed it to one of the stage management team and told him that he was on no account to open it but just to put it on the lectern. Afterwards, I told him, he was to collect it and give it to absolutely nobody but me.

When the time came I went to the Royal Box and escorted the Queen down to the stage. The Commonwealth children were in position and the Princess Royal had just made a short speech about Save the Children.

The audience were taken completely by surprise by the Queen's arrival on stage and jumped to their feet. Had they looked at the programme carefully they might have guessed something would happen. But no one did, and more importantly I had insisted that only press cameramen were to be allowed in, no reporters.

During the Queen's speech one of the smaller children started to wobble with his large yellow flag. But suddenly a hand grasped it from behind, and all was well. Afterwards, going back to the Royal Box, the Queen gave a little skip of relief and said she had thought the child with the yellow flag was going to hit her. 'You weren't the only one, Ma'am,' I said. After the show the Queen met all the cast. Roy Castle had led the Twelve Days of Christmas brilliantly, which was admirable because he was very ill with cancer. He told me that people kept asking him if he was afraid of dying. He said, 'I just tell them no; millions of people have done it and there's never been a complaint!'

After the Queen had met everybody, Bill Heseltine came up to me in mock dudgeon. He had kept his eyes on the file with the Speech and had asked the stage manager for it. But the stage manager had been told he could only hand it to Major Parker. Bill remonstrated, 'But I'm the Queen's Private Secretary.' The stage manager stood his ground stoutly. 'I don't care who you are, Sir. I'm only going to hand it to Major Parker.' I recovered the speech, congratulated the chap, and handed it over to Bill.

The show had been a great success but to me the greatest success of all was that there was absolutely no leak of the Speech in the press afterwards.

* * *

Each year we got bigger and bigger. One year I decided that the Seven Deadly Sins should be part of a 'triumph of good over evil' scene. Roger Moore agreed to play the Devil, an amusing take on his previous role as the Saint. I had intended him to wear large red horns until I saw the gossamer work of art that was his hair, so we left them off. Later, in a packed and stiflingly hot dressing room, he asked if I had a tea-bag because if I had he could have put it under his arm and they could all have had a cup of tea.

I persuaded the Royal Marines to provide six men to abseil out of the roof as angels appearing from the sky to overcome Satan. I was less than honest about what they were going to wear, but as I was running the Royal Tournament at the time they didn't ask any questions. When I showed the chaps the natty silver lamé hotpants, wings and winged boots they were to wear, they were somewhat nonplussed. I could hear them thinking: *I didn't join the effin' Royal Marines to dress up as an effin' angel in effin' tinfoil knickers.* The Senior NCO said, with a pained expression, that he thought the costumes were 'a bit much'. However, he said, they would wear them as long as they could wear their green berets as well. I told him that of course they could. I don't think that I have ever before been saluted by someone in silver lamé hotpants and a green beret. In fact, the boys enjoyed themselves a great deal as did a number of the young ladies in the cast.

Tickets always went very fast. In 1989 the box office telephoned to say that the Queen of Greece wanted tickets, and I had to tell them that we were sold out. All I could do was send a message advising her to book early next year. This she did, and bought about sixteen in the middle of the stalls in front of the Royal Box. Our control position was on the arena floor just in front of her. As I walked up in the interval to meet Princess Margaret she asked if she could come with me in order to use the Royal retiring room – not unreasonably, as she did not want to have to queue for the ladies. I took her into the box and Princess Margaret sank into a low curtsey and said she would be delighted for the Queen of Greece to use the Royal retiring room.

Every year for the Nativity Scene we would have a real baby playing Jesus. It was something of a challenge to find a willing mother with a baby of about three months old, which we discovered was about the right age, not too small and not too large. Experience taught us that baby girls are better behaved than boys, so equal opportunities came early in the manger stakes and swaddling clothes covered up any evidence.

We always invited the Choir Boy and Choir Girl of the Year as part of their prize for winning. On one occasion we had Antony Way, who went on to do other events. He also sang for us at the Fiftieth Anniversary of VE Day. Many of the other children also went on to greater things, including the now-famous actor Chiwetel Ejiofor, who we knew as 'Chewy'!

After five very successful years, Gary handed on the baton to Alan Jacobi of Unusual, and although my designs were nowhere near as good as Gary's the show continued to be a great success and a money-spinner. Dougie Squires took over as Director, and Maureen Mele was the brilliant administrator, ably assisted by Emma Bagwell Purefoy who had worked on several of my shows since 1991, and who took over from Catie Bland as my PA.

It was a challenge and a joy to try and find a different way of doing the Twelve Days each year. Once we did it as a circus and once – with Prunella Scales – in the form of letters written (by John Julius Norwich) between a girl and her boyfriend. The exchange began: *My dearest darling, that partridge – in that lovely little pear tree!* then escalated through chaotic quantities of unmanageable gifts, culminating in a lawyer's letter arranging for *the return of much assorted livestock*. One year Paul Scofield read for us – without sliced cabbages. Everyone from Michael Ball to the Dankworths took part and gave their time freely and generously.

But after ten wonderful years we began to think that it might be time to stop. I had done Christmas in so many ways that I was somewhat 'Christmassed-out'. I always think that one should stop doing things before they turn stale, so we pulled the curtain down. Every year I had been promising to have a Gothic cathedral as a set and for the last year, in 1997, we eventually managed it. In the Finale Gary Withers, an amateur actor and I came down dressed as the three Kings in magnificent costumes and offered up our gold, frankincense and myrrh, to a very startled baby girl Jesus, for the last time.

CHAPTER TEN

Bureaucrats and Other Headaches – G7, VE Day, VJ Day and EXPO

In my line of work I have discovered that it is seldom, if ever, a good idea to contract to work with the government – any government – for a national event. With one or two notable exceptions, it has meant dealing with civil servants who have no idea what they are doing, yet are certain that they know everything about conceiving and producing events. With the arrogance of complete ignorance they dislike taking advice from those who have spent a lifetime producing such things, and who may have picked up a few lessons along the way.

The brave exceptions to this rule have been the initial G7 Summit in Buckingham Palace in 1991, the VE Day and VJ Day fiftieth anniversary celebrations in 1995, and the Golden Jubilee celebrations in 2002. But the 1992 EXPO in Seville, the Millennium celebrations and the Royal Military Tattoo in 2000 were copy-book examples of how not to do things. In fairness to those involved with the Royal Military Tattoo, it was only the MOD Contracts Department who earned the Olympic medals for stupidity. The rest of the MOD support was very good – but then they were also mostly military.

*　　*　　*

In early 1992 the Foreign Office asked if I could think of a way to entertain the heads of state at the G7 Summit after their dinner with the Queen at Buckingham Palace. This would be during the run of the Royal Tournament which would cause me problems, but none were insuperable.

I suggested using the quadrangle inside the Palace so the heads of state could watch from the balcony above the Grand Entrance, and suggested that we should have the Massed Bands of the Household Division, including the Mounted Bands and Pipes and Drums, and that we should project images on the walls of the quadrangle with lasers and projectors. More controversially, the roof and balconies would be covered with fireworks and we would also, of course, have a large lighting and sound system. The Palace agreed in principle, subject to us convincing the Master of the Household that we would not damage the fabric of the building.

Alan Jacobi and I produced a budget and submitted it to the Foreign Office, who agreed immediately and asked how I would like the money. A dispatch rider came round to my house that afternoon with a cheque for half the sum, and not a single piece of paper had yet been signed! This has always been my preferred way of doing things – i.e. by gentlemen's agreement. I was just somewhat amazed by the speed at which it had happened.

The crucial meeting with the Master of the Household was set up, and I told my brilliant firework expert, Wilf Scott of Pyrovision, to bring his plans to the meeting. Wilf's usual style was that of an 'ageing hippie', so I impressed upon him the importance of making a good impression, and asked him to come looking respectable and in a suit. When Wilf turned up at the meeting in the Chinese Dining Room, I looked at him with horror.

'But I told you to wear a suit!'

'It is a suit – it's a boiler suit.'

'The Household' looked slightly surprised, and even more so when Wilf took out his tobacco (or possibly something similar) and started to roll a cigarette. He put it away when I thumped him, and the meeting went well. Wilf's charm and enthusiasm won them over.

The Deputy Master, Michael Tibbett, now Sir Michael, could not have been more helpful and soon everything was agreed.

I asked if we could have a room for the boys to use as a base which also had access to the roof. Michael offered us the Ball Supper Room. When I saw it I was amazed. It was very grand, all gold leaf and heavy mirrors, with huge chandeliers, hardly a normal riggers' rest room.

Michael said he would find 'some old furniture' for us which turned out to be late eighteenth century. A large table covered with an immaculate linen tablecloth was set up with silver urns of tea and coffee. Silver dishes of biscuits were put out, and a footman waited on the crew. The riggers could not believe it. After a few days Michael told me the riggers had eaten the Palace out of biscuits and could we please ask them not to take quite so many.

The music was rehearsed at Chelsea Barracks. The famous flautist James Galway came to the barracks to rehearse, and kept the bands in fits of laughter with endless jokes interspersed with musical magic.

I went to great lengths to ensure that the least number of people possible would know what was going to happen. In particular we needed to keep the fireworks a secret, as we didn't want the public gathering outside the Palace to watch.

I thought it important that the Royal Standard should continue to fly in spite of the fireworks. One day I stood on top of the Grand Entrance and had the flag man run up the different sizes of Standard so I could choose the best. I became aware of someone beside me and turned to find it was the Queen. We discussed the sizes of the Standards and she thought the State Standard, the biggest at thirty six feet by eighteen, would be the best. I agreed totally but pointed out the fireworks situation.

She laughed. 'Do you think it would be very significant if the Standard was burnt?'

'Oh, yes, Ma'am,' I replied. 'The End of the Dynasty!'

I reassured her that one of our boys would be sitting at the base of the flagpole with a strong black string attached to the Standard so it could be pulled in quickly if necessary.

Everything seemed to be going well – probably rather too well – when the telephone rang very early one morning. The caller introduced himself as 'Special Agent Wilson' of President Bush's security team. I stifled a laugh.

'Is it true,' Agent Wilson enquired, 'that you guys intend to fire off over a ton of fireworks from the Palace roof?'

'Absolutely!' I confirmed cheerfully.

'Well, I have to tell you that it is quite unacceptable to have our President stand so close to the fireworks.'

'Look,' I said. 'Your President is going to be standing next to my Queen, and there's no way I'd put her at any risk. In fact, the safest thing would be for him to stand as close to her as possible!' But he did not have a sense of humour and demanded to talk to the 'person in charge' of the fireworks. I reluctantly gave him Wilf's telephone number, then quickly rang Wilf to tell him this Special Agent would call him and that it was not a joke; Agent Wilson was for real so Wilf was not to take the mickey out of him. We heard no more.

The Tournament was in full swing so rehearsals had to be arranged for late at night so I could get there from the Tournament which normally finished just after 10pm. I explained to the Queen when she came to take the salute that evening what we were going to do and I have a feeling she watched the rehearsal that night. The rehearsal went surprisingly well but we fired no fireworks.

On the night itself I had to leave the Tournament performance to my Signal Sergeant to run which, apparently, he did annoyingly well, leaving me feeling slightly redundant.

We all waited in the Ball Supper Room. Just outside the door stood President Bush's 'man with the nuclear code suitcase'. He also did not have a sense of humour and looked on impassively as wheelbarrow loads of dirty gold plates from the dinner were pushed past.

In the end the whole event went really rather well. Nothing caught fire and no one was burnt. The Dynasty was safe! And so was the President of the United States.

The Queen greeted me immediately as I went in to her reception afterwards. She had obviously enjoyed it enormously and said I must come and meet the President. So I was introduced to the President of the United States of America by the Queen of Great Britain – quite something!

Afterwards I wished so much that I had asked the Queen and the Duke of Edinburgh to come and meet the riggers in the Ball Supper Room. The boys were an extraordinarily scruffy sight, filthy with cordite and oil and general roof dirt. They were draped over the elegant 'old' chairs and the perfect linen cloth was covered with black handprints. The silver biscuit trays were of course empty.

A couple of days later I was woken by the postman. 'Do I need to sign for something?' I asked sleepily.

'No, guv,' came the answer. 'Just that it's the first time I've ever delivered a letter from the President of the United States!'

The President had written, 'I just wanted to say personally how very much Barbara and I enjoyed the spectacular evening at Buckingham Palace.'

*   *   *

Some eight years later a further Summit was held in this country. A large production company asked me to help put forward a proposal to fit the criteria of the Foreign Office brief. I came up with a plan which was bigger and better than the previous one and we went to present our ideas to the Foreign Office. One official said beforehand how honoured he felt to meet me as he had been an admirer of mine for years. How nice, I thought; there's one who's going to be on my side. I was to be disappointed.

The 'Chair' announced that the last Summit's entertainment had been a great success and they wanted to do it better this time. That sounded hopeful.

I started to present my ideas when I was stopped by a lady asking why I wanted to use the Massed Bands of 'the Guards'.

'Because they play very well, they look very smart, they do what they're told and, most importantly, they're prepared to play in the rain!'

The lady answered that it was quite unacceptable to use 'soldiers in scarlet jackets' as it would 'remind everybody of our colonial past'! 'If it's really so important that we use then,' she added, 'can't they just perform wearing their ordinary clothes?'

The people from the production company surreptitiously moved their chairs away from me; I was clearly no longer an asset to them. No one else supported me in any way, so I excused myself and walked out, saddened to have it confirmed that political correctness meant that our pageantry, ceremonial and tradition, which most of the world admires, even envies, were now something of which we should be ashamed.

In the end, apparently, a girl with green hair sang in the Ballroom. I don't imagine the President of the United States sent too many thank-you letters afterwards.

*　　*　　*

The following year, 1992, would see the International Expo in Seville. In 1989 the Prime Minister, Margaret Thatcher, had been determined that it was going to be a far greater success than the previous one which had taken place in Vancouver. My old friend Simon Arthur, now Lord Glenarthur, then a Minister at the Foreign and Commonwealth Office, asked if I was interested in getting involved and I said that I would be delighted. Responsibility for mounting the British contribution to the Expo was suddenly moved from the Foreign and Commonwealth Office to the Department of Trade and Industry, so I went to their dreary offices in Victoria Street.

We were working from a blank sheet of paper but not knowing anything about a subject has never stopped me having strong views about it. The main parts of any Expo are the national pavilions, with each country vying to make theirs the best. I tried to impress upon the civil servants that the important thing was to have a concept first and then build a building around it. 'Do *not* build a building and then try to work out what to put in it,' I warned. They nodded sagely and produced a brief to put out to tender.

A number of production companies sent in proposals, which I was allowed to look at and comment on. One or two were great fun, in particular one from Terence Conran which suggested that the whole pavilion should be built as the White Cliffs of Dover with real sheep grazing on real grass on top. I thought that was marvellous fun. I wrote a number of points on all the submissions, all of which were ignored. The two main civil servants were Brian Avery, who had now become the 'world's greatest expert on Expos', and Peter Lambert, who was much more laid back and imaginative and would look after us all marvellously on our repeated visits to Seville.

However, disregarding all my advice, they chose an empty building. A very striking one designed by Nicolas Grimshaw with a huge water wall down one side but only a lot of escalators inside. I kept asking what would be the theme of the Pavilion, and was told, 'Great Britain'. How was it going to be portrayed? I asked. They didn't seem to know, so I removed myself from anything further to do with the actual pavilion.

It eventually consisted of two pods with 'mixed media' shows – in other words, people performed in front of a screen with other action on it. In the rest of the large space there was a Land Rover hanging up and some Marks and Spencer underwear. Outside stood a Rolls-Royce and Sir Francis Chichester's *Gypsy Moth*, with Union Flag sails which added some much-needed colour, and that was about it. There was a white tide mark on the glass at the bottom of the Water Wall which looked terrible, so I offered to jump in and clean it myself. Oh no, I was told, that would breach the working rules on the site.

The whole thing was such a waste of a very impressive building. I ended up refusing to take the VIP visitors round as I was so embarrassed by it.

Every country had a national day during which they could do very much as they wanted within a loose framework, and I took on the job of conceiving and producing this major event for Britain. We had available our pavilion, naturally, but also the use of the Palenque, an outdoor theatre in the round holding about six hundred people and a large marble theatre called the Auditorio, which seated about three thousand; it was all very splendid.

Brian said we needed somebody to pull together the substantial numbers of cultural events that were going to be running during the year. I was much against bringing in what I rudely called 'an 'arty-farty type'. I could not have been more wrong, just as I had been about Rosemary Anne Sisson. Luke Rittner was a joy. He had been Director General of the Arts Council and was extremely knowledgeable about all things cultural. We were to become great friends.

Together Luke and I put together a pretty impressive programme. I gathered military bands, pipes and drums, choirs, fanfare trumpeters, dancers and about three hundred other participants. We were going to do the Opening Ceremony in the Palenque and a further four shows there during the day and evening, all of which ended up playing to highly enthusiastic packed houses. As the main event in the Auditorio, Andrew Lloyd Webber's Really Useful Company had agreed to mount a major concert of tunes from his musicals with a large cast of stars including Sarah Brightman and Michael Ball. It had all the makings of a marvellous show. The evening before, the Royal Liverpool Philharmonic Orchestra and Chorus would perform Mahler's Third Symphony in the Cathedral.

We had huge problems getting all our scenery and technical equipment out to Seville, not least because of the 'handling charges' to move about the site. It cost more to move the lorries five hundred yards from the gate of the site to the theatre than it had to drive them out from England.

The Prince and Princess of Wales were coming to our National Day, which immediately put it at the top of Seville society's 'must do' list. Their imminent arrival had attracted immense press attention, and the excitement nearly reached hysteria. The Palace had wanted to split the couple and get them to take different routes on the site. I said I was having difficulty organising one Royal route, let alone two. I also thought it was likely that, if they did split, the press would follow the Princess rather than the Prince and I suspected this would not have been popular.

The evening before Britain's national day arrived. The Liverpool Philharmonic had been held up at the airport and got to the Cathedral with little time to spare. Moments before the Waleses were due to arrive I popped in to the conductor's dressing room to find him still in his underpants. To give him time, I told the Prince and Princess that there was a very fine gold altar in the Cathedral and that they might like to go and have a look at it. So Sir John Ure, the very urbane and charming Commissioner of the British pavilion, duly took them off while I rushed back to see how the conductor was getting on.

The concert started with Handel's Coronation anthem 'Zadok the Priest', for which I had lent the orchestra six of my fanfare trumpeters. It was simply magnificent. The Opening Ceremony the next morning went quite well, except for the firework finale; that was to go off uninvited some time later during one of the other performances, much to everybody's surprise. But at the time no one noticed – again a case of 'Never tell people what is supposed to happen. Then they won't know when it doesn't.'

The Red Arrows Air Acrobatic Team had come over to do a display that covered the whole of Seville and looked and sounded wonderful. Too late, I realised that it could not be helping the rehearsals for the Andrew Lloyd Webber's show that night. I understand there were quite a few hissy fits.

At the end of the Waleses' tour, at the Spanish pavilion, I had arranged for a free-fall parachutist to drop into the lake nearby with a message of greeting to the Royal couple. At this stage the Princess disappeared for what seemed like an eternity. I was surprised how little concern the attendant Household seemed to be showing; years later, of course, we found out about the 'problems' there were at the time. The parachutist waited, dripping, to deliver his greeting. The evening concert was excellent and Andrew Lloyd Webber gave a party afterwards at which we all got very relaxed indeed. My task was done, and I was glad it was over.

A couple of months later, I was in Stockholm looking at the King of Norway's Royal Guard who were coming to the Edinburgh Tattoo later that year. I was in my No. 1 Dress with scarlet hat, gold cross belt and spurs, and an American general was heard to remark, 'If that's the way their majors dress, what the hell do their generals wear?'

After the parade I had lunch with the King. Everybody was speaking English to each other even though I was the only Englishman there, which I thought was extremely polite. The King asked what I had been doing and I told him about our National Day in Seville. 'Oh, so you are the person to blame!' he said. 'The Norwegian National Day was the day after yours, and everybody spent the entire day talking about the British one, and not ours!' He smiled. 'I was very annoyed!'

*   *   *

In 1993 I was beginning to take note of anniversaries, both to use them in my current regular shows and as opportunities for new events. I had been looking ahead to what I might do at the Royal Tournament in 1994 and 5 to mark the fiftieth anniversaries of D-Day, VE Day and VJ Day, and it became clear that John Major's government was intending to mark them only in some very minor way.

However, the new President of the United States, Bill Clinton, had different ideas. Presumably seeking the veterans' vote he decided that D-Day would be marked with a massive American naval presence and a large number of events in Normandy.

Our Government madly tried to catch up and produced a plan for a great celebration in Hyde Park which would include amongst other things 'spam fritter mountains'. Our veterans were up in arms immediately and quite correctly pointed out that many thousands of men had died on the beaches and inland, so the anniversary of D-Day should be not a 'celebration' but a 'commemoration'.

I received a telephone call one day to say that Ian Sproat wanted to see me. He was Minister of Sport at the time, and I had difficulty in understanding quite how, in that role, he was going to be responsible for a national event. I told his assistant I was rather busy, but he persisted so I said that if the Minister would come and see me I would give him breakfast.

Ian Sproat tried to persuade me to revive the Government's plans. I said that I was willing to help but that there was no way any of the things they were expecting to do would ever work. They must rethink their ideas completely. Later I was asked to go to the House of Commons for what turned out to be a full meeting of the Committee in charge of whatever might happen. I was completely unprepared for such a presentation, but produced a few half-baked ideas. They fell on them with glee, even though I was not yet ready to finalise anything.

That was the last I heard of Mr Sproat, but the MOD had found a very good project leader, Brigadier Tom Longland, with whom I was to work closely in the near future.

D-Day was the first priority. Although the main events were to be in Normandy, the Government was keen to host the President and other 'Allied' leaders in Portsmouth. We talked through all sorts of ideas, but settled on a dinner in Portsmouth's town hall followed the next day by a drum head service overlooking where so many of the assault craft had left for France.

However, the general public wouldn't be able to see anything much. I told Tom that the cheapest way of entertaining the maximum number of people, over as large an area as possible, was some sort of firework/pyrotechnics display. He asked me to present my ideas to the Steering Group, which was chaired by Lord Cranborne (now the Marquess of Salisbury) who was then the Lord Privy Seal and Leader of the House of Lords. This committee was in a completely different league from others I had met. I suggested a multi-media event using very large video screens to cover two main sites in Portsmouth that would allow around eight thousand people to watch something worthwhile. We would tell the story using archive film, readings, pyrotechnic battle effects and stirring music. A lady at the end of the table got very enthusiastic about the whole thing; I discovered later that she was Dame Sue Tinson of ITN. We became friends and she was a great supporter and help during the rest of our time working on the anniversaries. I went away encouraged and wrote the script, and my lighting designer Robert Ornbo put together a brilliant series of images.

I went back to the Committee and, with some pride, told them that I had actually managed to tell the whole story of World War Two without mentioning the Germans once. I think they were highly amused.

At about the same time General Sir John Mogg, an old friend from my time in Germany, asked me to do something for the D-Day veterans at the Royal Albert Hall. He asked me to a meeting of the Veterans Association in the Union Jack Club. 'You might find the whole thing a little strange', he warned. I did – it was so democratic that it was difficult to work out who was in charge. Afterwards, Major General Peter Martin, a leading veteran, and John Mogg and I sat down and decided what we would do.

I came up with the idea of building the front of a life-sized landing craft on the stage of the Albert Hall. The ramp would lower to let various displays and stars walk or march on. With the help of Charles Messenger, my military historian friend from Sandhurst, I wrote a narrative script and a mass of generous stars again agreed to donate their services. It all went off well, and Dame Vera Lynn brought the proceedings to an end as only she could. I went straight down to Portsmouth and the D-Day event there that evening went as well as could be expected, although we did set light to a number of things that we should not have. Tom Longland seemed very pleased so that boded well for our proposals for the VE Day anniversary celebrations.

A wonderful civil servant (a rarity!) now appeared on the scene. Peter Young was urbane, extremely polite and very switched on. He had been seconded from the Foreign Office to the Department of National Heritage who were the organising ministry. He had a great sense of humour and I think was rather thrilled to be doing something more exciting than writing dry ambassadorial letters.

The Department's brief for the VE Day celebration was quite specific about what they wanted and they laid down a series of instructions. But I looked at them and decided we needed to do something completely different. Even the Silver Jubilee Celebrations, the largest since the Coronation, had been on a smaller scale than what we had in mind. The ceremonial side, which of course would be magnificent, was outside our remit. We were going to try to re-create some of the actual VE Day celebrations, and I hoped to capture some of the spontaneous excitement that I had seen on the newsreels. 'Commemoration' would play an important role later.

But I couldn't find any precedents to help me, so I had to invent a new way of doing this sort of thing. We had a blank sheet.

Alan Jacobi and I went to present our plans to Tom Longland and Peter Young, and to representatives of all the interested bodies such as the Royal Parks, the Metropolitan Police and London Transport. My proposal was materially different from what we had been asked to do but I managed to persuade them that my ideas were better.

We got the job and started planning and designing in earnest. No sooner had we started than things began to go wrong. The Royal British Legion had booked Wembley Stadium for a huge concert. Normally this would not have mattered, but it was going to be in direct competition with what we were planning in Hyde Park. So I was asked to try to get them to cancel or move it.

In the meantime I was asked to address a full meeting of the Steering Group, which consisted of all the Ministers of the Departments involved. It was headed by Lord Cranborne, for whom I had by this time developed a huge respect. It was fascinating to watch him finessing the multitude of political problems that beset us.

It was a daunting meeting of some seventy people. I started by saying, 'So this is what the Great and Good look like,' which broke the ice as they all laughed. When I finished my probably too-flowery presentation Robert Cranborne said, 'Well, that all sounds fine. It's very ambitious, though. Just out of interest – have all the previous things that you have done been a great success?'

'Well,' I said, 'most – except trying to teach the Minister for the Army tank gunnery, which I failed to do completely!'

Nicholas Soames, whom I had taught at Lulworth and who was now a junior minister at the MOD, jumped to his feet and remonstrated loudly, and the meeting dissolved in laughter. It was a good start.

The Royal British Legion was not impressed with my pleas to cancel their concert. They had, they said, lined up thousands of male voice choristers, and a number of stars had agreed to take part. This was, of course, exactly the sort of event that I wanted to do, so I tried to persuade them to join us. At a press conference in the Banqueting Hall in Whitehall the Prime Minister, John Major, outlined what was to happen at our event. This included the Opening Ceremony in Hyde Park, and the Heads of State ceremony at St Paul's followed by another in Hyde Park, the lighting of a nationwide beacon chain and a final concert. He also mentioned the Royal British Legion concert at Wembley. As I was driven away from the Banqueting Hall I received a call to say there were some serious financial problems with the massed choirs for the Royal British Legion event. I went straight to RBL's offices in Pall Mall and tried again to persuade them to join us. They were still reluctant but I later recruited the help of Bob Reader, whom I knew slightly and who produced the Festival of Remembrance in the Royal Albert Hall each year, just as his father Ralph Reader had done before him. He was a great help and the RBL eventually agreed to join us, which was a great relief.

Everything seemed to be on track, until I got a telephone call early one morning from Tom Longland. The Prince's Trust wanted to mount a big concert outside Buckingham Palace during the run of our event. This was the same problem all over again, but more so because the Trust had great clout and could call upon virtually any star they wanted. That would have completely sunk us.

Tom asked what we could do. Probably very little, I replied, unless Ministers were prepared to stop them. I suddenly had an idea, and suggested that we reproduce the Royal balcony appearance of the actual VE Day, with the Queen, Queen Elizabeth the Queen Mother and Princess Margaret. We could march the massed bands down from Hyde Park, and have some stars singing on a stage at the centre gate. In one minute flat I had conceived a brand new event.

Dame Vera Lynn and Harry Secombe immediately agreed to come and sing, and it was all looking good until an 'expert' told me that we wouldn't attract a big crowd – forty thousand at most, he said, and that would barely make a mark in the area outside the Palace. I simply could not believe that, but he held firm. So I telephoned Cliff Richard. He had far more than forty thousand fans, so if he sang that would double the crowd immediately. As always, he was very generous and agreed at once. I got permission to put daylight fireworks on the roof and got agreement for a fly-past of about twenty-four aircraft. A World War II Swordfish would precede the Battle of Britain Memorial Flight with a Spitfire, a Hurricane and a Lancaster bomber, and the Red Arrows would bring up the rear.

The plan was to get the massed bands to lead people Pied-Piper fashion down from the park. The MOD would not allow me to put a proper sound system down the Mall because, they said, 'nobody will come' and it would be too expensive.

The preparations in the Park were going well. An enormous Veterans'

Centre was set up by the MOD and was extremely successful, not least in reuniting old comrades who had not seen each other for decades. The stands and performance areas were brilliant, and best of all was the World War Two Museum Pavilion. The National Army Museum and the Imperial War Museum had declined to lend any meaningful artefacts as they said, not unreasonably, that security would be a big problem. So Jonathan Park, the brilliant pop designer, and Bill Harkin had devised a 'World War Two Experience'. My friend Charles Messenger provided the historical input. Using acting groups and clever sets, they led visitors through the Blitz, through 'Battle in the Air' and 'Battle at Sea', ending up with a full blown VE Day street party where everybody was given a balloon, a flag and a bun.

Jonathan had designed a remarkable stage, with an original Spitfire and Hurricane mounted on tall cranes at either side, which would accommodate a choir of three thousand for the first concert, and also ballet dancers and orchestras for the Heads of State ceremony. But we still had no idea what the last concert might be. I set about trying to persuade the Prince's Trust to come in with us and use their pulling power to draw on a younger generation of stars. Tom Shebbeare, who was running the Trust at the time, was enthusiastic and imaginative and had masses of good ideas. Eventually the Trust agreed to come on board and immediately got a marvellous number of very big names. They asked George Martin, the Beatles' producer, to direct their show. But almost at once things seemed to go slightly adrift. The Trust's liaison officer said that 'his stars' would not like the military connections of the event. I pointed out that it was a WW2 Veterans' event to celebrate the end of the war, but he said, tellingly, 'We don't want any old men with medals there.'

So that was the end of that. Robert Cranborne skilfully extricated us from the arrangement, and I was left to instantly invent a second concert. As always, Dougie Squires came up trumps as did Rosemary Anne Sisson; they wrote a show around fifty years of British musicals. After the event I mentioned to the Prince of Wales how sad it was that the Prince's Trust concert had not got off the ground. I repeated the 'no old men with medals' remark and he was horrified, and most annoyed that people frequently said things in his name without him knowing anything about it, and most certainly not agreeing.

Meanwhile, the administration of the whole event was not going well. There were too many willing but inexperienced service officers in key roles. We gradually replaced them all with women who, despite their extreme youth, would have been able to move an Army group without any problems. More than a hundred stars would perform over the three days, and just sorting out their transport, reception and welfare needed a genius. But they were all performing for nothing, not even expenses, so the least we could do was look after them well. The bits of the military that worked really well were at the top, namely Tom Longland and the officer running the Heads of State service at St Paul's. The rest of the jobs we took over with the exception of the Royal Box seating. When the MOD told me that they had got a computer programme to organise the seating which was 'infallible', I groaned. To me, the words 'computer' and 'infallible' did not sit well together.

Once the construction was finished, I drove Robert Cranborne around the site in my golf buggy and he seemed pleased. All we needed now was actually to do the show.

All events were free but in order to keep control of numbers tickets for the concerts had to be applied for and issued. Where events are concerned, there are always arguments between local authorities – in this case Westminster City Council – and the organisers. The authorities need to be certain that an event is safe and that all necessary facilities are provided. We worked from what we called 'the pop code', which told us things like how many people we could have per square metre, and how many loos we needed. It's all fairly sensible stuff but sometimes one is unfortunate enough to have a really stupid local authority official. In this case we were lucky; Brian Blake was someone I knew well and respected, so we were going to be all right. However, they would only allow us a total of sixty thousand for the concerts in the park. We disagreed, pointing out how enormous the site was. Finally Alan Jacobi stopped the argument by saying that we would agree to their now increased number of seventy thousand. He then, with a perfectly straight face, told them that the tickets would all be numbered but that for 'security reasons' the numbers could not be consecutive. The council were happy with that and Alan printed a hundred thousand non-consecutively numbered tickets and fortunately everything turned out all right!

The night before the opening we had our one and only rehearsal for the first concert. Three thousand singers including 'my' choir, the Morriston, of which I'm a Vice-President, turned up in fine voice and good humour. They would be conducted by Owain Arwel Hughes. The Tri-Service Massed Bands would be conducted by the Principal Director of Music of the Royal Air Force. We had a fantastic cast of over fifty stars which included Cliff Richard, Lionel Bart, Honor Blackman, Ute Lemper, Elaine Paige, David

Clark and of course Dame Vera Lynn. We also had almost a thousand participants ranging from wartime veterans and Chelsea Pensioners to the Land Army and Bevan Boys.

Dances and complicated excerpts from various musicals required exact timings from the band. Everything had to work perfectly as it was being televised live. It became immediately obvious that the military conductor could not cope. All the other performers were getting very annoyed as the cues weren't working at all well.

I had a swift conference with the BBC and my key people. We would have to change conductors. Tom Longland agreed to back me. I took the conductor to one side, and explained that we were going to have to replace him as we had no time left to get things right. He was very upset, and started arguing. Suddenly from above us a voice said, in a marked Welsh accent, 'You've got to go, boyo – you're effing useless!'

Owain Arwel Hughes agreed to stand in, without any preparation, and immediately things improved. Fortunately we had a short window on the Saturday evening for another rehearsal before the gates opened.

That morning we were thrilled by how many people turned up for the Opening Ceremony. Queen Elizabeth the Queen Mother and Princess Margaret were the Guests of Honour and the Prime Minister, John Major, was going to make a speech followed by a few words from Queen Elizabeth. I went up to the Royal Box to check everything. In the centre of the front row were two large gold chairs for Queen Elizabeth and Princess Margaret. As I was standing there a young naval officer walked past carrying the two specially bound and gilded programmes for them. He put them at the very end of the front row. I asked him who the hell they were for – had he not noticed the two gold chairs in the centre?

'No,' he replied, 'the computer says that seats 1 and 2 in Row A are the best in the box.'

'And who,' I asked, 'is going to sit in the big gold chairs?'

He looked at his list and said, 'Oh, the Lord Mayor of Westminster, I think.'

I groaned. 'And where, just out of interest, will the Prime Minister be sitting?'

The 'infallible' computer had put the Prime Minister somewhere that would have meant him walking in front of Queen Elizabeth to get to the microphone. It was not the poor chap's fault, but it didn't help me very much just as we were about to start. We decided to seat them all as they came with the obvious ones going in the front row; even so the Lady Mayoress of Westminster was in the second row somewhere, and the Chief of the Defence Staff was sitting behind a pillar.

Queen Elizabeth arrived and as usual radiated sunshine wherever she went. All our troubles were forgotten and the ceremony went off perfectly. Even the parachutists came in on time, no easy matter with Heathrow Airport just down the road. The Prime Minister, who perfectly understood the seating problems and was more than happy to be placed to one side, spoke very well, to be followed by Queen Elizabeth who touched everybody there by her simple memories of the war and all the sacrifices people made. We started to clear the crowds at about five o'clock so the concert audience could come in. Even those with tickets for the concert had to go out and come in again so that we could keep control.

Just before the Princess Royal arrived my head policeman came up to say he was very worried. There was a large contingent of about two hundred and fifty Hells Angels in the audience, and he didn't know how they would behave. I was too busy to worry so I just said I was sure it would be all right. The audience was very mixed and did not look like one that was going to get out of control. The concert was really rather good. The German cabaret artist Ute Lemper did a fantastic Marlene Dietrich impression, singing 'Lily Marlene', and all my old friends from stage and screen did their pieces immaculately. Afterwards I went back to my policeman and asked about the Hells Angels. He said, 'Oh, they behaved immaculately throughout, and when Vera Lynn came on they all stood up, sang and cried!'

On the Sunday the fifty-six Heads of State or members of foreign Royal families all went to St Paul's for a service and in the afternoon came to us for a Celebration of Peace and Reconciliation. The security boys caused us considerable problems by demanding that the audience be kept well away from the Royal Box. This made a complete mess of my plans which were supposed to involve all the public in the celebrations.

Vice President Gore was representing the USA. The President did not come because he had yet to do a State Visit. Thank goodness he didn't; even the Vice President's protection squad totalled twenty, in all shapes and sizes from good-looking girls to heavyweight bruisers. My orderly, Lance Corporal Stokes of the Welsh Guards, had the time of his life. Firstly, he was probably the first guardsman ever to stand on the balcony at Buckingham Palace and secondly, the Vice Presidential team took a tremendous shine to him. He went off with them one evening and came back in the morning looking very, very well-scrubbed, with a large box full of personal gifts – cuff links, pens, tie clips, paperweights – from the Vice President. That certainly made my job easier as they calmed down a lot.

I needed a focal point for the Heads of State ceremony and had decided to build a very large geodesic dome some thirty-five feet high. On this globe were drawn all the countries of the world, their shapes made up of their national flowers. Inside the dome, the night sky had been done with fibre optics, and in the centre a 'Table of Peace and Reconciliation'. Around the outside of the table was a laurel wreath; its leaves came out and were going to be signed by each of the Heads of State, as a token of their desire for peace in the world. They would then be put back into the wreath by the young children to whom the pledge had been made.

Sir Ian McKellen introduced the celebration and was so taken with the massive crowds that he sent one of the stage managers off to buy him a throw-away camera so he could record the scene from where he stood.

It was a very hot day and I was worried about the children being out in the sun, so I passed a message to the Queen to say that we were shortening the event and explaining why.

Chicken Shed, an inspirational theatre company of mixed-ability young people from north London, performed 'A Peace Worth Having' by one of its founders, Jo Collins. Each child had on a t-shirt with the national flag of one of the Heads of State present. They were supposed to take 'their' Head of State to the globe and invite them to sign the laurel leaf for the peace table. A child came forward to collect the Queen and that worked well. The second most senior Head of State was King Hussein of Jordan (the seniority of Heads of State is determined by the length of their tenure). Nothing seemed to happen so, knowing King Hussein quite well, I took him down to meet 'his' child. The rest got the message until we got to the High Commissioner of New Zealand. It transpired that the High Commissioner for Australia had gone off with the New Zealand flag. 'Bloody typical,' said the New Zealander, and I rushed off down the line to rescue his flag for him.

All the children had learnt a few words of welcome in the language of the person they were escorting, in some cases so well that some of the Heads of State thought the children were from their own country and engaged them in animated conversation, which did not get them very far.

The next day was the Buckingham Palace balcony appearance and Sing-Song. I was really worried, and praying that the experts would be proved wrong. The Massed Bands prepared to march down from Hyde Park to the

Palace and we just hoped that the people would follow. But I need not have worried; the police told me that there were at least four hundred thousand people there already.

The bands managed to struggle through the crowds and take their place in the Palace forecourt. We had built a stage in the centre gate, the stars (who had all got changed at the Palace) were on it, and the Fly-past was forming up somewhere above Essex. The doors on to the balcony opened and the Queen, Queen Elizabeth the Queen Mother and Princess Margaret came out to massive cheers as Cliff Richard led everybody in singing 'Congratulations'. The moment my technical boys saw the balcony line-up, with the Queen in red, Queen Elizabeth in yellow and Princess Margaret in green, they said, 'Ah, traffic lights!'

Bob Holness was supposed to commentate on the fly-past as it went over. Unfortunately, I had stood him where he could not see anything because I had not allowed for the fact that the Queen Victoria Memorial would completely block any view down the Mall. It must be one of the worst-sited memorials in the world as those in the Mall cannot see the balcony, and those on the balcony can see only some of the Mall. So we had someone relaying the names of the aircraft to Bob who had to pretend he was watching them. The singing went well enough but the MOD had not allowed me to put up enough speakers in the Mall because 'nobody will come', so the hundreds of thousands that had come could hear very little.

The daylight fireworks were a mixed success and a number of them fell still burning into the band in the forecourt. The Queen kept looking over the balcony to see where they had landed. She told me afterwards, 'You know, you almost set light to my mother!'

After it was all over I presented the stars to the Queen, then went to prepare for the evening. By now the crowd outside the Palace had reached eight hundred thousand (those were the police figures, so it was probably more). I stood on the Memorial for some time and vowed that if I ever did anything else in that area I would do it properly. I made a mental note of where the stages and speakers should be, and where the large television screens would be mounted, and decided that we would also have screens in the parks and in Trafalgar Square.

I actually designed the Golden Jubilee there and then, and wrote it down when I got back to my office. Seven years later we did everything exactly as I had envisaged.

That night we had another full house in the park. Before the Queen, the

Duke of Edinburgh, the Princess Royal with Commander Timothy Laurence, and Princess Margaret arrived, we warmed up the crowd with bands, dancers and pipes and drums. On the arrival of the Royal family Robert Hardy would read an extract from the Churchill papers, then a single maroon would signal the start of the two minutes' silence. I was worried that such a large crowd would not be able to keep silent so, in a 'wise virgin' decision, I had a piper hoisted to the top of one of the masts with a piece of string attached to his ankle. I reasoned that if the silence did not hold we would tug it to start him playing, which if nothing else would make people stop talking and look at him out of curiosity. In the event the huge crowd was eerily silent.

The Queen was handed a torch by Emily MacManus, the great-granddaughter of Sir Winston Churchill, who had lit it from the peace torches that had travelled from London, Edinburgh, Belfast and Cardiff.

The fuse the Queen lit was supposed to set off a small laser beam to the main stage where a much more powerful laser would illuminate the Post Office tower which would then burst into spectacular firework displays on all levels. Gary Withers of Imagination had done all this with his usual panache. Unfortunately the fuse spluttered up in front of the Queen, and nearly burnt her. She stepped back rapidly. The small laser never worked at all, so the big one on the stage just shot at the tower when it thought it would. So there was no visual link between the Queen and the tower; however, no one seemed to notice.

We all went back to the Royal Box and Dougie Squires' second great concert of British musicals took place. It was brilliant, all the more so considering that it had only been set up one month earlier and had had only one rehearsal. The line-up of stars was hugely impressive – Dame Vera, of course, Michael Ball, Christopher Biggins, Bernard Cribbins, Robert Hardy, Anita Harris, Gloria Hunniford, Ron Moody and thirty other stars including Anthony Way, the little chorister who had sung for us in the Royal Albert Hall. I had him put on a crane high above the stage and only afterwards did he let on that he was terrified of heights. We also had the original casts from a number of West End shows including the *The Boyfriend* and *Salad Days*, with Julian Slade playing.

After a massive firework display over the Serpentine, all the stars gathered to be presented. This went quite well except that Danny La Rue tried to buy the large white hat Princess Margaret had worn on the balcony, which did not go down well. Celia Lipton, the American multi-billionairess, asked if I could get the Queen to pose with her for her Christmas card. I declined.

Everybody seemed thrilled with the whole four days. The Veterans' Centre had been a particular success. One afternoon, I saw an elderly gentleman with rows of medals standing looking a little lost. I asked him what the trouble was. 'Oh, I'm fine, thank you,' he said. 'It's just that a little boy came up and asked to shake my hand. And he said, "I want to thank you, Sir, for all you did for us". Well, I didn't know what to say, so I just cried.'

We had had a fantastic crowd, particularly on the last day when the park was so full we had to close it. Later Field Marshall Lord Bramall told me a lovely story against himself. He had been trying to get from the Dorchester Hotel, of which he was a director, into the park and had been stopped by a young policeman. The conversation went something like:

'Sorry, Sir, you can't come in here.'

'Do you know who I am? I am Field Marshal Lord Bramall.'

'Well, Field Marshal, you can go and find another bloody Field to Marshal, because you're not coming into this one.' He got in in the end.

At the end of it all, Peter Young was thrilled that he had managed to finesse the Ministers, and Tom and I were just relieved that it was all over.

*　　*　　*

The next problem was the fiftieth anniversary of VJ Day. We had not actually been contracted to do this and there was talk of bringing in another production company. We were never quite clear why, as VE Day had been judged to work very well. However, the Steering Group, under Robert Cranborne, decided that we should do it, which was a bit of a relief as I had thought of most of the plans already. However, my health was deteriorating quite rapidly and I had some doubts that I would actually be able to finish it at all.

VJ Day was always going to be more difficult. We all agreed that it was a commemoration and not a celebration. Veterans who had fought in the Far East had always felt that they had been given a rough deal, and I believed they had. There were no great homecoming victory parades for them; the country was too busy picking up the pieces after the war in Europe.

The veterans' groups were wary of what might be done. I think my major objective was to give them, as far as possible, the same as we had given the VE Day veterans. Most of our arguments over the next couple of months were occasioned by this desire. We were greatly helped, though, by having Field Marshal Viscount Slim's son John on the Steering Group; he gave us very valuable advice and kept us on the right track.

The overall plan was for a service outside Buckingham Palace, a large parade down the Mall in the afternoon and a Final Tribute on Horse Guards Parade that evening. I wanted to add a balcony appearance at Buckingham Palace to the programme, but that took some time to be achieved.

The parade in the afternoon we had nothing to do with at all, which is probably why it went so well. In fact, it was brilliant and the Duke of Edinburgh even came down from the Royal Box to march past with his old comrades. We were to have little to do with the service in the morning either, except that I suggested a massed poppy petal drop from a Lancaster bomber during the Silence. The Lancaster is an excellent and very impressive machine with the most wonderful-sounding engine roar. The only trouble is that it only seems to have two speeds, flying or crashed. So it's very difficult to plan for it to arrive at an exact moment. Its course and take-off time had to be worked out to the nearest thirty seconds. On the day of the service at Buckingham Palace it had probably started its run-in before anybody had got up. I had timed the service precisely, every word and every pause, and the plan was for the Lancaster to drop the poppies at the beginning of the second minute of the two-minute silence. What could go wrong?

It was a very hot day and we were all busy ensuring that the veterans were getting plenty of water when suddenly everybody stood up. I looked at my watch in horror. Through no fault of her own, the Queen had been shown to her seat two minutes early and therefore the service was going to start two minutes early. In the normal way this would not have mattered at all but the Lancaster was on course and could not be speeded up. This meant that the poppy drop and the engine noise would come after the two minutes' silence, in the middle of the prayers that followed.

I went round to the front of the Royal Box and desperately tried to catch the eye of the Archbishop of Canterbury, George Carey, but could not attract his attention. In the end I stood there with two fingers in the air to indicate that we were two minutes adrift, hoping that he wouldn't misunderstand the gesture! As we came to the beginning of the silence, I could still only just see the plane in the far distance. Fortunately, the Archbishop must have realised that something was amiss because he waited, and waited. Eventually the aircraft came down the Mall, dropped the petals perfectly and roared away. In the event there was actually a four-minute silence. I think the only person who noticed was the Queen.

The service completed, I went to Horse Guards for a quick rest. I was feeling pretty rough, and was beginning to think my decision to delay my operation may not have been a wise one.

The Queen's speech that evening at the Final Tribute on Horse Guards would be shown live at other tributes around the country, in particular on the Esplanade in Edinburgh during the Tattoo, and the whole ceremony would include live television links with Scotland, Ireland and Wales. This all meant that the timing had to be precise because we also wanted a second, nationwide, two-minute silence that evening. I was thankful that I had just handed over the show to Brigadier Mel Jameson, so it was going to be his problem.

My plan was to have a large choir conducted by Sir David Willcocks and an orchestra, military bands and pipes and drums. The seating for the Final Tribute was to be on Horse Guards but facing the building. Some of the Queen's Birthday Parade stands had been left up but those in front of the building had been removed and on the park side of the parade ground new seating stands had been built with a big covered Royal Box in the middle.

I was keen to get as many children involved as possible, as I saw them as a symbol of the future; so we planned to fill the parade ground with children with torches as well as the military bands, pipes and drums and two guns from the King's Troop, Royal Horse Artillery. As always, the stars were willing to come. Sir John Mills, Dame Judi Dench, Edward Fox, Keith Michell, Joan Plowright, Saeed Jaffrey, Dennis Quilley and Iain Cuthbertson, Mark McGowan and even the former Speaker of the House of Commons, Viscount Tonypandy, had all agreed to read. Rosemary Anne Sisson had chosen the readings and, as always, gave the whole tribute some much needed shape.

The Fanfare Trumpeters were going to be on the roof of the stage, which they weren't keen on as it meant they had to sit to attention forty feet in the air throughout the whole tribute.

It had been an uphill struggle to secure the balcony appearance after the lowering of the Commonwealth flags, as the Palace were worried that there might not be a large enough crowd. I felt very strongly that we should do everything we could to make the VJ veterans feel that they were every bit as appreciated as those who had fought in Europe, but the Palace was reluctant to agree. At one stage someone pointed out that the Queen was not actually in residence at the time, as the Palace was closed for August; she would actually be staying on the Royal Yacht on the Pool of London.

The arguments went backwards and forwards. Eventually it was agreed that they would decide by looking at the crowds as they drove to the Tribute whether or not to appear on the balcony. The BBC were not best pleased as they had to book all the satellite links. But I told them that this was as good as it would get.

The invited audience was streaming in and the Royal Box was filling up with VIPs. Tony Blair came up to me and introduced himself and congratulated me on the VE Day celebrations. I thanked him and asked which one he had enjoyed most. He didn't seem to be programmed to tell me that, so we had a non-conversation. Even when the Royal cars arrived the Private Secretary, Sir Robert Fellowes, told me no decision had yet been made about the balcony appearance. The BBC were even less pleased.

The event went very well with wonderful music and wonderful readings. Maria Ewing just rescued Andrew Lloyd-Webber's 'Pie Jesu' as the young boy drifted off tune a bit. We'd had a weird conversation with the BBC at midnight the night before about whether we would use 'the prettier boy' with a slight tendency to drift or the plain boy who stayed in tune. They even discussed getting one to sing and the other to mime. I was amazed by this until I saw the opening of the Beijing Olympics, when they had the same problem. It would be unfair to divulge which boy was which!

We had issued the audience with little torches, and the thousand children also came on with torches to form a giant cross over the whole parade ground. I walked behind the Queen with the equerry and Private Secretary as she and the Duke of Edinburgh walked through the singing children to get to the stage for the speech, where the flags of all the Far East veteran groups formed a backdrop behind her. The Queen's speech was followed by a young cadet reading a tribute, then the Last Post, and one round from one of the King's Troop guns. Two minutes later the second shot was fired and we all processed back to the Royal box. I asked Robert if the decision had yet been made about the balcony appearance. The answer was still that it hadn't.

I asked again as the Royal party got into their cars after the ceremony, and the answer was still 'not yet'.

The Tri-Service Massed Bands processed down the Mall in front of the Royal car and the choir followed, while the children with candles came directly after that; I had wanted to put them around the Royal car but was not allowed to. As I walked just behind the car with my orderly I was feeling terrible, and it occurred to me that it would indeed be poetic justice if, having insisted that we should all go back to the Palace, I should expire on the way.

There seemed to be a lot of people on either side of the Mall which was heartening. We had asked the audience on Horse Guards to remain in their seats and watch the large video screens. In retrospect, I think that was a mistake and that it would have been far better if they had come down with us.

When we got to the centre gate of the Palace the Queen and the Duke of

Edinburgh went on to the dais. The BBC were pestering me for a decision. It still had not come.

The choir, who all had to get on to the Queen Victoria Memorial quickly, sang the remainder of the service, the bands played, and the Commonwealth flags all around the Queen Victoria Memorial were lowered. Finally, from high on the roof of the Palace, the Gurkha Pipes and Drums played 'The Heroes of Kohima'.

After the Anthem the Queen stepped off the dais and walked into the Palace. At last Robert said to me, 'OK, we're going to do the balcony.' The BBC man nipped off. 'But we haven't told the Queen what to do, so you'd better rush off and tell her.'

I was in no fit state to rush anywhere. I struggled upstairs and along the corridor to the Centre Room. Halfway along I heard loud cheers and realised that they must have gone out on to the balcony early. Prince Edward was at the door and saw that I was a little perturbed. I explained the problem, and he said it didn't matter – better early than not at all.

Suddenly the Queen and the Duke came back into the room just as the bands and choirs launched into 'Land of Hope and Glory' – the original cue to go out in the first place.

I went up to the Queen and told her. They were clearly very reluctant to go out yet again, not least because the police had unilaterally decided not to let the public into the area around the Memorial behind the children. I had only just noticed this, and it was too late to change it.

I pleaded with the Queen and the Duke of Edinburgh to go out again, if only for the television coverage which was going live to the whole Commonwealth. They did, to tremendous cheers. On the video recording the gap is not noticeable at all as the television producer had cleverly slipped in some archive footage to cover the fact that the balcony was empty for a while.

The Queen came up to me afterwards, smiling broadly, and said jokingly, 'I'm surprised you didn't have another heart attack after all that! You'd better have a large drink.'

So some kind person put a large drink into my hand ('large' at the Palace is very large indeed). The Queen said good night and left to go back to the yacht.

*   *   *

I went in to hospital the next day for an operation to give me a new metal heart valve. A few days later Sir Kenneth Scott sent me a lovely silver box from the Queen with the Royal monogram on top, and the hope that I was feeling better.

I recovered surprisingly quickly, helped by my friends Francis and Liz Gradidge, who allowed me to stay and recuperate with them, and by other great friends, Guy and Sarah Norrie, who all made very good nurses and helped to wean me back onto alcohol. As I had this bit of metal in my bloodstream I was going to have to be on Warfarin for life, which apparently made drinking a problem. I canvassed as many opinions as I could until I came up with one that I could live with. Basically, I could drink so long as I drank roughly the same amount each day and did no 'binge' drinking. When I asked how much 'roughly the same amount' was, the answers varied from one glass to – in a slip of the tongue – one bottle. I decided I would keep between the two.

I was very touched that during this time Rosemary Anne Sisson wrote a poem for me:

For M.J.P. – Perfectionist

> *"Ah, but a man's reach should exceed his grasp," said Browning,*
> *"Or what's a Heaven for?" That theory stinks,*
> *For he who follows it may arrive in Heaven*
> *Much sooner than he thinks!*

*　　*　　*

The next year at the Tournament we used massive lasers in the show. Towards the end of the run I had a problem with one eye and thought that I must have been hit by a laser. My eye specialist consulted the RAF Medical Branch who were the experts on laser damage, and told me it wasn't laser damage; I had a clot in the back of my eye. He then said, 'If you weren't on Warfarin I'd put you on it.' What he should have said was, 'You're on Warfarin but you still have a clot, so obviously the dose is too low.'

One weekend shortly afterwards, down at South Lodge with my aunt Maggie, I suddenly collapsed and was sick a number of times. She managed to call an ambulance, and Liz and Francis Gradidge. I lay on the ground unable to move. The ambulance drivers decided that they could not possibly take me back down the very rough track, so called in a helicopter which took me to Odstock Hospital in Salisbury.

There I was left for what seemed like hours in considerable pain. No-one seemed to know what to do; they only seemed interested in the fact that I had arrived by helicopter. Eventually a young lady doctor arrived and had me taken to a ward.

I could not bear light or sound, and I could not move the left side of my body, but no one seemed too concerned. The first night was agony, not improved by the chap in the next bed shouting very loudly every ten minutes or so, 'Does anybody know the way to Blandford?'

I told the night nurse that I could not stand the noise and the light, and she very kindly pushed me into a single room, displacing some poor chap who would wake up in the morning to find himself in the main ward. It was bliss, dark and quiet.

No-one seemed to know what was wrong with me. The food was terrible – I remember a supper of 'grated carrot sandwiches' – and Sarah kept me going with plates of smoked salmon. It was clear I had to escape. My London doctor booked me in to King Edward VII Hospital for Officers (Sister Agnes'), and Sarah borrowed a wheelchair, gave me dark glasses and ear-plugs, and wheeled me out to her car where my godson James was in the back with a broken leg in plaster. We absconded to Sister Agnes', where as usual the first thing they asked was what newspapers I would like in the morning. The medical staff were horrified that the hospital in Salisbury had done a lumbar puncture, because of the anticoagulant Warfarin. The next day I was told that I had had three small strokes and probably had encephalitis. The good news was that the strokes were in unimportant parts of the brain, so 'new routes' would be found for my movement, and in fact a week later I could move everything. The bad news was that the encephalitis was not treatable, but as it was 'very slight' it might go away of its own accord.

The side-effect was a constant blinding headache. They tried every type of pain-killer on me but none worked except for Dihydrocodeine, which helped for a bit. In fact, it sent me on a 'trip' with the distinct impression that my head was floating around the room. Sadly after a few days this effect wore off leaving me with just the pain. Then I had a new American drug, which was amazing, but it caused even stranger side-effects so I stopped taking that as well.

Sixteen years later the headache is still with me. It varies a bit in severity, but when it is very bad I am incapacitated and have to lie down in the dark. I feel sometimes that people think I am being rude when I am actually just distracted by the pain. I am so used to it now that I can disappear without anybody realising. I spent quite a bit of the Tournament, the Royal Military Tattoo, the Queen Mother's hundredth birthday, and the Golden Jubilee in my bed on site, but I don't think anybody noticed.

CHAPTER ELEVEN

❧

How I Almost Met My Waterloo
– The Edinburgh Military Tattoo

The Edinburgh Military Tattoo is the most famous in the world; whenever we went overseas for new acts for the Royal Tournament we would always be asked whether the Tournament was 'anything like the Edinburgh Tattoo'. We found it slightly irritating, but Edinburgh had a far higher worldwide reputation than the Tournament. Its setting, high up on the Esplanade in front of the ancient castle, is unequalled, and it attracts audiences from all over the world. Every country has people of Scottish descent, and some form of Caledonian Society. There is even Scottish dancing in the jungles of Papua New Guinea.

In the 1950s, under Brigadier Alistair MacLean, the Tattoo was in a class of its own and streets ahead of any other military show. Since then, though still highly popular, it had got slightly stuck in a rut.

In 1991, the Tattoo's business manager, Major Brian Leashman, asked if I had considered applying to replace the then producer, Lieutenant Colonel Leslie Dow. Surely, I countered, the Tattoo was such a very Scottish event that they wouldn't want an Englishman to produce it. But Brian said it was worth a try so I applied to Headquarters Scotland and went up for an interview, with no very high hopes, to be grilled by a growl of Scottish generals. 'What would you do with the show?' they asked.

'For a start, I'd make it more Scottish,' I replied. They blinked furiously at this. 'The thing is that the show isn't really very Scottish,' I explained. 'The beginning is Scottish and the end is Scottish, but the middle's just a mishmash of school bands and irrelevant foreign acts.'

'And what do you think about the music?' they asked. I said I thought the choice of music for a show was far too important to be left to musicians, so I always chose ninety percent of the music for my shows myself. That clearly went down well.

To my amazement I was offered the job. I suspect I had a lot of support from Brian Leashman, who saw that it might be in his own interest if the producer were away from Edinburgh much of the time. He had not got on well with Leslie Dow.

They asked to see a copy of my current contract, and were surprised when I said I'd never had a contract for anything – I'd always worked on a 'gentlemen's agreement'. So they drafted a two-year trial contract which I was happy to sign, and I went up to Edinburgh in 1991 to understudy Leslie Dow in his last year.

He had already told everybody that he didn't mind who took over as long as it wasn't 'that bloody Michael Parker!' I sat at an extra desk in his office and he did not say a word to me for two weeks. His lovely kind PA, Pixie Campbell, hovered in embarrassment trying to break the ice. She never succeeded.

I watched what he did, determined to do everything quite differently, and started to plan my 1992 show from a completely blank sheet. Each show would be devised around central themes and all would be predominantly Scottish. Foreign acts would be invited only if they both fitted into the theme and had a significant connection with Scotland.

The theme of my first year was to be the 350th anniversary of the Scots Guards, marking all the Regiment's achievements past and present. From Leslie Dow I had inherited the Mehta Band from Turkey, who had a very strange way of marching – two paces forward and face to the left, two further paces forward and face to the right. Heaven knows what their enemies made of it. I was about to cancel them when I realised that there was a really good connection – in the eighteenth century our military bands used Turkish percussionists for drums, cymbals and tambourines, so we could have a Scots Guard band in eighteenth-century uniform playing with the Mehta Band. I confirmed their invitation.

For about sixteen years Leslie Dow had used what he called 'The Voice of the Castle', which sounded like a sort of Scottish Boris Karloff reading dreadful McGonagallesque verse. He asked one day whether I would continue to use 'the Voice'. I found a – I hope – gentle way of saying No.

I lived in the Officers' Mess, which was the old Governor's residence. It was freezing cold with wind penetrating from every direction, but it did have an amazing view over Edinburgh. At night when I was all alone in the castle except for the guard, it could be very atmospheric and spooky.

I decided we needed giant gas torchères on the edge of the old moat and on the Half Moon Battery. Historical Scotland, who ran the castle (we called them 'Hysterical Scotland'), were not keen, saying they would never be used again. Twenty years later they are still a major feature. I brought in my sound designer, John Del'Nero, to redesign the terrible sound system, and my lighting designer Robert Ornbo did the same with the lighting. I put hydraulic lifts in the moat to bring up the fanfare trumpeters and built a stand for the Kevock Choir.

The Esplanade is actually on quite a slope and some acts, particularly the pipes and drums, tend to march more slowly uphill than coming down again. The main gateway is not central to the arena, so once over the drawbridge acts have to wheel left to get on to the centre line. I once suggested to 'Hysterical Scotland' that it would be great if they could move the main gateway to the right (they had, after all, replaced all the 'uneven' original cobbles with flat modern stones, and a lot else besides), but they were not amused.

We normally had two days' rehearsal at Redford Barracks then two under lights on the Esplanade, which I felt wasn't nearly enough. In the past, the producer had always done the commentary. I certainly wasn't going to, so I looked around for a professional commentator. A TA officer called Alisdair Hutton was suggested. He had a splendid voice and was fun, which fitted the job description perfectly. The first year he was accused of having an English accent, I suspect because people thought it was me talking and not him. The second year he acquired a much more pronounced burr.

All the cast had to be up in the rest areas well before the audience were let in, which meant a long wait before the performance. The Army's answer was to provide 'packed tea meals', which thrilled nobody. These always included an apple or an orange. At one performance the Massed Bands surreptitiously took their oranges on parade and, at a privately pre-arranged cue, released them. Two hundred oranges rolled down to the hill to the total mystification of the audience.

The other problem we had from time to time was that pipers tend to be fond of a 'wee dram'. I used to have one of the Officers' Mess staff give the Lone Piper a large whisky when he had finished each night. But it was surprising how many 'wee drams' they managed to get down in one short evening. If there was ever any suspicion that we had a few 'relaxed' pipers on parade we would place military policemen at the bottom of the Esplanade and as the Pipes and Drums countermarched the offenders were whisked away without, we hoped, anybody noticing.

In the second year the theme was 'The Kings of Scotland' from Macbeth to George IV. We brought the Scottish state coach up from the Royal Mews, to live somewhat incongruously in a humble-looking garage on the Royal Mile. The carriage horses were brought up from the Palace of Holyrood stables and hitched on before the steep climb to the arena. The Household Cavalry Musical Ride and Mounted Bands also took part, which was quite a challenge for them on wet sloping tarmac.

That year we also had the King's Guard from Norway. These exceptional young National Servicemen were very impressive and immaculately drilled. In honour of this Viking connection we started the show with Up Helly-Aa, which includes burning a Viking longboat. Naturally 'Ealth'n'Safety did not think it a good idea, but we ignored them.

I thought it would be fun for the Norwegians to start their act by skiing down the Esplanade. They enthusiastically had skis made with small wheels underneath, and about ten of them achieved impressive speed as they shot off down the arena. One day the inevitable happened – the arena team, who were supposed to stop them under the stand, missed one of them who sailed straight under the stands and continued right down the hill until he contrived to fall over before he hit the traffic.

I wanted to fire all the cannon on the Half Moon Battery. 'Hysterical Scotland' complained that they weren't made for that. I said I thought that was exactly what they were made for, so we were allowed, in the end, to put our pyrotechnics in them. The end of the show was difficult to get right and I tried a number of ways of doing it before we finished with the famous Lone Piper. We even wrote a verse of cobbled-together Scottish lines which is still in use today and is probably thought by many to be by Robbie Burns as supposed to Hutton and Parker.

I had changed the Tattoo considerably and made it much more theatrical. Ticket sales were up, and I believe many more local people came than had for some years. I wanted to do much more but, depressingly, some members of the Board kept querying why we needed to improve things, or spend more money at all. It came to a head when one member said, 'There's no need to improve or change anything – people will come no matter what we do.' I decided then and there that my time at the Tattoo should come to an end, although I had enjoyed it enormously and loved the town of Edinburgh itself. I had, by now, been given a new contract which had a six-month let-out clause. So I gave in my notice, which horrified them. I pointed out that had I been there on my normal 'gentlemen's agreement', I could not have resigned so easily.

In a way I had found it was not challenging enough. I always try to do things differently and better each time; I may not succeed but I need to try. On a 'difficulty of production' scale of one to ten, I suppose the Royal Tournament scores about eight. The Edinburgh Tattoo scores about five.

As it happened that last year, 1994, was nearly *my* very last year – ever. My heart had 'gone' at the Tournament and I was feeling terrible. I came out of hospital in London and went straight up to Edinburgh to start rehearsals. I took my Royal Signals Assistant from the Tournament, who by now knew the ropes and understood how I worked, and of course I had John Del'Nero, Robert Ornbo and the excellent Director of Music, Barry Hingley. I warned them all that I might not last the course. My Arena Master was the extremely good WO1 Steve Walsh who, after I left, was to take on more of the role of a director, a role that he still fulfills today having retired from the Army.

We had an ambitious programme, themed around the Queen's Own Highlanders and the Scots Dragoon Guards and including the Scots Greys capturing one of Napoleon's eagles at the Battle of Waterloo – no mean feat on slippery tarmac. In the Finale the whole cast would form the Stag's Head cap badge of the Queen's Own Highlanders, a hundred dancers in white dresses making up the 'antlers'. We normally had two days' rehearsal and I would split the acts between them. This time I insisted on doing the whole show in one day. I asked my team to follow me around closely and note everything I was doing and ask questions if they did not understand what I was trying to achieve.

I went back to the Castle to change for the evening rehearsal, and collapsed, rather embarrassingly, in the anteroom of the Mess. Pixie rushed over, put me in an ambulance and came down with me. I remember hearing the pipes warming up all around the ambulance as I was driven slowly down through the Castle, and thinking that this was a very smart funeral for a mere major. Once in hospital I was put in a casualty ward, where the beds were so tightly packed together that you had to be put on them from the foot end. Pixie sat on my bed, distracting me when they came to take away prone – presumably dead – bodies. It was all rather bizarre. I eventually made it up to the ward, and my team came and told me that everything was actually going quite well and that they had been able to make it all work. It seemed that they had not missed me at all!

Three weeks later I was well enough to be taken up to the Castle, and was carried up the stairs by two soldiers. In the control box I watched as 'my' show materialised, just as I had imagined it and looking pretty good. My boys had done an amazing job. I was carried down again and went straight to London. My consultant wanted me to go in for an operation immediately but I told him it would have to wait until after VJ Day in August the following year.

My old friend Brigadier Mel Jameson took over as producer and did a great job. He couldn't believe his luck when I resigned, as he was expecting me to go on for at least another nine years. He is now doing shows in Australia and Russia. The Tattoo has been renamed the Royal Edinburgh Military Tattoo, and is going from strength to strength and raising serious amounts of money for military charities, not least for the Army Benevolent Fund – The Soldiers' Charity, of which I am a Trustee.

*   *   *

One of the pleasures of producing 'the most famous Tattoo in the world' was being approached by other countries who want to do a tattoo themselves. By far the best approach I had was in 1993, from a lovely lady called Cynthia Ham with a wonderful Tennessee drawl, who telephoned to ask if I would be interested in helping to put on a show as part of the 'Memphis in May' celebrations. I invited her and her team to come to the Tattoo and have dinner. I liked them immediately and agreed to go over to Memphis to see what the possibilities were.

Memphis, home of Elvis Presley and *Beale Street Blues*, is a typical inland American city. Large parts of it were torn down, presumably because they were tenement buildings, so the centre, or downtown, seemed to be mainly car parks. A few gems stand out in this sea of tarmac. The Peabody Hotel, where I stayed, is a magnificent Edwardian edifice still famous for its daily Parade of Ducks. At eleven o'clock a fanfare would sound in the main foyer, and six ducks would waddle out of the lift to a Sousa march. Their very own red carpet led down to a fountain in the foyer where they stayed, being fed and pampered, until five in the afternoon, when the fanfare sounded again and they marched back into the lift to be taken back up to the Duck Palace on the roof. A wonderfully wacky American tradition. Duck is not served in any of the restaurants in the Peabody Hotel!

The first Tattoo 'saluted' Russia, so we did the 1812 Overture (naturally). However, the fire chief was so wet about the pyrotechnics that we were only able to use pathetic ones for the cannon fire. It would have been more exciting if we'd got the orchestra and band to stamp their feet and shout 'Bang!'

Otherwise everything went very well and I was most impressed with the efficiency of the stage technicians and production company. Everything cost half what it would have back home, and was achieved in half the time. Cynthia and her friends were so hospitable and kind that it was very difficult, when the time came, to leave.

The second year we 'saluted' Côte d'Ivoire, the Ivory Coast. We all went over there and found the place quite an experience; the BO needed to be experienced to be believed – it was so solid you could almost sculpt with it! The Ivorians could not have been friendlier, and we soon found the amazing Rose Marie Guiraud, who had built a dance school with huge dance studios and classrooms for about four hundred children found abandoned on the street. Apparently any child after the tenth in a family was just left out for someone to pick up. We went to some of the villages, where hundreds of local dancers danced for us. At one village they drugged the very young children, painted them in white stripes, and threw them around like juggling clubs. The ladies of Memphis did not think this would go down well at home.

We found a pair of classically trained musicians who were trying to recreate some of the ancient music of the jungle, with five-hundred-year-old mouth bows and a sort of zither made from varying lengths of metal which were plucked by hand. It sounded very strange and I asked if they were able to play western tunes on them.

'Oh yes,' they said. 'What tune would you like?'

I immediately said, 'I Got Rhythm', which they proceeded to play perfectly. We booked them, and over a hundred of Rose Marie's dancers, wonderful kids who had the time of their live in Memphis.

We had a slight hiccup when someone suggested that 'I Got Rhythm' was racist, so I hastily I telephoned Dougie Squires in England. He told me that the song, from the musical *Girl Crazy*, had been sung first by Ethel Merman and later by Gene Kelly, and that the songwriters George and Ira Gershwin were New York-born Russian Jews! So we were all right. A brilliant local musician produced a unique arrangement, which went from Stone Age mouth bow via three hundred children on xylophones and a military band of three hundred, then to fifty pairs of timpani and finally a full symphony orchestra and a choir of five hundred. It was the most extraordinary sound, and totally marvellous.

A few years later, I returned to Memphis to produce the opening of the new Symphony Hall. I was at a loss as to what to do, so I wrapped the orchestra, like a huge parcel, in gauze which was ripped away when they started playing. The conductor was not initially very keen to do this, until I told him that the alternative was for him to be lowered from the roof by parachute. We did the 'parcel'.

After the concert we gave an Ice Ball, with all the drinks bars made out of solid ice. A team from New York sculpted a nine-foot block of ice into a conductor using chainsaws, all done to pop music. It was the most extraordinary and fascinating scene, even if it did make the dance floor a little damp.

I am longing to go back to Memphis with Emma, a serious Elvis fan, and show her Gracelands. I have had many VIP tours around that extraordinary house. On my first one I was conducted to the grave beside the swimming pool, looking for all the world like a sun-lounger. The 'Everlasting Flame' at the head of the lounger had gone out. It always does that, they said, when it rains.

CHAPTER TWELVE

Setting the Middle East Ablaze

At a reception following the 1985 Royal Tournament, when the Jordan Band and Pipes and Drums had performed, I met General Zaid bin Shaker, whom I had encountered on my first visit to Jordan, and his wife who was known to us only as Umm Shaker, or 'mother of Shaker' – their son was Shaker bin Zaid. They were a wonderful couple. He had been at Sandhurst and was, like the King, extremely polite and considerate but, also like His Majesty, there was obviously an iron will just beneath the surface. When the General asked if I would like to produce a show similar to the Royal Tournament for King Hussein's fiftieth birthday, I said I would be delighted.

'And when is His Majesty's birthday?' I asked. November, I was told. 'So we'll have just over a year to do it,' I said. 'That's fine.'

'Oh, no,' came the answer. 'This November.' It was now the end of July, and November was only three months away. So I travelled back to Jordan on the Shakers' private aircraft to see what the form was.

There was no 'form'. They had no acts except the bands and some pipes and drums. They had some horses available but they had never done a show. I had to think fast. I asked immediately for a switched-on liaison officer; Lieutenant Colonel Riad al-Turk was produced, and he became a great friend. We toured Amman looking for a suitable site, but there wasn't one. Eventually we found a flat piece of land by the military airport with a suitable road. I asked if we could build an arena there looking out across the airfield. 'No problem,' said Riad, so I did a sketch and work started immediately. In a remarkably short time a stadium suddenly appeared, complete with a marble-lined Royal Box.

I immediately asked the British Ambassador and the Military Attaché for their support in getting the MOD to send out suitable instructors. This they did and, once home, I speedily identified suitable instructors in riding, parachute, motorcycle and continuity drill, and a Musical Director as well as a piping expert. They all turned out to be first class and in no time at all we had made huge progress. The Corporal Major from the Household Cavalry had the horsemen doing a musical ride within a few days, though when I told him I wanted to add some camels, he was not best pleased.

In just a few days the Red Devils' parachute instructors had the enthusiastic Jordanian Special Forces freefalling and doing 'relative canopy work', which is when the parachutes hitch together on the way down. I was given a thousand men for the drill display, which was quite a challenge for the Sergeant from the Queen's Colour Squadron who was used to dealing with ninety, but he made a fantastic job of it, even if at times he might have felt like shooting them. The Bands and Pipes and Drums improved considerably. The Special Forces under the excellent Brigadier Tahseen Shurdom were outstanding. Tahseen was a huge bull of a man who was reputed to have killed eighteen people by his own hand in the Six Day War. He was a great and lasting ally who understood better than any what I was trying to achieve. I also had at my disposal the entire Royal Jordanian Air Force, commanded by Tahseen's brother Ihsan, or 'Sam'; he was a great friend of Patricia Salti, who was to prove an invaluable help as she knew every level of Jordanian society from the King down. All the Jordanians are really lovely people and they could not have been kinder, more generous, or more forgiving of my hectoring them during the long days of preparation.

From the beginning we had a problem with the concept of 'time'. Most Arabs are quite unconcerned about when things happen – 'See you in an hour' could well mean a day later. The idea of doing anything in 'three minutes precisely' was completely alien to them, but we came to an arrangement – we would have 'Jordanian time' and 'English time'. The two seldom agreed.

I wanted thirty fighters of the Royal Jordanian Air Force to do a fly-over at the beginning of the show, to be timed to coincide with the show commander paying tribute to the King. We were talking about seconds, not minutes, to make it work properly. They all clearly thought I was mad. We did a trial which was in my opinion terrible, but they were rather pleased that they had actually turned up on the right day. I worried that they would arrive several minutes late, or – worse – early which would have drowned out the speech. The other problem I had was the timing of the King's arrival. Like most rulers in the area he could turn up very late for engagements. Security was always the excuse given, and in his case it was not unreasonable as at least twenty attempts had been made on his life so far. But it was vital to me for him to arrive precisely on time.

The Special Forces were staging a 'battle' which involved abseiling from helicopters. Prince Abdullah, the King's eldest son, was then a Captain in the Special Forces, and every day I would remind him to impress upon His Majesty how important it was to arrive precisely on time until it became a running joke.

At a reception the King asked why it was so important to turn up precisely on time.

I replied, 'Well, Sir, most of your Air Force will be in the air waiting to do a fly-over, and if Your Majesty is late they will run out of fuel and crash.'

'That is a very good reason,' he agreed with a huge smile.

The parachutists became brilliant, and surprised even themselves. Meanwhile, the Corporal Major in charge of the camel and horse rehearsals had got a hundred of each doing some impressive movements. The 'experts' had said that camels and horses would never work together. I ignored them and, in fact, once the two had got used to each other it did work very well. I was watching one rehearsal when everything seemed to come to a sudden stop.

The instructor rode over, jumped off his horse and said, 'That's it, Sir, I give up!'

I told him not to be so wet – what was the problem?

'One of the bloody camels has just given birth, and now my numbers are uneven!'

The little newcomer was immediately ushered away and I am sure was quite delicious. Baby camels are much prized as a delicacy.

Two days before the Celebration, I casually mentioned that the airfield side of the arena looked a little boring and that it was a pity that we couldn't have a few armoured vehicles. The next day two whole tank regiments turned up. The commanding officers were not amused as they had been on training at the time.

The day of the Celebration arrived. The generals were all in the Royal Box, shoes off and feet up on the marble handrails, drinking Turkish coffee. I told Field Marshal (he had just been promoted) Zaid bin Shaker that His Majesty would be here shortly. He laughed and said he doubted it, but I pointed out the cloud of dust which was the Royal cavalcade coming across the airfield. They were all amazed, and jumped to their feet to put their shoes on. As the King walked up to the Royal Box, next to my control box, he gave me a large wink and a broad smile.

The general in charge of the show spoke, then the Air Force thundered over in perfect formation. Everything, in the event, went perfectly. It was the forerunner of four more national celebrations that I was to do for them.

*   *   *

A year later the Palace called from Amman. Could I please come immediately? No one seemed to know why, but my ticket would be waiting at the airport. I asked Alan Jacobi of Unusual Rigging to come with me as I had a feeling that, whatever we were going to do, I was going to need him.

I was sure someone from the Royal Court would meet us on arrival, but there was no one. I expected to find instructions at the hotel, but there were none. Patricia Salti suggested we simply go to the Palace in the morning; she thought it might have something to do with forthcoming marriage of the King's second son, Prince Faisal, to Alia al Tabbaa.

The next day I was welcomed by the Chief of Protocol, Faisal abu Tayi (grandson of Auda abu Tayi, the hero of the Great Arab Revolt played by Anthony Quinn in the film *Lawrence of Arabia*). He was as mystified as I was as to why I was there, so he took me to see the Chief of the Royal Court, the second most important person after the King. After a moment's thought, he said, 'Ah, it must be the wedding of Prince Faisal – would you organise it, please?'

With that comprehensive briefing, and in only two days because I had to go to Berlin, Alan and I invented the wedding from scratch. On the first day a thousand people would come to a reception at the main Palace in Amman. We would cover the car park with Turkish carpets, and build a false extension to the Palace, a large revolve in the woods for a symphony orchestra, and an eighteenth-century topiary garden with tall box hedges. There were more plans for subsequent days. The Palace were delighted, and told me to go ahead. I asked if they were interested in the cost. 'Perhaps you'd be kind enough to let us know in due course,' was all they said.

Alan and I flew back to London and within days everything had been drawn up and finalised. The budget was running into high six figures but that didn't seem to concern anyone much. Not a single contract or piece of paper was ever signed; it was all done on a 'gentlemen's agreement'. The first instalment was paid immediately, and the remainder as soon as it was asked for.

We flew a 747 cargo plane to Amman, with a large sound system, a large light system and acres and acres of simulated box hedging. The Royal Jordanian Air Force sent a C130 plane to collect the fireworks and special effects, as no civilian aircraft would carry them. Within days our team of forty had got the Palace extension and the topiary garden built. I also got them to make a pond with fountain in the centre. The idea was that a fanfare would sound, the fountain would stop playing, a very large wedding cake would rise up out of the pond, and a walkway would extend over the water to allow the bride and groom to cut the cake. As usual, nothing complicated.

But first there was to be a lavish firework display to music. Unfortunately the firework company sited the fireworks too close to the Palace, and we were too busy to notice. Large pieces of burning debris fell into the VIP audience, dresses were spoiled and someone's hair actually caught fire. Our own control box went up in flames, as did one of the royal garages.

I was wondering what the hell to do. There stood the Prince, and his bride in a lovely white dress with a long train. The King was just behind them. On the spot I invented another of my Rules for running shows – 'Always stand as close as you can to the principal guest so you can be the first to get in with your excuses'. So I went to stand beside the King. 'Michael,' he asked, 'is it supposed to be like this?'

'Oh yes, Your Majesty, good firework displays are always like this,' I said, crossing my fingers.

He nodded. 'It's very impressive'.

I just prayed that nothing would land on the bride's train. It didn't, and the cake was cut immaculately. The control box fire was out by this time, so we had sound and light again.

The revolve kept turning to bring out the orchestra/band and the effect was only slightly spoiled by the conductor hanging onto the side and waving like a child on a roundabout as he disappeared into the trees.

Prince Faisal's mother is HRH Princess Muna al-Hussein, who met the King while – as Toni Gardiner – she was working on the set of *Lawrence of Arabia*. For the second evening we had designed a 'Nightclub in the Desert' to fit onto the double tennis courts at her house, on the roof of which would be a huge falcon – Prince Faisal's security code name. The falcon looked terrific and the forty foot fountains in the swimming pool were pretty impressive. The garden looked strangely splendid. It turned out that, unknown to us, the Palace florist had flown a planeload of cut flowers over from Holland and had stuck them stem first into the ground.

My technical boys, used to working off 'cue sheets' and having everything written down, had found it difficult to adapt to my strange way of doing things. I explained that we were having to make most of it up as we went along. My point was proved when the King turned up early and was given the Queen Mother's fanfare. When the Queen Mother arrived she got the full works – His Majesty's Fanfare. 'Well,' they said defensively, 'that was what was written down.'

Dinner seemed to be going well, until the head chef came to me in tears, quite inconsolable. His great finale pudding had been designed to feature spun-sugar Hashemite crowns on each plate plus sparklers. But the truck bringing these works of art had hit a bump in the desert and the whole lot had shattered to bits. Just cut up the spare wedding cake, I told him, stick a sparkler in each piece and pretend nothing's wrong. No-one noticed. Which goes to prove another of my Rules: Never tell people what is supposed to happen. Then they won't know when it doesn't.

Before the dancing there was to be a laser and firework display. Queen Noor asked if we could bring it forward a bit as her young son Prince Ali had to go to hospital to have his appendix removed and he was refusing to go before the laser show. I'd noticed an ambulance outside but thought it was just part of the set-up. So we did the show early, to thunderous applause.

Later, as Princess Muna danced with one of her very obviously 'fey' elderly friends, one of my boys remarked, 'Look, two old queens dancing together!' Afterwards she kindly gave me one of the tiny gold coins that the bride and groom traditionally throw amongst wedding guests.

After the success of that wedding, the Commander in Chief, Zaid bin Shaker asked me to organise the wedding of his son. Not only was Zaid known as bin (son of) Shaker, he was also abu (father of) Shaker. I went to meet the Field Marshal and his wife to discuss what we might do. Bill Harkin designed a brilliant and very large tensile structure to hold a thousand dinner guests, and we levelled the helicopter landing pad at the Shakers' house and put up three-quarters of a huge geodesic dome covered with transparent polythene. This seated three hundred people for the dinner and the fireworks afterwards. The fireworks were fired from all around the dome and looked wonderful from inside. I had realised that nights were very cold in Jordan, which is why we built the dome in the first place, but I hadn't reckoned on it being so cold that the warmth inside produced condensation which started to drip onto the Royal Family.

That afternoon I had received a surprise invitation to the Palace, where the King presented me with the magnificent insignia of a Grand Officer of the Order of Al Istiqlal (Independence). We then had our photograph taken, flanked by the King's two Cossack bodyguards. Now, in the dome, the King asked me to sit with him for a while. I was praying that nothing would drip onto us while we were talking.

*   *   *

I organised His Majesty's sixtieth birthday celebrations and two coronation anniversaries. The last of these was in 1993, and of course it was bigger and better than all the others. All the Jordanian acts were by this time first class and could have held their own in any show in the world. But in 1993 there was a terrible accident which very nearly turned into a national disaster.

A mock battle was staged, with almost a full brigade of troops, including four C130 Hercules aircraft dropping two hundred parachutists. The battle started with recce helicopters carrying Special Forces in to abseil by rope to the ground. Prince Abdullah was first out of his helicopter and as he reached the ground a second soldier, who in his excitement had failed to get on the rope properly, plummeted down and was killed instantly. Only by inches did he miss the Prince, who would certainly also have been killed.

I felt utterly wretched, and so did the Prince, who reluctantly agreed after some discussion that we should treat it as a minor accident. I had already told the Arena Master to send on a stretcher to take the chap away. I could not believe that I could be so cold-hearted, but it was the best we could do in the circumstances. There was nothing we could do to help the poor chap now and I knew from experience that if we were to stop the show it would never start again and His Majesty's celebrations would be further marred. Later that afternoon the Prince went to the poor young man's funeral.

*   *   *

A few months later I received another call from Jordan. Prince Abdullah was to be married, and would I go over and organise it?

At least this time we knew why we were going. I came up with a variation on Prince Faisal's layout but with a more modern look. In the centre was a magnificent cake in a soaring Islamic equivalent of the Albert Memorial. The Prince was still in the Special Forces so we thought it might be rather fun to have his grandfather's gold sword delivered by a free-fall parachutist for him to cut the cake. This was no easy matter at night, but that was the whole point – it had to be difficult, otherwise it wouldn't be worth doing.

So it was vital that the bride and groom should rehearse. The bride, Rania al-Yassin, was not too keen but we persuaded her, and I closed and cleared the whole site so no one would see them except me and the sound expert. We paced out precisely with the music and tied bed sheets behind the bride-to-be so she could get used to the train.

On the night itself it was fortunately very clear. I asked the King, who was receiving guests on the main stage, if he would let me know when he wished to finish receiving and go on to the cake cutting. I said, 'Shortly after you tell me, Sir, I shall give you a little signal to go to Prince Abdullah immediately and ask him to process to the cake.'

The King asked, 'Why immediately?'

'Because, Your Majesty, the parachutist with the sword will have just left the helicopter, and we won't be able to put him back in.'

'A very good reason – again!'

I gave the signal and the Prince and Princess proceeded to the central edifice. You could see the parachute circling slowly in the sky overhead. On the 'wise virgin' principle, I had another golden sword hidden behind a bush, just in case. The officer carrying the real sword landed heavily on the tarmac – rather too heavily, I feared – but he got up after a moment and painfully made his way to present the sword to the Prince. The cake was cut, and from the distant hills a spectacular firework display covered most of Amman. At least this time I didn't have to worry about burning the bride or the Palace.

My work in Jordan was over. But I kept in touch with my friends there and was happy to see that Prince Abdullah later became King in his father's place. Of all the King's children, whom I knew, he was the most like his father and had earned the affection and respect of his men and all who knew him. I was not to see him again until his State Visit in 2001, when I was asked to the Lord Mayor's Banquet at the Guildhall and was able for the first time to wear the decoration King Hussein had given me ten years earlier.

*   *   *

After the embarrassment of the Omani pipes and drums not being invited to the Royal Tournament, I was surprised to be approached in 1990 by Charles Kendall, the Sultan of Oman's procurement agents, who asked if I would go and run a very large equestrian show for an anniversary celebration. My lack of knowledge of horses did not inhibit me at all and, having met the Commander of the Royal Stables in London, I went on a recce to the stables in Seeb, outside Muscat. There they had over three hundred and fifty horses of virtually every breed, from rarefied racehorses in air-conditioned stables to eight circus horses that been brought out by Mary Chipperfield for a one-day show some years previously and left there. Ever since, they had come out every day with their groom and, complete with ostrich feathers, had performed their routine before the sun became too hot. Yet no-one had ever watched them since that single show all those years ago.

My immediate contact was Abdul Razak al Shahwarzi, known to everybody as Abdi. Now a Brigadier in command of the Royal Cavalry, he was very jolly with a very English sense of humour. He and I set about devising the largest horse show we could. Finance was not a problem – I could ask for whatever I wanted, so we bought a great many more horses.

I had asked to bring instructors from the Household Cavalry and the King's Troop to help train the very willing horsemen available. Both were actually very junior non-commissioned officers, but I told the Omanis they were very senior instructors and we dressed them as captains in the Royal Cavalry. One of them, Lance-Corporal of Horse Waygood, was an outstanding young man who was to end up as a Major (real) and Riding Master of the Household Cavalry at Knightsbridge Barracks.

I asked for the King's Troop instructor because I wanted to replicate the Troop Drive, but using carriages instead of guns. Six magnificent specially-built carriages came from Germany and twenty-four Haflingers to pull them. I dread to think what it all cost. We also brought another set of circus horses and Mary Chipperfield came over with them. When she arrived we found yet another lot that she had brought over years previously, which they had forgotten, so we now had three sets. We also bought twenty Shetland ponies for the children to ride but sadly they did not fancy it so they were never used. From my 'well of equine ignorance', I devised rather a good show and they were very pleased with it.

In the midst of all these preparations I received a fax from my friend Sarah Norrie. For some time I had been looking for a house to buy in England. I knew exactly what I wanted. Sarah said she had found a lovely little cottage up a long track in the woods near where she and her husband Guy lived. She thought it was just what I wanted. So I bought it unseen, and never regretted it – South Lodge was a joy for twenty years.

The weather was always extremely hot, so we could only rehearse before the sun came up and after it had gone down. It made for rather a strange working day, but at least the country was not 'dry'!

Punctuality is always a problem in Arab countries and the Sultan was known for being up to two hours late for a parade. On the day itself everyone wanted to be mounted and on parade at the appointed time. No, I said, we'd wait until we actually heard the helicopter. The Commander of the

Mounted Band knew the Sultan's pilot, who promised to give us due warning. The audience of six thousand or so had been in their seats for an hour and half whilst we were still drinking tea. When eventually we got the message from the pilot we were on parade, ready and fresh, just as the Sultan appeared. Apparently I was considered something of a miracle worker by the Omanis, who were used to sweltering as they waited for hours.

Afterwards I was presented with a large wooden box from the Sultan. I thanked him very much and got back into my huge car thinking I had been given an ornate cigar box. I went through layer after layer of wrappings and eventually discovered that it was actually an 18 carat gold Rolex watch. I mused that it was probably worth what I had just paid for the new conservatory at South Lodge!

*   *   *

I had first been to Saudi Arabia in the early 70s when the Crown Prince, later King, Fahd wanted to give his brother a special present for use when they went hawking together. I came up with an idea for a mobile throne-room cum *majlis* for use in the desert. I went over to show him the plans, but he obviously did not like them as I never heard another word. So when I was contacted by Brigadier David Bromhead and asked if I would come to lunch at the Dorchester with a Prince Faisal I was less than keen. However, I went and was very pleasantly surprised. Firstly, the Prince, Faisal bin Mohammed al Saud, was charming, very jovial and enthusiastic, and secondly he drank wine. We had a marvellous lunch and he waxed lyrical about his idea for the largest exhibition of 'The Horse' ever mounted. He had already persuaded major museums worldwide to loan priceless artefacts, models and paintings of the horse through the ages. He wanted me to help with the exhibition itself and the horse-related entertainment to go with it. Again, drawing on my zero knowledge, I was able to provide plenty of ideas. In fact, it occurred to me that I might soon actually begin to know something about horses, which would put my 'amateur status' at risk.

In conversation the Prince mentioned that it would soon be the 'centenary' of King Abdul Aziz al Saud. They did not normally 'do' celebrations but had decided they would on this occasion. Would I like to help them with that as well? I flew again to Riyadh, and stayed with David Bromhead. He had been part of the Defence Attaché's team, but now worked directly for Prince Miteb, Deputy Commander of the National Guard which was more powerful than the Army. The Commander was his father Crown

Prince Abdullah. King Fahd, whom I had met all those years ago, was now very ill and Prince Abdullah, his half-brother, was in effect ruling the country.

Prince Faisal greeted me like a long lost friend and introduced me to Prince Badr. There are thousands of princes in Saudi Arabia but they have to be directly descended from King Abdul Aziz or a very close relative to be really important. My Prince Faisal was descended from Abdul Aziz's brother, and Prince Badr is a grandson. Tall, amusing and very talented, he is a renowned poet in the Arab world, also a composer and musician. My only problem was that being a very devout Muslim he did not drink, but apart from that I got on with him immediately and we started hatching plans.

We decided that the Prince would write an 'Arabic opera' about Abdul Aziz and the founding of the Saudi Kingdom. Poetry, music and prose would be interspersed with action scenes and battles. It was to be performed in an indoor arena at Janadriyah, where an effort had been made to recreate some historic sites from the interior. I decided to build a desert landscape with rolling dunes. There would two big video screens, each forty feet by twenty, on tracks so that they could form one big screen or two smaller ones. I went to the cavalry barracks and found six hundred horses that were scarcely ever used. I had brought out with me the very young but excellent Household Cavalry Lance Corporal of Horse Semuschion, telling the Saudis he was a very senior expert from England. Within a few days this young corporal had sorted out all the brigadiers and colonels, and had chosen a hundred horses and riders for the battles. I brought over from the Ukraine the eight Cossack riders we had used at the Tournament, and dressed them as Arabs to lead the others. My excellent team of lighting, sound, video and stage management was there, Dougie Squires came to direct, and Barry Hingley of the RAF wrote the music. It was brilliant and sounded totally Arab, only with catchy tunes.

Prince Badr wanted me to go to Riyadh every weekend which, even with First Class gold-plated seats, did not appeal. However, he owned a hotel just off the Champs-Elysées in Paris, so I took the Eurostar and stayed there instead. That was much more satisfactory; it also meant that I could meet his wife, the daughter of the last King, and his daughters whom I was not allowed to meet in Saudi.

I asked for fifty camels for the battles, and was told it was impossible as camels and horses would not work together. After my experience in Jordan I was now an 'expert', so I told them to stable them together for a month. In the end the camels were far less trouble than the horses; they looked at us disdainfully, and humoured us by doing what we asked.

Rehearsals were a nightmare, as it was Ramadan and the Saudis only worked after sunset. We found ourselves working during the day as well and eating meals at very strange times. Dougie did a brilliant job, but it was very difficult to keep up morale. Then one of the senior officers asked if we would like to go to his home for a drink. Expecting yet more orange juice we were tempted to refuse, but thought it impolite. When we got to the house, and all his staff were out of the way, he pushed a button in the wall and a fully-stocked bar motored out. We all became more cheerful immediately.

I had been trying for weeks to get generators for the theatre as there wasn't enough electricity. They were promised daily but did not arrive. I told Prince Badr that the show would have to be cancelled, and they arrived within the hour. But with no fuel.

'Fuel – very difficult,' I was told.

'This is bloody Saudi Arabia!' I retorted. 'Go and push a stick into the ground; the bloody oil will gush out.' The fuel arrived.

Then I asked for seven hundred tons of sand for my desert scene. We were surrounded, as far as the eye could see, by sand dunes. But, 'Sand – very difficult...'

The final straw was the unloading of the two Jumbo jet cargo planes that had brought our equipment from England. We could see them on the tarmac beside the runway. 'Why,' I demanded, 'have they not been unloaded?'

'Customs men very tired,' apparently. In other words, they wanted paying. I told Badr that our budget did not allow for bribes. They persisted, and so did I. No kit, no show, I said. The kit appeared.

The opening of the show was 'The Creation of the World', no less. A huge burning sun descended from the roof, acres of blue silk covered the 'desert', and video and pyrotechnics and Barry's marvellous music completed the picture. Prince Badr asked if he could bring his wife and daughters to a rehearsal. I agreed, not appreciating the ramifications. We had to empty the whole building of the three hundred extras, one hundred horses and fifty camels, and only I and one sound engineer were allowed to stay. When everything was considered clear, a large luxury coach with blackened windows appeared, and a number of women totally unrecognisable in black chadors got out. 'Hello, Michael, how are you?' they greeted me cheerily.

The show coincided with the end of Ramadan, when about ten of us, with fifty or so guards, were taken to the desert for a 'picnic' with the Crown Prince. A great roaring fire of cedar wood was lit on a hilltop, which seemed incongruous until you smelt it, and we sat on fine Turkish carpets in a tent.

Set before us were four sheep, eight goats, dozens of chickens and in the middle a young boiled camel, looking slightly surprised. There was also a huge pile of vegetables and fruit, and only ten of us to eat it all. Our hosts pulled pieces of meat from the various carcasses and handed them to us; the young camel was delicious. We found it hard to make any inroads at all into the immense heap of food. But when we left to go back to the fire, the guards descended like gannets and demolished the whole lot within minutes.

Afterwards I was given a gold and silver letter opener in the shape of a sword, and bid Saudi Arabia good-bye with a certain relief. Everyone had been immensely kind and generous, and we had made some good friends, but I found the way of life strange, to say the least.

CHAPTER THIRTEEN

A Miracle of Rare Device
– The Millennium Disaster and a Success

Just after the VE Day and VJ Day fiftieth anniversary celebrations a meeting was called on the South Bank to brief production companies on the requirements for the main Millennium celebration.

The Minister, Virgina Bottomley, and Jennie Page, the civil servant in charge of delivering the event, were there. I took Alan Jacobi with me and we introduced ourselves to the Minister and Ms Page, both of whom recoiled as though we were infectious. The fact that VE Day and VJ Day had been judged by most to have been great successes was obviously to be held against us. It was made clear that my 'sort of thing' – ie, something traditional, something historic, with pageantry and ceremonial – had no place in their idea of what the Millennium celebrations should be. They wanted something 'forward looking' and 'relevant', what was later to be known as 'Cool Britannia'. The briefing was rather like a cheap necklace made up of pearls of cliché, one after the other. I began to feel that this was not something with which I really wanted to be involved.

Later, Gary Withers, who had started the brilliant production company Imagination and ran it with a ferociously creative talent, was briefed. I went to have lunch with him, as I did from time to time, and he showed me his proposed plans for the main event. He had been to enormous trouble, devising a series of pavilions with 'Time' as the main theme – 'Past Time', 'Future Time', 'Play Time', 'Work Time' and so on – in a coherent journey through time. I thought it was great and suggested forming the pavilions in a circle rather like a clock. We ended up with twelve pavilions marking the hours, and a tall 'Tower of Time' in the middle which would act as a sundial gnomon to tell the time when the sun was out, and be augmented with a powerful laser for night time and sunless days.

Gary's design turned the angular pavilions into geodesic spheres and the

Tower of Time into an exciting central feature with lifts all the way around it, each with video walls, so that your journey up to the viewing platform started in the core of the earth, and went up through the oceans to the land into the sky and finally into space.

The briefing papers said that the sites for consideration included East Stratford, Greenwich and Birmingham. The only site that fulfilled the mandatory requirements of access by road, rail and air was Birmingham. But I was sure, from some of my contacts, that the Government really wanted to go to Greenwich which, with the Observatory and the Greenwich Time Meridian going through it, is already linked to the 'story of time'. Gary made it clear that his event could easily be adapted for Greenwich, but at a cost. He won the competition and was immediately told that it would be moved to Greenwich.

This suited me very well, as I had been working on plans for an Opening Ceremony. My concept was to join up the two icons of time – Big Ben and the 'pips' of Greenwich – using a huge river procession from Westminster to Greenwich, with Royal barges and floating orchestras and masses of small boats in attendance. The procession would make a 'journey in time' from the past to the present, and look forward to the future. Each of the bridges was to be decorated with Shakespeare's Seven Ages of Man, but in reverse order. So as the Queen travelled with her entourage down the Thames she would leave the past behind in 'mere oblivion'. The old millennium was the 'lean and slipper'd pantaloon', growing younger as the Justice, the Soldier, the Lover and the Whining School-boy, until the journey to the future paused at the rebirth of the Infant of the new millennium.

At the Royal Naval College, Greenwich there would be a seated stand on the opposite side of the river. From her Royal Barge the Queen would watch a brief firework display set to Handel's Music for the Royal Fireworks, then zoom down to 'the future' in a modern fast catamaran. At midnight a very strong laser beam would fire down from the Greenwich Meridian at zero degrees longitude and set off a series of inter-visible beacons across the whole country.

At the same time a 'River of Fire' would unite Greenwich and Westminster in a continuous stream of flame. This idea was later 'borrowed', and not in the end done properly. I was going to use thirty boats to produce a pyrotechnic extravaganza; in fact, they used far fewer and it failed, as it was bound to.

In the early stages, the police and local authorities were worried about letting the public onto the bridges at all because they were not stressed for sideways pressure for very large numbers of people. They wanted everybody to watch from the embankments, with the bridges being used only as crossing points until shortly before the display began. So we would also be putting the fireworks on the bridges as well as on the barges. This official advice changed later and they did allow people onto the bridges.

Whilst our planning was going on the Government changed, and the whole project became an ego trip for Tony Blair and Peter Mandelson. At the same time Ms Page was trying to cut the budget, so one by one our ideas were discarded until our whole concept was disappearing fast. Eventually someone asked: what was the cheapest way of covering a very large area? Someone else suggested a dome. So a dome it was to be, and I resigned.

Later I was approached by Cameron Mackintosh, the famous producer of *Les Miserables* and *Phantom of the Opera*. Would I be interested in joining him and John Napier in producing the central show in the Dome, something that would happen two or three times every day? John had come up with a brilliant idea for a circular theatre, with seated segments which could motor back to turn the stage from a small area into a very large one. This would be fed from underneath the seating and we would be able to do some pretty spectacular effects. We worked on it for a bit, and went to another meeting with Ms Page. It was bizarre, to say the least. Again, all our ideas were subjected to the 'expert' view. I have no problem with experts as long as they know what they're talking about. But this was not the case.

Everything the real experts said was second-guessed by the resident team. In one exchange I remember well, we said it was vital to have good changing rooms for the cast of a thousand. Cameron's idea would involve thousands of people, particularly the young, coming from all over the country a county at a time, who would take it in turns to be part of the daily series of shows. 'Why,' they asked, 'couldn't they arrive already in costume?' It didn't seem worth explaining yet again that they would be changing costumes many times during the show.

During a break, Cameron, John and I walked round the block trying to make sense of it all. The project as we envisaged it was dead, so I resigned for a second time from the Millennium celebrations, a fact of which I am rather proud! But I was very sad to have missed the opportunity of working with Cameron who I greatly admire.

A little later I was summoned to Peter Mandelson's office. Mandelson curled up on his sofa and kicked off his shoes to reveal bright red socks. I think he was trying to be coquettish. If so, he failed miserably. He questioned me about Cameron's plans for the central theatre and complained it was too expensive. I said it was marvellous and well worth the money, and anyway there was little else of quality on offer. He simpered that the Dome would be a 'wonder of the world'. Well, it certainly turned out to be just that but not, I expect, in the way he was hoping. The banal crassness of the contents and ceremonies was indeed world class. Every piece of advice was ignored and, sadly, huge sums were wasted on very little. The only good pavilions were the two produced by Gary and 'Imagination'.

Mandelson ended up with a show that could have been quite good but looked hopeless in daylight. Jennie Page's Millennium Experience Company had been advised that blackout was desirable for theatrical effect, but they had chosen to stay with the 'white' roof to save money on lighting. The seating, in speckled yellow, orange and red, looked as though someone had vomited across it.

The Opening Ceremony was 'multi-cultural', which appeared to mean that every culture was represented except for Anglo-Saxon English. Christianity, the anniversary of which I thought we were celebrating, was quite side-lined. The Blairs bounced up and down as though they were enjoying it, and Her Majesty was forced to link hands and sing Auld Lang Syne. All in all, a triumph of bureaucratic non-creativity, and a huge wasted opportunity.

I had one other stab at doing something for the Millennium, and came up with a very stupid idea for Salisbury Cathedral. I designed a fantastic sunburst effect with the spire and nave, the choir and the transepts all coming together to reveal a vast golden sun, which would rise on the dawn of the new millennium. The Cathedral Close would be turned into the four seasons and the months of the year, and the spire would be used as a vast sundial to tell the time. I thought this quite an original idea until someone pointed out that Sir Christopher Wren had had exactly the same idea a little earlier. I was shown the mark he made on the wall in the Close where the shadow of the spire falls at noon on mid-summer's day.

Fortunately the whole thing was shelved, as I am certain that if I had been allowed to do it the spire would have fallen and the cathedral would have been ruined.

*   *   *

One idea which did come to fruition was the Royal Military Tattoo on Horse

Guards. The MOD had decided that it had to contribute something to the Millennium celebrations and this was what it was going to be. It all came about in a strange way, as I had been thinking for some time about what event might succeed the Royal Tournament which we knew was going to finish in 1999.

I thought about trying to replicate what had originally made the Royal Tournament so successful – pageantry, ceremonial, music and action – but in a different way. The first three were relatively easy, but action was a problem.

I came up with a two-part scheme to replace the Tournament. The traditional bands, music and ceremonial would feature on a famous outdoor site – Horse Guards or Windsor Castle – while 'action' would be created in a large mobile 'Experience Theatre' which included a series of interactive aptitude tests, which young people could 'swipe' into at any even remotely military event. Depending on their test results they would get email messages suggesting they consider a career in whichever branch of the services the computers indicated as being most suitable.

Much to my surprise, however, the MOD chose only the Horse Guards Pageant. So I devised a massive show to tell the story of 'Defence of the Realm' over nine hundred years, with a cast of fifteen hundred people, two hundred horses, and sixty aircraft and helicopters plus parachutists. We would also use massive video screens like the ones we had used in Saudi Arabia, and huge projections all over the buildings of Horse Guards.

However, this was an MOD contract and would have to be put out for tender. I was in the strange position of being the producer/creator of the show but with no production company to deliver it. At that stage, I believed Alan Jacobi of Unusual Rigging was the only person who could do what I wanted, but it became clear that Mark Wallace's company Caribiner were infinitely superior in virtually every field, so my beloved old Technical Team had to stand aside and I acquired a new and excellent lighting designer, sound designer and production management team. No one could have done it better than they eventually did. Jacobi never forgave me.

Rosemary Anne Sisson, Charles Messenger and I would meet for dinner two or three times a week to hammer out the very complicated script. Sometimes we would advance one or two centuries during dinner, sometimes we would go back and start again. Rosemary eventually produced a wonderfully succinct script that took us through the nine hundred years in a way that everybody could understand.

The show was going to have a full running narrative with music, stars, video screens and projections as well as aircraft, fireworks and special effects. Because it had to be done in such a short time it all had to be computer controlled which meant everything, including the massed bands, had to keep exact time. Given that we had to go through nine hundred years of history in ninety minutes, anyone who was more than thirty seconds late would find themselves in the wrong war.

I was very lucky to have Lieutenant Colonel Richard Waterer of the Royal Marines and his excellent team of WO2 McDermot and Colour Sergeant Peers who wrote and arranged all the music. Because of everything being computer controlled the conductor had to work to a 'click track'. I had been wondering how we could make a massed band sound balanced, with all the instruments at the right volume. Normally one instrument is drowned out by another, so you usually hear only the front rank. And in the countermarch, when the band doubles back on itself, the music suddenly goes 'quiet'. I was determined to avoid this. Sound designer Paul Keating came up with the answer. For the first time, a massed military band was covered with radio microphones and amplified, and computer controlled which made them sound exactly balanced at all times Everyone in the large cast was double-used. I explained to a company of Royal Marines, who would be re-enacting their exploits in the Falklands later in the programme, that I wanted them to play invading Vikings being fought off by King Alfred wearing helmets and black cloaks. A deep murmur rose from the ranks, very much along the lines of: 'I didn't join the effin' Royal Marines ...'

'But you are, of course, on your way to rape and pillage,' I added. That cheered them up considerably.

The King's Troop enacted the Charge of the Light Brigade, which was almost too real for comfort. Some of them headed for the cheap seats with lances lowered, giving the impression of not being totally in control. The men had to dismount quickly, be covered with stage blood, and come back hanging over the saddles of their horses.

In the end we had over fifty aircraft taking part, including the Battle of Britain Memorial Flight, a Tornado, a Jaguar and the latest Eurofighter. I felt really sorry for anybody trying to use Heathrow Airport on those evenings.

The stars included Dennis Quilley, Martin Jarvis, Timothy West, and Dame Judi Dench who did a brilliant part-read part-sung version of *I vow to thee my country*; her husband Michael Williams also took part. David Montgomery, son of the Field Marshal, was very keen to do his father's voice and was uncannily good. We set fire to Horse Guards in a Blitz scene, and had it put out by World War Two veteran fire engines, except on one night when a real fire engine was called out by some passing busybody only to be told to 'eff off' by a Lance Corporal on one of the entrances.

The Queen came with other members of the Royal family and I was amused afterwards to present to her the WRAC officer who played Queen Elizabeth I. QE II meets QE I.

The Prime Minister, Tony Blair, also came with his wife. Afterwards when I spoke to him he kept repeating, 'It wasn't what I was expecting.' I asked what he had been expecting, but he couldn't say. Interestingly, when I later took him to meet the Boys he couldn't connect with them and they were totally uninterested and ignored him.

I doubt there has ever been a technically more advanced or more ambitious tattoo, but sadly tattoos are no longer a growth industry, and I doubt if anything like it will ever happen again. However, as we 'executed' Charles I for the last time, I was pondering the Queen Mother's hundredth birthday celebration, which would take place on the same arena a few days later.

CHAPTER FOURTEEN

A Small Party for the Prince
– The Royal Wedding Fireworks

Kipling described power without responsibility as 'the prerogative of the harlot throughout the ages'. But if you're running a firework display you have responsibility without power. The only control you ever have over such an event, having designed it, is giving the cue to start. After that, you are in the hands of fate.

I love fireworks. They are a good way of entertaining a lot of people in a large area at a modest cost per head. I have been responsible for a lot of displays over the years; quite a lot have been successful, quite a lot have not. Some have been plain disastrous.

My first big display in the Regiment nearly burnt down the Colonel's house; my second one set light to a wood and almost ensured that the French won the Battle of Trafalgar. In Berlin I scorched a reasonable number of the audience in the Olympic Stadium and destroyed Moscow in a few seconds.

Just before their wedding in 1981, the Prince of Wales and Lady Diana Spencer came to the Wembley Musical Pageant. We played Music for the Royal Fireworks, with a large set piece hanging from the scoreboard. When ignited it looked magnificent for about two minutes, then the whole stadium filled with smoke, so that the fifteen hundred musicians completely disappeared from sight and the lights dimmed as though there had been an eclipse. The Massed Bands walked off under cover of the smoke.

In fact, I had had great trouble in getting Wembley Stadium to agree to fireworks in the first place. I offered a small demonstration to show them how safe they were. We hung a frame under the scoreboard and set light to it. It looked great and they seemed to be pleased. But after they had gone I noticed that the mechanical hare used for greyhound racing had been burnt to a cinder and looked a little sad.

The finale was the 1812 Overture (again!). Twenty Household Cavalry horsemen dressed as Cossacks galloped round the outside with large yellow Czarist flags, whilst the band played and the guns fired. One horseman fell off and lay prone, right in front of the Royal Box.

Someone shouted, 'Get the doctor!'

Someone else called back, 'That *is* the doctor!'

The medical officer had apparently become quite 'relaxed', had ordered a trooper off his horse and had taken his place. I think Diana enjoyed it, and giggled away afterwards as I explained the slight problems we had had.

But they were nothing compared to my really big disaster. The engagement of the Prince of Wales to Lady Diana Spencer had been talked about for so long before it was actually announced that I had already had a plan in mind. I had been longing for years to recreate in full the Royal Fireworks for which Handel had written the music in 1749. This seemed to be the perfect opportunity.

I suggested to Desmond Langley, the Major General Commanding the Household Division, that instead of giving the Prince of Wales a boring old desk, why not give him and some of his friends a fantastic spectacle as a wedding present? Using the Massed Bands of the Household Division and the King's Troop, Royal Horse Artillery we could reconstruct the Firework Palace that had been built in Green Park to celebrate the Peace of Aix-la-Chappelle and send up a ton or two of fireworks. It would be mainly for the Prince and his friends on the eve of his wedding, but could be viewed by the public as well.

Desmond Langley thought this was an excellent idea and sold it to the Palace. As I wanted everybody to be able to see it for nothing I now had to raise a considerable sum of money. We also moved the site to Hyde Park where there was more room for the public. Denys Randolph of Wilkinson Sword, who then owned Pains Wessex, very generously donated the fireworks. Barratt Brothers, the construction part of Earls Court Olympia, agreed to make the 'Palace' at cost price. Boring but vital things such as fencing, seating, lights and so on would have to be paid for with real money.

My original intention was for a VIP audience of about eighteen. The Prince of Wales then asked if he could bring the rest of his family, which took the numbers up to about sixty-five. Then the Foreign Office said that they really needed something for all the Heads of State and members of foreign Royal families to do on the evening before the wedding. The Queen had agreed to give a supper party; could they then all come to the Royal Fireworks? This was getting ridiculous – there would now be a hundred and eighty guests in the Royal Box. I told them I simply could not afford this, and that they would have to pay. They agreed, and sent a cheque immediately.

In the meantime, in order to raise money for the boring bits, I had unilaterally sold exclusive television rights to the BBC for £25,000. The Queen's Private Secretary, Sir William Heseltine, whom I had got to know quite well by then, telephoned to say that I couldn't possibly sell the rights only to the BBC. I explained my financial problems, and he agreed to support me in what I was about to do. So I told the BBC that they now had to share their 'exclusive' rights with ITV, and I told ITV I wanted £25,000 from them for the shared rights. They also agreed.

I worked out that the original budget for building the Firework Palace in 1749 came to about £2.5 million in today's money. I thought it unlikely that I could match that but I would try. I designed it to resemble the original and drew plans for the 'windows' to be filled with set-piece firework pictures in lance work to reflect the Prince's life to date. The windows were twenty feet by thirty, which is extremely large for lance work pictures. His arms, titles, orders and decorations would all be in stars thirty feet high on the 'roof'. The arms and logos of his schools and universities, all the regiments of which he was Colonel in Chief, and all his main charities would be in the windows. All this took a long time to research and even longer to make. I laid out the performance area on the Gallows crossroads in Hyde Park.

An added complication was that it was taking place at the same time as the Royal Tournament, but at least it meant that I had a number of assets to hand. I had the Massed Bands of the Household Division, the Guns of the King's Troop, Royal Horse Artillery, the Choir of the Welsh Guards and 'my' choir, the Morriston Orpheus. Searchlights came from the Royal Engineers Territorial Army and the Scouts agreed to provide six hundred torch bearers. On arrival, the Prince of Wales would light the first of a national chain of beacons with the 1948 Olympic torch, the very one that had been used – with mixed success – at Windsor for the Silver Jubilee Beacon; it would be presented to him by a disabled member of Queen Elizabeth's Foundation. There were to be a hundred and one beacons, all inter-visible, on sites surveyed by the Royal Institute of Chartered Surveyors covering all four countries of the Union. Many sites were the same as those for the Silver Jubilee, with an additional 'leg' to take in Diana's home, Althorp (incidentally, the only one to send in a bill afterwards for the bonfire). Unfortunately the Royal Parks would not allow a very large fire; in fact, they insisted on a pretty pathetic brazier on a pole, so we had to send the message

Emma and me at Music on Fire.

Cardinal Hume being told about his crocked cross!

Music on Fire! Sandhurst 2008.

Emma and I surrounded by 2 million of our closest friends – Golden Jubilee 2002.

Finale "All The Queen's Horses" Windsor 2002.

Royal Tournament Field Gun Run.

The Defence cuts beginning to show at the Queen Mother's 100th birthday.

My very stupid idea for Salisbury Cathedral at the millennium.

Queen Elizabeth II meets Queen Elizabeth 1 at the Royal Military Tattoo 2000.

Projections on the front of the Palace and Fireworks –
Golden Jubilee.

The Commonwealth Children's Balcony Hanging – Golden
Jubilee.

Rigging a new 'Throne' on the roof of the Palace for the
Golden Jubilee.

The Queen leaves in the Gold State Coach in blue…

And she returns dressed in red.

A Singular 'Honour' – The Spam© Lifetime Achievement Award.

The Walpole Cultural Achievement of the Year Award-2002.

The Gold State Coach at 'All The Queen's Horses' Windsor 2002.

Anton du Beke making use of the limited rehearsal space in Buckingham Palace –'Not Forgotten' 90th Celebration.

The setting for 'All the Queen's Horses' at Windsor 2002.

Dame Judi Dench, Nickolas Grace and Peter Duncan – Not Forgotten Association 90th celebration.

Minerva ship naming – Tower Bridge 2003.

My patriotic and practical headdress at the Army Benevolent Fund's 'Music on Fire' 2008.

The 106 year old World War I veteran Bill Stone at the Not Forgotten's Garden Party at Buckingham Palace.

The Ballroom with one of the hundred images projected during the 'Not Forgotten' Celebration'.

The last time my uniform fitted – July 2000

by lasers from a nearby building.

I wanted something really special to end the display, so I hired a hugely tall crane and designed a thirty-foot Catherine Wheel to go on top, with the letters C and D and 'Vivat' in the middle. Pedants said it should have read 'Vivant', but I didn't have room for the 'n'. When the crane got to its full height the wheel would be turned by hand by a brave fireman in a flameproof safety suit and helmet. As usual the 'experts' said that no one would come – we might get fifty thousand if we were lucky. Also, as usual, I didn't believe them.

I was worried about getting all our VIPs from the Palace to their seats; I couldn't possibly cope with over a hundred limousines. Sir John Miller, the Crown Equerry, came up with the answer. Except for the Queen, the Duke of Edinburgh and the Prince of Wales who would come by car, we would put them all in charabancs, as he called them. They had done it for Princess Alexandra's wedding and it had worked perfectly.

The list of VIP guests kept being added to, as the wedding was obviously very popular. Amongst those coming were the King and Queen of Tonga; they were of substantial size, to say the least, and we had to have two special double chairs made for them.

President Reagan was not coming, as he was yet to do a state visit, but his wife Nancy would be. I had many fruitless meetings with the President's security guards at which I kept explaining that they could not put six protection officers around the First Lady as there was simply no room. In the end I said, 'Look, I'll put the First Lady next to me, right behind the Queen. And if she's shot, I hope I am too.' That did not go down well.

Tens of thousands of fireworks had been put in place and the firework pictures looked great. Pains Wessex said they had never seen such a vast area of lance work before. It was all going to look splendid. The Massed Bands arrived, as did the two choirs. The King's Troop, Royal Horse Artillery, with their guns and limbers, rode from Earls Court having just finished their Drive for the Royal Tournament. But through no fault of their own they were directed up the wrong path in the Park and the heavy metal wheels sliced cleanly through all the firework control cables. The firework men tried desperately to repair them and inevitably connected many cables incorrectly – there were almost a thousand of them – the result of which was to become only too obvious later. Fortunately at the time I was unaware of the problem.

Meanwhile, at the Palace they were loading the guests into the coaches; each coach had a member of the Royal family as its 'tour guide'. The King and Queen of Tonga, we were told, had decided not to come so we removed the double chairs.

The crowds were vast. In my caravan was a monitor from a BBC camera high up on a building somewhere, so I could see virtually the whole of the park. When I went back for a quick afternoon nap, it was mainly green; when I woke up it looked entirely grey with people. The police reckoned there were at least eight hundred thousand there.

The coaches began to arrive, through an avenue of six hundred Scouts with flaming torches. We had arranged for the guests to be put into the buses in the order that they would enter the stands. But Mrs Reagan arrived on the wrong coach, far too early, and was shown to her seat in the centre of the stand where she sat for some time in splendid isolation in a bright red coat and hat. A perfect target.

Suddenly there was a slight commotion. 'That's the King and Queen of Tonga arriving now, Sir,' a senior policeman told me.

'Impossible,' I declared. 'They're not coming.' But they were. Their large limousine was coming down the flame path at that very moment. I turned to an officer and asked him to show the King and Queen to their seats, knowing full well there weren't any. To this day I have no idea who he was (fortunately, he has never come to thump me). And I have no idea where he put the substantial King and Queen.

The royals were now arriving thick and fast. Those who had been in buses before were not so enchanted by the experience but those who never had thought it was all great fun. A man I vaguely recognised came up and said, 'How do you do? I am the King of the Belgians.' I couldn't think what to say, and heard myself blurting out, 'Well done, Sir. I'm afraid we're running late so we'll have to hurry,' and off he went quite happily. He was the Senior Head of State present so at least I knew exactly where he was sitting.

Eventually the Royal cars arrived and the Queen and Prince Philip went to their seats whilst I took the Prince of Wales to light the beacon. I apologised for the pathetic size of it but as it was lit and the flames leapt up, the four hundred Massed Bandsmen of the Household Division marched on looking splendid. I walked Prince Charles back to the box and stood beside Mrs Reagan. I had said hello to her on arrival but she never said a word to me all evening.

After the King's Troop, Royal Horse Artillery had galloped on and put their guns into action, I attempted to do my only positive act of the evening; I had to give the cue for the show to start. The officer was supposed to keep looking at me and fire the guns when I sat down. I sat down but nothing happened, so I stood up and sat down again, very deliberately. Still nothing happened so I stood up again. The Queen turned round and asked, 'What on earth are you doing?' I explained, and tried yet again. This time it worked. But if you watch the video of the event, you will hear an offscreen BBC stage manager shouting, 'He's given the bloody cue, you idiot!'

I had had special silk programmes made, as in Queen Victoria's day, for each guest. They had been designed by the artist John Piper and his son Edward, and were very beautiful. However, they told the guests how and when the fireworks would be fired, and it became immediately obvious that none of what was written down was actually happening. All my carefully planned sequences were completely ruined, and the story of the life and achievements of the Prince of Wales had turned into a barely controlled bonfire. It was still quite impressive, but as soon as you could see something special it would immediately be masked by something else going off wrongly.

Fortunately the Queen seemed to think it funny and turned round from time to time to say, 'Those don't look like violet star bursts to me,' or 'Was that a flight of chrysanthemum shells?' I could only smile thinly. We were supposed to replicate the 1764 event, when one of the wings of the palace caught light, and had organised an ancient fire engine to come and put it out. But by the time it actually arrived, the fire effect was over so the firemen had to mime putting it out, and it all looked like a scene from a Laurel and Hardy film.

Eventually the crane went up and the vast Catherine Wheel sun ignited and turned. The flameproofed fireman obviously had not been burnt to a cinder as it kept on turning and looked rather good.

At last it was all over. As the Queen and the senior Royals left, I presented to them the key people involved. When I got to the firework people I could barely restrain myself from throttling them, but in all fairness it was not their fault and they had done brilliantly to get anything to go off at all.

Finally, after everybody had gone, the Major General, the Commissioner of the Metropolitan Police and I sat in the box drowning our sorrows. After a bit it became clear that the crowds were not dispersing properly. Policemen came rushing up to tell the Commissioner that someone had padlocked all the gates. Fortunately the crowd did not panic, still being in a very happy, if mystified, mood. The gates were cut open and eventually the crowd trickled away. Although it was never proved, there was a serious suspicion that London Underground staff had padlocked the gates because they did not want people to crowd the trains. Earlier in the evening the platforms had been so full that people could not get off their trains so had to go on to the next station.

I went back to the relative calm of the Royal Tournament to nurse my bruises. St John Ambulance later told me that they had dealt with three thousand casualties that night, slightly fewer than normal. Some people even thought the event was a great success, which just proves my point: 'If you don't know what is supposed to happen then you won't know when it hasn't.'

The ITV commentator Alastair Burnet, rather accurately, described the evening as 'A triumph of hope over experience'!

And the Household Division still gave the Prince and Princess a desk as a wedding present.

CHAPTER FIFTEEN

❧

A Surprise for the Queen, and Another Shot at Lord Nelson

Presumably working on the hope-over-experience principle, Peter de Savary asked me to go to Antigua again to do a display. In 1984 he had revamped a rather unattractive Holiday Inn into the ultra-luxurious St James's Club, and the opening ceremony was to be on New Year's Eve. I planned to build a pirate galleon in the lagoon and have its cannon fire on the chimes of Big Ben. There would then be a massive firework display to music, produced by Zambelli – the only American firework company I knew. I flew out four times to Antigua where, apart from the plans for the galleons, my main task seemed to be trying out the Club's range of cocktails. Of course I had to try each one several times just to make certain they were all alright.

On one visit I was met at the airport by Sir John Mills, a sort of honorary chairman of the Club. He announced gleefully that my galleon had sunk, but that he would get me a drink to help me get over it. We had to build another one immediately.

Peter apologised that I would not be staying in the Club for the opening, but would stay at the Copper and Lumber Store in English Harbour. I was thrilled, as it was a hotel that actually worked, unlike St James's which we had all dubbed Stalag Luft because nothing worked. The hairdresser Leonard, who was in the same hotel, had come to set up a new salon at the Club. But everything was so shambolic that he swore his Avocado Face Cream had actually been served as avocado mousse for lunch.

Everybody had insisted that it never rained at that time of year in Antigua, so Zambelli took none of the precautions they normally would, such as keeping everything dry with cooking foil and firing the fireworks through it. Liza Minnelli was there with a new boyfriend. Michael York and his wife were also there and Liza, who was in recovery mode after recent problems, kept coming up and giving me a big cuddle and telling me how 'marvellous' I had been in *Cabaret*. I kept trying to explain that I was the wrong Michael, but gave up. It was Liza who told me about the Club's twenty-four hour room service – it took twenty-four hours to get anything! I was glad I was staying over the hill.

I also met, and was surprised to like, Paul Raymond of Raymond's Revue Bar. He was there with a 'niece' whom we never saw during the day, so we ate together frequently. The food was less than excellent – one day we were given lobsters and sprouts – but it was plentiful and it was free. I also had lunch from time to time with Joan Collins, who was there with her latest fiancé, Peter Holm. They were constantly surrounded by paparazzi, particularly after it was rumoured that she had thrown her engagement ring into the sea. Once everything looked ready for the show I went for a drink with Joan, by this time reunited with her ring, on somebody's yacht, and we ended up lying on a bed together looking through the windows at a lot of black clouds that seemed to be coming in fast.

I went to my hotel to change and on the way back it started to pour with rain. Water was bouncing back at least a foot off the ground. At the club we found that the tables laden with food had been washed away and the swimming pool had overflowed because lobsters were floating down the drains. Some of the richest people in the world were scavenging for something to eat.

By eleven o'clock the rain had stopped, but I had a gloomy feeling inside. Midnight was approaching and everybody was gathering by the lagoon. When the Prime Minister of Antigua, our guest of honour, arrived I gave the cue for the show to begin. A radio announcement was broadcast from London, followed by the famous chimes. I waited expectantly for the first 'Big Ben' cannon shot, but it didn't fire. Neither did the next one or the next, or in fact any of them. The music continued but there were absolutely no fireworks going up. Then suddenly one went up, to a big cheer. The music came to a triumphant end accompanied by absolutely nothing. There was a long silence. The Prime Minister had obviously written a speech telling us how impressive and exciting he thought the firework display had been. All he could do was stand in front of the microphone spluttering out a few words about nothing in particular.

Liza came up and gave me a great big kiss. 'Darling, don't worry – sometimes *my* life seems to go like that. Have a drink!'

Peter was surprisingly kind. Had I been him, I think I would have had me shot.

*   *   *

HMS *Excellent*, the Royal Navy Gunnery School, where the Royal Navy Field Guns for the Royal Tournament came from, wanted me to help them celebrate their 150th anniversary. I was not keen as I had so much else to do, including the Household Division Retreat. But I agreed and they sent a helicopter each day to take me from Chelsea Barracks down to Whale Island, where I would do the show and then take a train back.

The show was so bad it was almost good. One scene showed Saint Barbara, patron saint of gunnery, who was imprisoned in a tower by her father who was struck dead by lightning after beheading her. On the first night her tower blew over, so it had to be made more stable. On the second night she was bewailing the fact that she was all alone on top of the tower, with twenty pairs of boots and gaiters perfectly visible underneath; this was pointed out loudly by members of the audience. Then, just to complete the shambles, her 'severed head' rolled out between the legs of the sailors.

The finale of the show was notable only for the fact that the fireworks managed to kill the two peacocks which belonged to the Officers' Wardroom. They were delighted, because the birds had made such a racket they could never get to sleep.

*   *   *

A rather more successful event took place in 1987. Every year the Queen and the Duke of Edinburgh would stay at Luton Hoo for their wedding anniversary, to shoot. Nicky Phillips, son of my friend Gina Phillips whose parents had lived at Luton Hoo, wanted to do a secret surprise for their fortieth, or Ruby, wedding anniversary. He no longer lived in the big house but in a smaller house in the woods and the dinner party would only be about twelve strong.

Wilf Scott and I designed a totally red firework display. Red is chemically quite a difficult firework colour, so you do not have a great deal of variety to use. I produced a design with the Queen's E and Prince Philip's P and the dates 47-87, but for security reasons we couldn't tell anybody what we were celebrating. One of the workers in the firework factory gave it as his opinion, 'Well, it's for Major Parker, so E P is obviously for his mother Ethel Parker!'

Nobody knew what was going to happen, not even Gina. Wilf and I had to hide when the Queen arrived preceded by quite a large van full of clothes. As soon as she was inside the house the curtains were drawn and we set up our fireworks. I told the butler to warn Luton Airport to close for ten minutes.

The idea was that just before dinner the guests would be asked to go outside. The Queen was first out onto the terrace; I didn't hide quickly enough and she saw me lurking there. 'Ah,' she said, 'I know what's going to happen!' The show was good and the set piece looked great. 'Ethel' would certainly have been pleased. The Queen seemed highly amused that Gina had not been told the secret, and Gina in return was rather miffed. I was given a bottle of pink champagne which I gave to the boys. Wilf said he would frame it.

*   *   *

Also in 1987, for P&O's 150th anniversary celebrations at Greenwich, the Queen was coming to dinner aboard *Pacific Princess* moored in front of the Royal Naval College. In order to look over the ship and plan what we might do, I had to go out to Madeira with Caroline Cousins and Richard Baker, who was going to choose the music and do the commentary. We all sailed home in her. I got on very well with Richard and his wife Margaret, who were great fun, and he and I started writing a possible scenario.

We decided to put the Massed Bands of the Household Division (again!) in a very large barge dressed to look like an old P&O paddle steamer. We would project lasers onto the College and the Queen's House and have floating firework barges at each end of the *Pacific Princess* which, by now, would be anchored in the middle of the Thames. A powerful laser would shine down the Greenwich Meridian from the Observatory, in its path a forty-foot globe on a hoist.

We did a run-through of the show aboard the cruise ship at high tide. It didn't go very well, so we headed for the nearest bar and just hoped it would be all right on the night. The night came and it was. The voices, the music, the lasers, the globe – everything looked marvellous. However, the fireworks, impressive to start with, were becoming more so, and the barge carrying them seemed to be getting nearer and nearer. I thought it was coming far too close for comfort, so I went to stand behind the Queen, in case anything went wrong (Rule 7).

The show just finished safely, everybody was very pleased, and I went to find out what had gone wrong. It transpired that the skipper of the tug with the main fireworks barge had had a row with his wife and had forgotten to fill up with fuel. So halfway through the firing sequence he had run out of diesel and drifted in on the tide. By sheer chance and good luck our timing was just right.

*   *   *

I did many other firework displays which were quite impressive, but none very noteworthy except for one in China.

P&O wanted a show at Shenzhen, just down the coast from Hong Kong, with the then largest container ship in the world, the *Shenzhen Bay*. We were going to do it at the huge container port which was also owned by P&O. We thought it would be wise to buy Chinese fireworks. However, in those days – despite the Chinese having invented fireworks – although very impressive they tended to have very dodgy fuses. They either went off straight away, or waited a few minutes and then went off. So we bought all the firework material and took it in a P&O ship to a Dutch harbour that allowed explosives to be imported. There we changed all the fuses and re-imported the fireworks back into China. There are advantages to working with a shipping company.

The whole length of the ship was covered with fireworks. I wanted a large P&O set piece firework on the side of the ship some fifty feet by seventy, but this proved too costly so I suggested they paint a very large P&O on the side. This they did, and liked the look of it so much that they painted most of the other ships in their fleet the same.

We built a seating stand for about three hundred VIPs under the path of two of the very high mobile cranes that motored down tracks to lift containers off ships. The idea was that at the beginning of the show the cranes would motor over the audience and, when in position, lift the fixing bar onto which we fixed many fireworks. This is not the sort of thing 'Elf'n'Safety' would allow you to do in Britain.

The container bars covered in fireworks looked splendid as they rose out of the water. Everything went well in spite of the fact that the Chinese tug skippers seemed to be unaware that the tide came in and out each day and forgot to take the barges out when planned. We also nearly wrote off fifty young children who crept in to watch the show and sat neatly on the line of explosives that we were going to set off on the dockside for the finale. We removed them just in time.

Afterwards the Chinese officials were very impressed by the way the fireworks had gone off exactly in time with the music, something they had not seen before. So we explained how we did it. By the time the Beijing Olympic Games came round they had certainly learnt about firework fuses and produced the most fantastic display.

*   *   *

P&O's cruise liner *Oriana* was named by the Queen in Southampton and then sailed to Sydney. The old *Oriana* had taken many immigrants to Australia over the years, and her name was still fondly regarded.

I planned a welcome show in Sydney Harbour, which is pretty famous for spectacular firework displays. As we sailed into the amazing harbour we were surrounded by literally hundreds of small craft including a scale model of the original *Oriana*, and fire boats jetting plumes of water. It was a fantastic sight. I could see from the bridge a large number of people continuing to sunbathe by the pool. The captain declined to draw the spectacle to their attention, saying, 'They've all paid; they can do what they like.'

We used a local firework firm who started off saying, 'What do you bloody Poms know about fireworks that we don't?', but progressed to 'Not a bad idea, mate; might steal that one.'

I very nearly didn't make the event at all. I went out in the pilot boat to tell the captain of the ship where I wanted him to stop for the display, and fell between the pilot boat and the ship. I was only saved by someone grabbing me at the last moment and throwing me up onto the ship. No mean feat, considering my size.

* * *

2005 would see the two hundredth anniversary of the Battle of Trafalgar. I had already removed myself from any role in this, much as I would have loved to have done it. Two people I had worked with over the years, and to whom I had given so many opportunities, were told by the Royal Naval Project Officer that they would not get the contract if I was running it, so they decided to cut me adrift but still take my ideas with them.

In fact, they did not get the contract in the end. However, when I discovered that the First Sea Lord had decreed that the English and French fleets in the commemorative re-enactment had to be called the 'Red' and 'Blue' fleets, I thought that was so wet and pathetic that I would have resigned immediately in any event. Even the captain of the French aircraft carrier that came over for the ceremony thought the whole thing rather stupid.

Later I was very happy to be approached by the Royal Yacht Squadron in Cowes, who asked if I would come up with ideas for their celebration of the anniversary. I said I would only do it if we were allowed to use an 'English' fleet and a 'French' fleet and on condition the French fleet would lose. They agreed totally and my old friend Sir Donald Gosling generously agreed to fund the exercise. We took over the usual Cowes Week fireworks and totally reorganised them. The Royal Yacht Squadron are the most marvellous set-up, very civilised and hospitable. We had a number of really good lobster lunches, and some seriously good dinners, most of which ended with delicious savouries, which I love.

Wilf Scott and his boys designed a pyrotechnic masterpiece and firework barges were hired for both fleets and loaded with tons of highly-combustible material. The display was going extremely well when suddenly there was an extra-large explosion from the 'French' fleet. Everybody thought it was marvellous, but I had suspicions that it was not intended.

At the height of the battle, the music was to reach a crescendo followed by silence. Then the French fleet was supposed to fire a signal maroon to represent the shot that killed Nelson. Nothing happened. So, probably for the first and only time, Lord Nelson had to commit suicide during the Battle of Trafalgar. When it was finished the squadron fired a *feu de joie* from its own cannons. Afterwards, when I apologised for the lack of the 'fatal shot', nobody had even noticed.

So, in all, I had three attempts at trying to re-enact the Battle of Trafalgar. The first one the French almost won, at the second one (at the Royal Tournament) nobody wanted to kiss Nelson, and in the third Nelson had to commit suicide.

*　　*　　*

On the day I covered the sacrosanct Parade Square at Sandhurst with tons of explosives, Academy Sergeant-Major Lord must have been turning in his grave!

I was organising 'Music on Fire!' for the Army Benevolent Fund and, as a trustee, I was anxious to raise as much money for them as possible. The concept was 'Fireworks and Music' rather than 'Music and Fireworks', with two hours of almost continuous pyrotechnics and stupendous special effects, including flame-bursts that went up thirty feet in the air and could be played from a piano keyboard. We had brilliant readers and soloists, and did wonderful projections onto the white Georgian building of the Old College. The military bands, orchestras and choir were outstanding and were shown at their very best in extremely demanding music that they seldom have the opportunity to play.

Unfortunately, although we drew very good crowds they were not enough to make it worthwhile, but we did raise the profile of the charity and achieved some useful headlines in the *Daily Mail* about how those returning wounded from Iraq and Afghanistan were being treated. In the same way that I believe the Royal Military Tattoo will never be excelled in this country as a tattoo, I think that 'Music on Fire!' will probably never be eclipsed by a better military musical spectacle.

* * *

I had made the first of the two best decisions of my life when I joined my Regiment. Now, forty years later, I was to make the second, which was possibly the more important.

Almost without noticing it, I had become more and more fond of Emma. I had known her since 1991 when she had worked on 'Joy to the World' and she had since worked on many of my other events. She became my PA in 1997, after Catie Bland went to help run the Royal Tournament, and we became closer and closer.

I have had much joy with all my god-children over the years (though they always had the great advantage that one could 'switch them off' and give them back at the end of the day!) but I had always discounted any possibility of marriage as my total absorption in my work seemed to preclude any distraction. I always admired those who could produce large shows and cope with the complications of family life at the same time. I could not, and anyway I reasoned that no one would want to put up with me. It was not until some of my friends began teasing me about Emma that I realised that perhaps there was someone who might.

Emma and I married in 2005 and she and her son Oliver, whom I had known since he was tiny, have been a joy ever since. I also acquired something I had never had until now, a lovely 'proper' family of parents-in-law, sister and brother-in-law and two nephews and a niece – the Gilroys and Wigans. It is wonderful watching the young ones growing up; Oliver did brilliantly in Technical Theatre at RADA and now, very annoyingly, knows far more about staging things than I do!

CHAPTER SIXTEEN

⚜

Buff Orpingtons and Barbara Cartland's Knickers – Queen Elizabeth the Queen Mother's Celebrations

The Queen Mother, or – as she was known by everybody – Queen Elizabeth, was Colonel in Chief of my Regiment and took a great interest everything it did. Sadly, during my time serving she did not actually visit us, but every Christmas she would send each of 'her' regiments Christmas puddings, which the boys tucked into for Christmas lunch.

The first time I met her properly was at the Silver Jubilee Beacon. By then I had left the Regiment but continued as an officer in the Auxiliary Emergency Reserve which entailed spending two weeks 'training' with the Regiment each year. On one such occasion a couple of years, later Queen Elizabeth visited us in Detmold. I met her before lunch and she said immediately, 'Ah, I know you; you set light to one of my family at Windsor!' I never did discover which member I had narrowly missed incinerating; fortunately she made it clear that she had found the whole thing rather funny.

I was thereafter to meet her quite frequently at the Royal Tournament. She had an amazing ability to make you believe that you were the only person to whom she really wanted to talk. Later, when I used to present representatives of the various acts to her after a show she 'did the line-up' quite differently from the rest of the Royal family. They would chat for a few moments to each person then move on to the next, which is a perfectly reasonable way of doing it. Queen Elizabeth, having spoken to someone and moved on to the next person, would suddenly bring the previous person back into the conversation, which caused a few amusing double takes. On occasions she might even bring into the conversation the next person whom she had not yet met, taking them completely off guard. It all made for a very much more relaxed and amusing way of doing things, and all those she met

191

became her devoted admirers.

In 1980 which, as she had been born in 1900, marked her eightieth birthday, I suggested that we stage a tribute to her at the Royal Tournament, bringing together representatives of all the regiments or units of which she was Colonel in Chief or Honorary Air Commodore, or Royal Navy ships that she had launched. I was helped in this by Major Andrew Parker Bowles who at that time was the Adjutant in the Household Cavalry Headquarters. Being one of her godchildren, he was the ideal choice. He did all the work and I just had a few ideas. On the day Queen Elizabeth came to take the Salute we did our little tribute which was very well received. Shortly afterwards the press got it into their heads that she was about to die, and for almost a year they followed her everywhere. Every occasion was going to be the 'last time' that she did something. They came to the Tournament that year for her 'last one'. Fortunately they gave this up after a bit which was lucky for them because she lived for another twenty years.

1985 marked the three-hundredth anniversary of the raising of a number of regiments of the British Army when, as a result of the Monmouth rebellion, a standing army was formed for the first time. The Royal Tournament decided to mount a special show in the Royal Albert Hall to allow all the regiments to celebrate, with Queen Elizabeth as Guest of Honour. Charles Messenger and I wrote the script, and I made good use of his extraordinary knowledge of weird, wonderful, unusual and useless facts. It was, with hindsight, madness to try and do something so complicated in one day with no rehearsal. However, having at this stage been confirmed as a total masochist, I was not going to be put off by a mere challenge.

I puzzled for ages about how to tell the story of some eighteen regiments over three hundred years, and decided the only way to do it was to sketch a simplified history of the nation during that period and choose one famous incident from each Regiment's history.

A huge chessboard was made to cover the Royal Albert Hall arena so that history could be played out with our kings and queens pitted against our enemies' leaders. Their identities would change to mark the passage of time. The knights were the military commanders; the bishops would represent religion or the causes of conflict, while the castles, being heavy, big and thick, would be the politicians. And the pawns were of course the 'poor bloody infantry' of each side. They worked particularly well in the representation of the First World War. By chance, one of the regiments – the Fifth Inniskilling Dragoon Guards – had fired the first British shot of the War, so the pawns advanced, with cannon fire and smoke all around them, and were mown down by skeletal machine gunners. The bugler who stood in the middle of the bodies and played the Last Post was showered with red poppy petals on a smaller scale than the Festival of Remembrance, though poignant nevertheless. It was a slight pity that 'Queen Victoria' appeared still to be on the throne!

Of course everything went wrong from the start. The wrong kings had the wrong generals, but the music kept going and most people were unaware. Those with historical knowledge must have been very confused by the bits we got wrong or left out altogether, but a lot were amused by it.

My own regiment enacted the Knighting of Trooper Thomas Brown by George II on the battlefield of Dettingen. Although severely wounded, and having had two horses killed under him, Trooper Brown still rescued his regiment's guidon. There was a lot of blood in this one.

The boys loved dressing up and hamming everything up, particularly the deaths which would have done credit to Morecambe and Wise. At the very end we were to give three cheers for Her Majesty. I chose a Regimental Sergeant Major to do this on the grounds that he had a very strong voice and would have the confidence and know what to do. How wrong I was. When the moment came he bellowed, 'Three cheers for Her Royal Highness, Queen Elizabeth the Queen Mother'. I was horrified and apologised profusely afterwards.

'Oh, please don't worry one little bit,' she said. 'I haven't been a Royal Highness for over fifty years; it made me feel quite young again!'

It was not long before the prospect of Queen Elizabeth's ninetieth birthday appeared on the horizon. I longed to do something special for it and as usual my idea was rather ambitious and involved the participation of as many people as possible. I always thought that on her birthday Queen Elizabeth drove to Buckingham Palace for lunch. My idea involved building a massive Cathedral of Flowers over Clarence House on the approach road up to the Mall. It would be put in position while she was away – or so I thought – at lunch. But I was wrong – the Royal Family always went *to* Clarence House for lunch.

Gina Phillips, later Lady Kennard, was a great friend from my days of helping St John Ambulance, of which she was the Chief President. She took me to see Sir Martin Gilliat, Queen Elizabeth's Private Secretary, whom she knew well. This was the first time I had been to Clarence House and I was very pleased when they said that I would be allowed to park in St James' Palace. The moment we got inside the door we were offered huge gins and tonic, certainly more gin than tonic, and our meeting was interrupted regularly by the pouring of fresh drinks. Sir Martin, a wonderful old-school gentleman with exquisite manners, pondered my ideas and after a lot of pleasantries and gin pointed out tactfully that there would be no 'return' to Clarence House, as they would have been there the whole time.

I was rather crestfallen, but he then asked me if I would do him a favour. The Headquarters of London District had had an idea for a tribute about which Clarence House was a little worried – would I be kind enough to go and talk to them and see if I could help? Of course I agreed. By this time we were all pretty sozzled, so I had to leave my car behind and take a taxi. I never drove to Clarence House again.

At our meeting the Major General and his staff outlined their idea. I could see immediately that there were problems, the main one being that what they planned was far too small for the huge expanse of Horse Guards Parade. Simply having representatives of the eighteen regiments and units, as we had had in the tiny arena of Earls Court in 1980, was just not going to be good enough. I told them as much and said I would go away and think about it. I did not leave the room a very popular person.

All my best ideas come when I am in the bath. This one was no exception. I suspected that many people would love to pay tribute to Queen Elizabeth and thank her for all she had done for the nation over the years, so whatever I suggested needed to involve very large numbers. Also, Clarence House was going to be inundated with requests for her presence. Could I think of a way of 'killing many birds with one stone'?

I asked Clarence House with how many organisations Queen Elizabeth was involved. The answer turned out to be well over three hundred. I asked for a list.

'Oh dear,' they said, 'we haven't got a list. All we have is little cards in a filing box.'

Could they please type out a list?

'Oh dear...' they said.

Two weeks later I went to collect an immaculately typed list on very stiff paper, obviously done on a steam typewriter. Just as they were about to hand it over, they said, 'As this is the only one we have, would you mind if we took a copy?'

I was amazed by the eclectic mix on the list, which was a complete cross-section of British and Commonwealth life and society. Apart from Service connections, it encompassed the Aberdeen Angus Cattle Society, Bible Reading Fellowships, the Poultry Club, the Royal Philharmonic Orchestra, the Colditz Association and the Salmon and Trout Association.

'Why don't we ask them all to take part in the tribute?' I suggested.

Sir Martin thought for a moment, and said, 'What a frightfully good idea, dear boy.'

I asked for the names and addresses of all the organisations and their officials.

'Oh dear,' he said, 'the Girls won't like that.' The 'Girls' were the Clarence House secretarial staff, who were ladies of some seniority.

Perhaps they had all the addresses on a computer? 'Oh no, the Girls wouldn't like that.'

Two weeks later a list arrived, again beautifully typed. I went back to Horse Guards with my ideas. The Major General was quite positive, while the then Garrison Sergeant Major was not quite as enthusiastic as I had hoped.

'We can't possibly have the King's Troop, Royal Horse Artillery parading with dachshunds,' he said. 'Or the Household Cavalry parading with chickens. And the Aberdeen Angus bulls would never keep in step.'

Oh dear, I thought.

Shortly after that meeting I met Sir William Heseltine, the Queen's Private Secretary, who asked how things were going. I told him what the reaction to my ideas had been, and elaborated on them a bit, and he said he thought it all sounded rather splendid. Well, if the Queen's Private Secretary says things are splendid then they are splendid. All opposition disappeared immediately and we started to contact all the groups.

To my amazement, virtually all of them agreed enthusiastically to take part. And without exception each one said how Queen Elizabeth had taken an 'extra special interest' in their organisation. With over three hundred organisations and only three hundred and sixty-five days in the year, that was quite an achievement. The Jockey Club, the Church Army, Barnardos, the National Trust, Shetland ponies, midwives – the list went on and on. What did amaze me was that the Royal Society, that august group of the great and the good, had accepted to take part in the Parade – they were to regret it later.

Now I had to raise the money to pay for it all, as I wanted all the seats to be given away free to the organisations and there was no other source of income in sight. A few years previously I had met Sir Donald Gosling, when I had given him a little help with an event he was doing for the White Ensign Association. With his business partner Ron Hobson he had given millions to deserving causes. I diffidently approached them and they sent a cheque by return. They were thrilled to be involved.

The rule was that participants had to pay all their own expenses; the only things we would give them would be free seats, a free programme for the representatives, and an airline meal kindly donated by Monarch Airlines. After the Parade there would be a reception in the Banqueting Hall, which was also sponsored.

We had the Massed Bands of the Household Division, the Royal Marines, the Royal Air Force and the bands of all Her Majesty's regiments, the King's Troop, Royal Horse Artillery, the Household Cavalry Regiment and contingents from eight cavalry regiments. We even had a real ring of church bells. It had been made for an Expo and was the only portable rig of its kind in the world at the time. Wing Commander Barry Hingley wrote two brilliant pieces of music, one for the pipes and drums and choir called 'The Sound of the Pipes' and another for the Massed Bands, the church bells and the King's Troop guns, a rather unusual combination.

The whole Parade was to be commanded by the now Lieutenant Colonel Andrew Parker Bowles, who was the Silver Stick Commanding the Household Cavalry.

The Minister of Defence at the time was Tom King, who seemed to take great interest in the Parade. It transpired later that what he really wanted was to sit in the Royal Box with Queen Elizabeth.

I struggled with a way of controlling the Parade without the rehearsals which would have normally been required. In the end we used well-briefed guardsman, who controlled everything beautifully.

Queen Elizabeth came with Princess Margaret who watched the Parade from the Major General's office. The parade itself went amazingly well, all things considered. The military part was immaculate, and the civilians did a great job and managed to arrive at their allocated positions almost correctly. It was clear that the Royal Society did not fully realise for what they had volunteered – marching was not quite their scene. The wonderfully multi-coloured group, all in Doctors' robes, wandered past looking a little bemused. When they arrived at their final position a continuous stream of stretcher-bearers was required to carry off what, from a distance, looked like a lot of brightly-coloured parrots.

Afterwards we moved across to the Banqueting Hall, where Queen Elizabeth spent an hour talking to all the representatives of the groups. The Guild of Glass Engravers produced two very beautiful glasses for Her Majesty to use at the reception, engraved with their idea of what the great procession would look like – a little optimistic as it turned out, but never mind.

Queen Elizabeth gave a little party afterwards for all those who had run it. She was very keen that we should admire the easel on which the painting of the Parade, that we had given her, was resting.

'This was made by my grandson; he's a carpenter, you know!'

Sir Martin Gilliat, who was rather exhausted by all the celebrations, said that fortunately he would not be around for the hundredth birthday – and very sadly he was not.

Following what most thought was a great success the Queen very kindly made me a Commander of the Royal Victorian Order, one of her personal awards, and Princess Margaret wrote me a lovely letter saying how much she had enjoyed it all and telling me that the Royal family called it 'the Buff Orpington Parade'.

After the celebrations I was approached by Richard Briggs who owns stables near Hyde Park and who was active in supporting the Park. Prince Michael of Kent had had the idea of putting memorial gates in Hyde Park to celebrate his aunt-by-marriage's ninetieth birthday, which I thought an excellent idea. Would I like to organise the Opening Ceremony when the Queen would unveil them? I readily agreed, and I suppose I was not too surprised to discover that there was virtually no budget for it.

So I told my team to pull in a few favours. I had seen the drawing of the gates and they looked quite good, but then drawings always seem to look better than the real things turn out to be. I had had an idea of using two very large cranes parked on the roundabout in Park Lane. They would hold up a huge rolled-steel joist on which would be hung very large drapes; however, the only free material I could get was bright pink. When the Queen pressed the button the cranes would raise the drapes and all would be revealed. But that seemed a bit too simple (Rule 4), so I arranged for the riggers to be hanging in harnesses inside the drapes armed with ninety-three thousand dried rose petals (Queen Elizabeth would be ninety-three when the Opening Ceremony came) gathered and dried by members of the Garden Society, one of her many organisations. As the beam and drapes were raised into the air the riggers would throw out the petals.

When I briefed them there was a moment reminiscent of many exchanges I had had with soldiers over the years – 'I didn't become an effin' rigger to throw effin' rose petals at effin' gates!' We did have a sort of dress rehearsal, and the drapes hung sixty feet above Park Lane, giving the riggers a great view, so they were quite pleased and there were no more complaints.

The day before the Opening Ceremony the gates arrived to be hung. They were stainless steel filigree with stylised flowers, and in the centre was an heraldic panel purporting to be Queen Elizabeth's coat of arms. For some reason it had been designed by a different artist from the main gates. We all thought they looked terrible. Once they were up we covered them so no one would see them, using sixty metres of the pink material attached to the steel beams. A passerby remarked that it all looked 'rather like Barbara Cartland's knickers'.

When they arrived, I briefly told the Queen and Queen Elizabeth what was going to happen and they moved to the unveiling switch on a little mahogany lectern. The lever was pulled, the fanfare sounded and Barbara Cartland's Knickers rose majestically. The wind, unfortunately, had just changed direction so all the petals were actually blown into Hyde Park Corner and not in our direction as planned. As the gates were unveiled, there was a gasp from the VIP guests – and I don't think it was one of admiration.

Fortunately, at that moment the 'knickers' caught on one of the spare bits of stainless steel sticking out of the gate. This caused everybody to laugh which broke the tension. A man dashed out and climbed the gates to free the snarled material – I have a feeling he might have been the artist. We repaired to the Hyde Park Hotel for a reception for all those who had been closely involved.

It was fascinating to hear Queen Elizabeth talking to everybody. She found at least forty different ways of not actually saying whether or not she liked the gates. Those who liked the gates, mainly those who had worked on them, imagined she also liked them. To those that did not like them (most of us), then neither it seemed did she. But she never actually said one way or the other, so everybody was happy. I wished at the time that I had made a recording to capture all those wonderfully different ways of saying nothing.

* * *

Queen Elizabeth's hundredth birthday started to appear on the horizon and I began to think about it. The year 2000 was going to be rather a full one. At least I did not have to worry now about the dreaded Dome at Greenwich. I was, however, producing a huge Royal Military Tattoo on Horse Guards, and I had it in the back of my mind that whatever we did for it would have to be used for the Queen Mother's birthday celebrations.

The main thing that I was determined to do was to change the Parade Ground around. Normally the main section of the audience faces the Park, not the beautiful line of buildings behind them. For years I had been trying to persuade the Major General that the Birthday Parade (Trooping the Colour) would look so much better facing the other way. Nobody agreed. I would beard every new Major General only to be rebuffed. Major General Desmond Langley told me that it would take the Archangel Gabriel to turn the Parade around.

At the Household Division 'Beating Retreat', which I was producing in 1982, the Queen and the Duke of Edinburgh came to take the Salute and at the reception afterwards I mentioned my idea to Prince Philip. With a twinkle in his eye he seemed to think that it might be quite a good one. I leant over and tapped the Major General on the shoulder. 'I think the Archangel Gabriel might just have arrived,' I said. But at that very moment a waiter tripped and poured tartare sauce all down the Duke of Edinburgh's frock coat. John Miller, the Crown Equerry, bounded forward to clear up the mess and the moment was lost.

However, my idea had been accepted for the Royal Military Tattoo, so that the stands would face the buildings and they would be considerably larger than the normal Trooping stands, seating some twelve thousand people. There were also to be about sixty hospitality boxes for sponsors and VIP guests.

The obvious time for the hundredth birthday tribute would be directly after the Royal Military Tattoo. This was not ideal from my point of view, as both were likely to be extremely mentally and physically taxing and rather difficult to do, but there was no option. Sir Donald Gosling had asked in 1998 if we could 'bear them in mind' to help with the hundredth – a lovely way of putting it. However, as my plans progressed it became clear that the hundredth was going to be considerably more expensive than the ninetieth, the infrastructure far more complex, and the audience more than double the size.

I kept my ideas to myself, sharing them only with Clarence House and the Major General, Evelyn Webb-Carter, who was an old friend. My general plan was to do much as we had done for the ninetieth but on a much more ambitious scale. Fortunately the new Garrison Sergeant Major, Perry Mason, was far more sensible and switched on than the previous one, and the whole of London District's staff joined in with gusto. Clarence House, with Sir Alastair Aird now in charge, was very supportive and all seemed set fair.

I had not taken into account the MOD Contracts Branch. We had been fighting a battle with them over the Royal Military Tattoo and this was going to be yet another bone of contention. I've never had to deal with a group of more highly intelligent but basically stupid people in all my life. I was trying to negotiate an extension of the seating and infrastructure hire from the Royal Military Tattoo which was 'owned' by the MOD. It had to be carried on for an extra week – not very difficult, I would have thought. But anybody listening in on our meetings might have supposed that we were trying to build an aircraft carrier, so complicated did they make it. We needed only to remove the large video screens, and build a covered stage for an orchestra and choir of about four hundred. Weeks of arguing went on, but at last we had a deal.

Then it was pointed out that I could not make a contract with the MOD unless I was being paid. I couldn't understand this at all, but they were the so-called 'experts'. So I said my fee would be £1 plus VAT. They looked slightly surprised but the contract was signed. We were going to have to pay them about £350,000 for the infrastructure. I went immediately to Sir Donald Gosling and Ron Hobson and told them the bad news – the hundredth was going to cost almost exactly ten times what the ninetieth had. There was only the slightest hint of an intake of breath before I was asked where I would like the money sent. A new deposit account was opened and Maureen Mele became the overall event co-ordinator, something she had done brilliantly for me in the past.

I took on extra 'girls' to help with getting all the organisations on board. It was a massive task but the whole situation was made far easier by Rear Admiral Rod Lees, the Defence Services Secretary at the time, who had also saved the RMT when it all started to go wrong. Most importantly, it was now – long before we were married – that Emma became my PA.

Once again the organisations were very keen to take part, although the Royal Society said that they would prefer not to march this time. All the plans for the changes on Horse Guards from RMT to the Queen Mother's hundredth, which we called QM100, were agreed with Mark Wallace of Caribiner, costed and put in hand.

The MOD asked for its cheque for £350,000 so I asked for mine for £1.

'Don't be so silly,' they said.

I said that I would not pay them until they had paid me. Obviously the MOD system could not cope with a cheque as small as £1. They got very ratty and eventually sent my cheque by courier. I sent theirs by second class mail; the money had been in the deposit account earning interest, so we made hundreds of pounds. Emma and I wondered if the £1 plus VAT – i.e. £1.17½p – would be rounded up or down. In the event it turned out to be for £1.18 – great excitement! – but I never paid it in and still have it as a souvenir. I imagine the MOD's books have never balanced since.

Don telephoned one day to ask about the hospitality boxes which each seated about twenty people. 'Why don't you sell them and give the proceeds to charity?' he suggested. I thought that was a brilliant idea. Don said that he and Ron would like to buy two each. I told him that that was ridiculous; they were already paying for the whole event. But he insisted and a cheque duly arrived. In the end we were able to give over £100,000 to some of Queen Elizabeth's charities, just from the sale of hospitality boxes. I was beginning to find the running of two such large shows in tandem quite a challenge, particularly as the officer initially in charge of the Royal Military Tattoo was proving to be less than effective and sensible. But the girls kept everything and me going.

Strange requests from participants kept coming in. One day Emma asked, 'Do you want camels?' It turned out that the Worshipful Company of Grocers, of whom Queen Elizabeth was an Honorary Freeman, had the camel as their badge and they thought it might be rather fun to come mounted on them. I said yes immediately, as long as they fed them, watered them, and picked up the proceeds afterwards.

Then Emma reported, 'The Chairman of the Hastings Winkle Club is on the phone.'

The Hastings Winkle Club! Now you would have thought, wouldn't you, that the Chairman of a winkle club would have a sense of humour. Not a bit of it. He was very dreary. I told him that the Club was not on the list that we had received from Clarence House, but he insisted that Queen Elizabeth was a member. As it happened I was going to a lunch, organised by Sir Piers Bengough, with Queen Elizabeth at the Ritz that day. I said I would ask her – at least it might be an amusing topic of conversation.

As we were sitting having a drink before lunch, I said, 'Your Majesty, the Hastings Winkle Club have been on the telephone.'

'Oh!' she exclaimed, half rising from her seat. 'I am a Winkle!'

We all gawped in amazement.

'Oh yes,' she went on, 'and when you meet another Winkle you have to shake your Winkle badge at him.' She flashed her lapel with what looked like a rather large diamond brooch on it. 'If you don't have a badge on to shake back then you have to pay a fine. That's how we make money for charity – I'll have to remember to wear my Winkle badge that day.' Well, that was that then; they were obviously on.

I continued to tell her about the other participants.

'Do we have any corgis?' she asked.

'Well, no, Ma'am,' I replied, 'since you are not actually the President or Chairman of any corgi organisation.'

'But I do have corgis, you know.'

I think that we all knew that. So I would obviously have to organise some.

When I got home I telephoned Mr Winkle Club to tell him the good news and suggested that it would be lovely if he brought a bucket of winkles with him as I loved them. He told me, with some distain, that they were a serious club and 'didn't do that sort of thing' but that they would be wearing their Winkle Suits. Well, that was all right then.

Alistair Aird telephoned and said, 'Tell me the worst', and I told him about the corgis. He groaned loudly and said that they were very badly behaved and not used to being on leads. I discovered later that one of Queen Elizabeth's pages, William Tallon (known as Backstairs Billy), had spent weeks dragging them on leads around the garden of Clarence House while he practised saluting bushes.

'There's a man with homing doves on the line,' said Emma.

He was offering to provide a hundred homing doves. I said that that would be great as long as they didn't cost me anything, but that I'd never actually heard of homing doves.

'Mine are definitely homing doves,' he said, so I said, 'Fine, thank you very much.'

By this time Emma and her assistant, Jane Charlie, had gathered together about ten thousand civilian participants which, together with the two thousand military ones, made the basis of a pretty good parade. Knowing that the rehearsals would be short and pretty chaotic I sent everybody very detailed instructions as to what they had to do. All the music was chosen and Lieutenant Colonel Richard Waterer Royal Marines was to be the Senior Director of Music. He had done a brilliant job on the Royal Military Tattoo so I was looking forward to working with him again. We had bands of the very best musicians from all the services, and the choirs from St Paul's Cathedral, Canterbury, Norwich, St Albans and St Magnus in the Orkneys with other choral societies under the direction of John Scott from St Paul's. There was also a Signing Choir from the Royal School for Deaf Children in Margate.

The Royal Philharmonic had asked, when invited, what they would be paid. I told them nothing, like everybody else, but said they could raise private sponsorship for themselves if they liked, which I believe they did.

One of the great treats of running this sort of event is choosing the music, so we had all my favourite pieces. I normally allow the Senior Director to choose one tune to keep him happy. It was not necessary in this case because Richard Waterer and I were in total agreement.

John Ward, the brilliant watercolourist, agreed to design and paint the programme cover as he had done for the ninetieth. Sir John Mills agreed to give a short address much as he had also done ten years earlier, but by now his sight had almost completely gone, which made it much more difficult for him.

We had an extraordinary cross-section of participants and I wrestled with how we were going to control them with the limited rehearsal time we had available. When I made the plans I had no idea just how limited that time would turn out to be.

I asked for a hundred Coldstream Guardsmen who were going to be in charge of the marching groups of societies and charities. I went to brief them in Wellington Barracks, and they all looked about twelve years old until they put on their bearskins. They looked at me with not-inconsiderable apprehension as I told them, 'You will be totally in command of your groups. You may be "commanding" anything from a Field Marshal to an Aberdeen Angus bull, and they will all do exactly as you tell them. Don't worry too much about the bulls; you need to get a grip of the keepers. You must form up and march at precisely one hundred and twelve twenty-three-inch paces to the minute.'

I had worked it all out to the last foot. The programme said they could 'march, skip or dance' past. I told them that whatever their groups did, they had to keep in line and in the correct position, and go at the correct pace. There was nervous laughter as I left the briefing room. In the event, they would all do brilliantly and we received many letters from participants afterwards, a number of which said things like, 'Do give our love to the Guardsmen in Rank 23 or any other for that matter; they were all gorgeous!' It was a tremendous tribute to these young men who cajoled and looked after the disparate groups that they all did so very well and that the timing worked out so immaculately in spite of all the trials and tribulations.

The Royal Military Tattoo was causing huge problems and completely draining me as we made the final preparations. I never knew quite what was going to happen or hit me next.

For her Birthday Celebration, Queen Elizabeth was to arrive by carriage with a large Household Cavalry Escort. Because there were obvious problems with her getting in and out of the carriage I suggested that she and the Prince of Wales should stop in front of the Royal Box, remain in the carriage to receive the Royal Salute, and for the National Anthem, then drive on to do the Inspection, after which they would alight, out of sight, underneath the arch. But just when I thought everything was sorted out I received a call from Alastair Aird.

'Her Majesty and His Royal Highness will not sit for the National Anthem; they will stand up in the carriage.'

I was aghast. I had always regarded landaus as little better than overgrown prams and very unstable. I begged Clarence House to reconsider and even produced evidence of a precedent set by Queen Victoria in the nineteenth century.

'Her Majesty is not Queen Victoria,' was the brief reply I received.

I was getting pretty desperate, until someone reminded me that on the Queen's Birthday Parade Queen Elizabeth drove on to Horse Guards through a gap in the ranks of the Guards and was received by a Royal Salute (the National Anthem), throughout which she remained seated in the carriage.

I pointed this out to Clarence House.

'Ah, yes,' they said, 'but Her Majesty was moving then.'

'Well,' I said, 'could we not play the National Anthem as the carriage is driving on?'

'Oh, yes,' they said, 'that would be fine.'... End of heart attack.

Whilst this was going on I was fighting on another front. The BBC had just told me that they would not be covering the celebration as they had in 1990. I was amazed and not a little annoyed. One snooty producer (who will remain nameless, although he has since turned into a right royal sycophant) said that it was an event of little importance and of no interest to the public, and anyway its timing clashed with 'Neighbours'.

I couldn't bear the thought that all the huge efforts that the various groups were making would not be recorded for posterity and that only twelve thousand people would see the Tribute. During the VE 50th Anniversary celebrations Dame Sue Tinson of ITN had become a friend and a great ally. I phoned her immediately and begged her for help.

'Surely the ITV might like to cover it?' I said.

She said she would do what she could. Others apparently were also on our side. A public relations executive at Carlton Television noticed the opportunity, and persuaded the ITV bosses that it would be very well worth covering. I have only just discovered from a friend, the intrepid journalist Robert Hardman, that the PR executive in question was a certain Mr David Cameron. In the event, ITV did a great job, achieving an audience of seven million viewers live and a further five million for the evening highlights. The sacrosanct 'Neighbours' achieved just three and a half million viewers. I introduced myself to Greg Dyke, Director General of the BBC, a couple of years later and he groaned and told me it was one of the worst decisions he had ever made.

ITV threw themselves into the challenge with gusto, and produced a great programme directed by Lawrence Vulliamy and presented by Sir Trevor McDonald. One of the other commentators was Hugo Vickers, now a very successful Royal biographer, who had worked with me at the first Great Children's Party. ITV put a news crew in to cover some of the background work during the build-up. Unfortunately, unknown to me at the time, they picked up my conversation with Mervyn Harridence, the great 'Merv' of Royal Tournament fame. I had asked him to build a huge birthday cake with a hundred candles. It had to be got on and off very quickly, so he decided that making an inflatable one was the only answer. I had organised fifty children dressed as icing sugar decorations to dance round it, and a little child dressed as a chef would pop out of the cake with a knife to cut it. Nothing complicated then!

For the rehearsal Merv drove it into position on his Land Rover and inflated it. It looked terrible, like a twenty-five-foot football with a leak. The candles were all flaccid and lying at suggestive angles, and it looked like an advertisement for failed 'French letters'. I had to tell Merv that there was no way we could we use it. He was devastated and went off in tears. That was bad enough, but it was all being covered live on television. After Merv had gone, the reporter asked, 'How do you feel about having to cut the cake?' I was mystified, as I clearly had not cut the cake. It then dawned on me that she meant: how did I feel about having to remove the cake altogether?

I telephoned Sir John Mills to warn him that he would have to change the end of his speech, written by Rosemary Ann Sisson, which finished with him presenting to Her Majesty 'the world's largest birthday cake'.

'Oh, my dear fellow, I can't possibly change anything now. I can't see, you know, so I've memorised it all.' I just hoped that no one would notice.

We had military rehearsals the day before with all the Massed Bands, Pipes and Drums, Colour Parties and Military Groups together with the whole King's Troop, Royal Horse Artillery and over a hundred Household Cavalry horses. It was very splendid and looked marvellous.

It was a hot day and the Massed Bands, unknown to us, had all brought water bottles with them. After a lengthy period of rehearsal I told them they could go off and have a smoke (you were allowed to do that sort of thing in those days). As they wandered off, there in perfect formation on that 'sacred' parade ground were four hundred water bottles. Even the Garrison Sergeant Major, the wonderful Perry Mason, had a sense of humour failure and berated the unfortunate musicians at the top of his voice until a little man appeared and said that he was from No.10 Downing Street with a message from the Prime Minister. 'Would whoever is shouting those obscenities stop immediately as it's upsetting the girls in the office.' I told him to go and do what they do to turkeys at Christmas.

The rehearsal had gone quite well so I was feeling slightly happier. My caravan, left over from the Royal Military Tattoo, was still in position overlooking the pelicans on the lake of St James' Park and I had used it quite a lot when my head got unbearable. We repaired to it now for a very large drink poured by Staff Sergeant Baynes who was still looking after me and was staying in my flat in Collingham Place. On the way to Horse Guards early the next morning, I noticed a newspaper seller in Knightsbridge, and said to myself, 'Gosh, I wish I was a newspaper seller.' I had often thought like that in the past when on my way to do something I was dreading. What I really did not want to do was to go and face thousands of people on Horse Guards, but obviously I had to.

When we got there, everything seemed quieter than we were expecting. All the Military were there but very few civilians. The Police Liaison Commander said that most of the main line railway stations were closed as there had been a number of bomb threats. As we were talking, there was a large explosion from the other side of the Horse Guards Building. It was a controlled explosion, as a suspect vehicle had been found in Whitehall. I told them not to tell anybody else, and also ordered all my team not to tell anybody, as I did not want panic to spread. There was a lot of sucking of teeth going on, particularly from the police, but I was determined to get on with the rehearsal. I told the Guardsmen that their 'charges' would probably not arrive in time but that they should form up and march past as if they were there. They all looked even more mystified. I had worked out precisely how long the civilian procession was and had marked out the start of each group on the ground with small numbered sticks that stretched halfway down Birdcage Walk.

The teeth-sucking was getting louder and louder. Eventually a police commander came over and said he was thinking of cancelling the whole event. I was furious and said that that was totally ridiculous. I then said, 'If you want to cancel Queen Elizabeth's hundredth birthday parade, you personally are going to have to walk down the Mall, turn right, and go into Clarence House and tell Her Majesty yourself, because I refuse to.' Fortunately Lieutenant Colonel Sir Malcolm Ross, Comptroller of the Lord Chamberlain's Office, who had been a friend for years, was with me at the time and supported me in this.

The policeman said, 'Well, perhaps...' and that was the end of it.

We staggered through the rehearsals as best we could. The marshals and directing staff were brilliant and pretended to be anything and everything that was not there. The music played, the Guardsmen marched past in perfect spacing, marshalling their invisible groups. At least it was all going to appear nice and 'fresh' for us when we saw it, if we ever did, that afternoon.

It was turning into a fine day and my worries centred as much on the children becoming too hot as on what we would do if it rained. Working on the 'wise virgin' principle we had ordered eight thousand see-through Pac-a-macs with the QM100 logo, the idea being that some of the costumes and uniforms would show through them if they were used. They were only for the civilian element; the Military would get wet as usual. Happily they weren't needed, and there is probably still somewhere, in some distant corner, a huge store of see-through Pac-a-macs.

By 12.30pm the sun was shining and about half of our groups had appeared. I decided we had to try and rehearse the Finale. The orchestra said they had to have a break as they had played through their 'statutory rest' period, but they were told to stay or, if they did not want to, then they should pack up and go home immediately. They decided to stay and played brilliantly.

The thousands of Monarch airline meals were distributed and the rising noise level from Birdcage Walk seemed to indicate that our numbers were growing. I had asked the police not to keep briefing me on the bomb situation as I was trying to forget it and get on with other things. By early afternoon the gates were open and the audience started coming in, so I repaired to my caravan and the pelicans and tried to sort out my head which was having a bad day. Staff Sergeant Baynes discovered that we had failed to bring my medals. There was no way he could get home and fetch them so I had to go on parade incorrectly dressed. Only about thirty people noticed!

As the audience piled in and the groups became more and more complete we had over twenty thousand people in a rather small area. The choirs and orchestras were in position, and the wonderful deaf children from the Signing Choir in Margate were obviously having a marvellous time. The audience seating was full, and the hospitality boxes were buzzing happily which indicated that alcohol was flowing freely. I longed for an invitation to go to one but none came. Staff Baynes and I paced up and down trying to be calm – he succeeded.

The Tri-Service Massed Bands marched on and the Massed Pipes and Drums, including the Black Watch of Canada and the Toronto Scottish Regiment, swirled into position with panache. The Mounted Bands of the Household Cavalry came on and then the Parade Commander. Colonel Toby Brown, Silver Stick in Waiting and Commander of the Household Cavalry, had assumed the task done by Andrew Parker Bowles for the ninetieth celebration. Toby had been a great help during the build-up. He also had a very good sense of humour, vital on occasions like these, and helped keep us going in the early parts of the day. He is now, some eleven years later, the Crown Equerry in charge of the Royal Mews.

Distant cheering meant that Queen Elizabeth was on the way. I took a deep breath and waited with some trepidation. As the carriage came into view I watched it carefully and thanked my lucky stars that Queen Elizabeth and the Prince of Wales were not going to have to stand up in it. They arrived at the beautifully decorated Royal Box. At the end of the Royal Salute the choir and orchestra launched into Hubert Parry's Coronation anthem 'I was glad'. It is quite my favourite piece of music, combining as it does everything that I most love about England and the Crown. We used the actual Coronation setting with the shouts of 'Vivat!' in the middle. It was pure chance that Queen Elizabeth's carriage arrived directly in front of the choirs at that exact moment, although I hinted that it had all been carefully timed. It was stunning.

After the Inspection the landau went into the arch where Queen Elizabeth alighted, then she went with the Prince of Wales into the Royal Box. This had been beautifully covered all over with British flowers by Margaret Ferguson, a great friend whose husband Iain had suffered me for years as the Vice Chairman and Director of the Royal Tournament. She was also later to build the garland of blue and yellow flowers around the carriage that Queen Elizabeth used on her actual birthday.

Queen Elizabeth's eyesight by now was not brilliant, but you would never have known; she acknowledged each group as it went past. Lieutenant Colonel Richard Waterer, the Principal Director of Music, had timed the music precisely so each group got its own regimental or service march at the moment it passed the Royal Box without a pause.

As soon as the Royal procession had cleared the Mall on arrival, the whole of the King's Troop, Royal Horse Artillery moved in. The Troop was particularly dear to Queen Elizabeth's heart, not least because King George VI had taken a great interest in them and given them their name. They ranked past in full splendour, the crunch of the gravel under the steel wheels adding greatly to the effect. They were followed by the Household Cavalry with their harnesses jingling and breastplates flashing in the sun. It was spectacular, and I felt a little tear in my eye (it went well with the nervous twitch!).

Then came the first dodgy bit – the release of the hundred 'homing doves'. Young Dominic Kraemer offered them to Her Majesty as a birthday gift, and sang Mendelssohn's 'Oh, for the wings of a dove.' The birds left their baskets rather uncertainly and showed no inclination to set off in any particular direction. It then seemed that one of them had spotted a mass of pigeons in Trafalgar Square and off they all disappeared in that direction. They must have had a very dirty weekend in the Square because very few were ever seen again. Their keeper spent the next couple of days trying to coax the few that were still around out of the rigging. I'm sure it was my imagination but there seemed to be an awful lot of white pigeons in the Square the following year.

'A Pageant of A Hundred Years' followed, paying tribute to the extraordinary span of Queen Elizabeth's life. Taking part were hundreds of children and young people in costumes, and mini-floats with models by Merv. The procession was led by Wendy Craig in 1900s nanny uniform pushing a pram with the baby 'Lady Elizabeth Bowes-Lyon'. Scores of stars included Dame Vera Lynn, Nickolas Grace, Hinge and Bracket, Barbara Windsor (with her recently presented MBE), Dame Thora Hird, and Patricia Hodge. Sir Norman Wisdom was trying very hard to fall off his float, and succeeding.

Then came the civilian organisations. My instructions said that they could 'march, skip or dance' past as long as they kept up with their Guardsmen guides. I was fascinated to see what might happen – I knew what was *supposed* to happen, but we had never rehearsed most of it. The Guardsmen did a fantastic job and an extraordinary mix of people, vehicles and animals came past, looking for all the world as though they had been rehearsing for months. The civilian parade was led by Billy Tallon; he was coaxing along two corgis on leads, who had arrived for the rehearsal in a huge Rolls-Royce, and all seemed to be going well until he dropped one of the leads. I had a sudden vision of the corgi rushing off and causing total chaos. Luckily he just managed to recover the lead and do a sort of bow-cum-curtsey to the Royal Box.

Racehorses, fishermen, dogs, chickens, bulls, nurses, lifeboats, gardeners, ballet dancers – it just went on and on. The Master and Court of the Grocer's Company, six of them in fur-bordered robes and black velvet Tudor caps, looked particularly splendid mounted on their camels. But suddenly the camels spied the expanse of sand, and obviously thought they had somehow been transported home. Two of them went down on their knees, and the others followed suit. The Worshipful Grocers were all abruptly flung forwards in a flurry of blue velvet, then lurched back again as the camels' back legs folded. To their great credit, they all managed to hang on, clinging on round the camels' necks for dear life, Tudor caps askew, as camel handlers in rather unconvincing 'Arab' dress (tea-towels, I suspect) hauled the beasts to their feet and persuaded them to move on. A few minutes later the camels obligingly repeated the whole performance, but this time the handlers – and the Grocers – were ready for them.

The National Trust did particularly well, with Jerry Hall dressed as a 'hall' with handsome arm candy, and beautiful floats showing their work – all were led by their Director General Martin Drury, who had been in my Regiment, mounted very elegantly and looking just like someone in a Stubbs painting.

In a prophetic view of future defence cuts, Massed Wombles went by dressed as Guardsmen. One fainted and lay prone on the ground. We thought it was all part of the act until a couple of hundred people had marched over him when we concluded that he really had fainted and went to rescue him. The real Guardsmen looked on with some surprise at the grey hairy Womble in scarlet tunic and bearskin being carried past.

The Winkle Club passed by but whether or not they and Queen Elizabeth 'winkled' at each other I didn't notice as I was too busy worrying about the Shetland ponies and the World War II vehicles behind them. Almost at the end of the parade were twenty vintage Rolls-Royces, provided by the Rolls-Royce Enthusiasts Club, and riding in them were holders of the Victoria and George Crosses, including the High Commissioner of Malta, representing the only country ever to have been given such a decoration. Without any prompting the entire audience stood up and clapped and cheered. The passengers' beaming smiles belied their outstanding courage and valour. Throughout the years I had met most of them; they were a wonderful lot of very special people, organised by their stalwart secretary Didi Graham. They had taken part in many of my events and had always impressed us by their modesty and refusal ever to talk about what they had done.

When most of the groups had passed, in the distance we heard the unmistakable sound of a Lancaster bomber. It flew over with the Royal Air Force Memorial Flight of a Hurricane and a Spitfire and a Bristol Blenheim. I think that was the first time that combination had ever flown over London.

At the very end came the In-Pensioners of the Royal Hospital Chelsea, resplendent in their scarlet coats; they also received great cheers. I found it rather amusing to note that virtually all those on parade were actually young enough for the Guest of Honour to be their mother!

All the groups had shuffled into place with varying degrees of precision when on to Parade drove the original Silver Ghost, kindly lent by Rolls-Royce, carrying Sir John Mills to give the address. Having done it for the ninetieth celebration he had asked if he could do it again. Johnny by this time had virtually no sight left. When we rehearsed it I briefed him and the driver exactly where to stop, and told him that if he stood up and turned exactly ninety degrees to his right, he would be facing Queen Elizabeth. He did just that and gave a charming speech written by Rosemary Anne Sisson, who had written a lot of wonderful scripts for me over the years. Because of his worry about his failing memory he had to leave in the bit about the 'biggest birthday cake in the world'. Knowing this, I had asked Dougie Squires, fresh from directing a camel battle for me in Saudi Arabia, to come up with something to fill the gap.

Using the children dressed as icing sugar, he devised a Cake Dance in concentric circles. In the centre was Alasdair Malloy, chief percussionist of the BBC Philharmonic Orchestra, with his tiny son dressed as a chef on his shoulders. I cannot think how we arrived at this solution but it's just possible that it might have been because young Malloy was such a character. In the event he overacted outrageously and nearly cut his father's head off, but everybody thought it was hilarious and forgot that there was no cake.

A special birthday song written by the RAF's Barry Hingley was followed by another special song and dance performed by the Chicken Shed Theatre, a remarkable group of mixed ability young people inspired by Mary Ward and Jo Collins. I had fallen in love with them when they first performed for me in 'Joy to the World' and tried to use them for everything I could.

I was also determined to make use of the huge metal grid put up above the seating for the lights and projectors for the Royal Military Tattoo so I asked the Royal National Rose Society, one of Queen Elizabeth's organisations, to provide one million dried rose petals. This they did, bringing in petals from all over the country. The only soldiers I could find to drop them were Gurkhas, who arrived with huge sacks full of petals and perched high up in the steelwork. As the whole audience sang 'Happy Birthday' they emptied the marvellous-smelling petals onto the crowds beneath. Their huge grins possibly masked their muttering, in Gorkhali, *'I didn't join the effin' Gurkhas to perch in an effin' grid and throw effin' rose petals.'*

Everybody on parade had signed the biggest Birthday Card in the world and this was brought forward. It had been no small feat to achieve all those signatures as a lot of the participants had only arrived minutes before they had to march on.

Queen Elizabeth now addressed the multitude. In 1990 we were told that the microphone height required was five feet three inches; in 2000 it had dropped to five feet precisely. Flanked by the Prince of Wales and Major General Evelyn Webb-Carter, she gave the most delightfully charming short speech. Three cheers were given, then a final Royal Salute before the car drove up to take her away. I had arranged that she should drive through the ranks of all the groups before leaving the parade ground. Staff Baynes had to rush round to make certain that the passageway had been left open for the car to get through. Her car had to go at a crawling pace because of the enthusiasm of all the groups. As she set off down the Mall to St James' Palace it was almost as though the sun had suddenly gone in, such was the loss of her presence.

After the parade I hitched a lift with the Chiefs of Staff to St James' Palace for the reception. Most of the Royal Family who had been watching the parade from the back of the Royal Box were there. Princess Margaret, although sadly not very well, was very enthusiastic and had obviously enjoyed everything very much.

After a short while Queen Elizabeth appeared, and spent the next hour walking round and charming everybody. After about half an hour she went up to Dame Vera Lynn and said, 'My dear, you're looking very tired – why don't you come and sit down over here for a bit?' So they both went over to a settee and sat on it with neither pair of feet touching the ground. It was her way of having a little rest without anybody noticing.

When she eventually left we realised just how exhausted we all were, but we went back to Horse Guards and watched the breakdown for a bit before repairing for a very large drink to Collingham Place. My head had been particularly bad all day so I was glad to get into darkness and silence. I reckoned I had probably earned my £1 that day.

*   *   *

I went down to South Lodge next morning and went into suspended limbo. Two days later I woke up to find a note from my postman saying that he had a 'very smart package' covered with seals and EIIR ciphers – probably the smartest thing he had ever been asked to deliver. Unfortunately, he couldn't because it needed a signature and he wasn't able to wake me, so I had to collect it from Salisbury. This was very sad as South Lodge was just over a mile off the proper road down a very bumpy track and no matter what the weather he always staggered down it even with junk mail.

I collected my 'very smart package' and opened it carefully. Inside was a lovely silver box with Queen Elizabeth's cypher on the top and inside was engraved:

For Michael Parker from Elizabeth R
Birthday Tribute on Horse Guards
June 27 1990 and July 19 2000

With it was a very touching four-page handwritten letter. Years later Sir Alastair Aird agreed that I could tell others what was in it. Amongst other things it said, '*The tribute was the most wonderful mixture of fun and discipline and was also very moving...I really think it cheered people up all over the country and made them feel patriotic...I loved seeing the very smart military contingents followed by an orderly rabble – it was all marvellous.*'

A couple of days later I received another letter, this time from Sir Michael Peat, Secretary of the Royal Victorian Order, telling me that the Queen was going to make me a Knight of the Order. I was so excited I had to tell somebody so I telephoned Emma, who told me that she was going to get the Royal Victorian Silver Medal as well. I was thrilled (on both accounts) and I remembered that Alastair Aird had questioned me so closely about Emma's role in the whole event that I thought she might be trying to get a job at Clarence House!

Evelyn Webb-Carter telephoned to congratulate me as he had been told before it was announced on Queen's Elizabeth's Birthday. He phoned back about ten minutes later, and said he was feeling frightfully foolish as further down his pile of mail he had discovered an identical letter written to himself. So we congratulated each other.

A few days later I also received a lovely letter from Princess Margaret. In it she said how thrilled she was that I had been given a knighthood, but '*actually I think it really should have been a Victoria Cross!*'

I was asked to a thank-you lunch at Clarence House and was greeted as a long-lost friend by Backstairs Billy, who kept apologising for dropping the corgi's lead. I told him that it could not have mattered less because had one of the corgis gone mad I had already given orders that it should be shot. He laughed uncertainly, and poured me another huge drink.

It was the last time that I was to speak to Queen Elizabeth, and we talked about the Golden Jubilee and how much she was looking forward to it. On Easter Sunday of the Jubilee year came the sad announcement that Queen Elizabeth had passed away, and like everybody else in the whole country and Commonwealth I felt a very personal loss. Her timing was, as ever, totally perfect. It was as though she was determined not to spoil the Golden Jubilee celebrations.

The day of the funeral came and the plans that had been worked on so assiduously for so many years went seamlessly into action. A few days earlier Emma and I had been allowed to go to the Lying in State on the private side of Westminster Hall. The scene was like a huge oil painting with shafts of sunlight on the slowly changing Guards of Honour. It was all very moving and I stood for a very long time just looking at the catafalque with her crown on top of her Royal Standard. I thought back to discussions twenty years earlier about the Lying in State. There was a feeling then that very few would want to come. I begged to differ and suggested a longer period would be required. The masses of people opposite seemed to bear me out.

I had been expecting to watch the funeral on television but very early in the morning Sir Malcolm Ross telephoned to ask if I had received my ticket for the funeral. There had been a slight slip-up and one would be waiting for me at the North Centre gate of Buckingham Palace. I put on my morning coat immediately and rushed around there. London was virtually at a standstill so I walked most of the way, picked up my ticket and walked on to the Abbey.

As I entered the Abbey I kept being ushered further and further inside. I was expecting to sit behind a pillar somewhere but when I was taken through the choir screen I began to suspect I had been given the wrong ticket.

'No,' they said, 'follow us.'

I ended up on the south side of the Quire, next to the Duke and Duchess of Devonshire, only a few yards away from where the Royal family were to be seated. I was amazed.

The whole sad pageant played out and I watched in awe as every immaculate piece fell into place. I was very glad that the worrying on this occasion was not mine, because I had become extremely emotional and had great difficulty in not crying. I looked around, trying to distract myself, and saw representatives of the whole of British and Commonwealth society. Opposite, in the top stalls, were Mr Blair and his wife; she was looking very bored and put out.

The music was wonderful, filling the whole Abbey with echoing chords. In a pause we heard the distant sound of the pipes slowly marching the coffin from Westminster Hall. To our slight annoyance the organ started playing again. On reflection I suspect that that was intentional, as it would have been too much to sit listening to that mournful approach. At last the draped coffin, with its standard and sparkling crown, slowly went past. On each side were the Colonels of Her Majesty's Regiments, most of whom I knew.

I remember little of the service itself as I was lost in deep thoughts. At the end the processions reversed themselves and before we knew it the whole Royal family had gone. We were then ushered out of our seats. To my surprise the Duke and Duchess of Devonshire, with me tagging along behind, went out before the Speaker of the House of Commons and the Prime Minister. When we got outside the whole area was completely clear, the crowds being held well back, so I was able to get a taxi immediately. It was all so surreal that I had totally forgotten how very bad my head was that day.

It was the end of an era for the country, and for me the end of twenty six years of wonderful memories of a truly remarkable lady.

CHAPTER SEVENTEEN

Concorde, the Commonwealth and a Cast of Thousands – The Golden Jubilee 2002

Newspaper articles have frequently described me as 'the Queen's official party organiser', or say that the Queen 'asked' me to arrange something. This is absolute rubbish. The Palace has never once asked me to do anything; I have always put forward my own ideas, which have been either accepted or rejected.

I first started planning the 2002 Golden Jubilee celebrations in 1995, after being so disappointed with what I had been allowed to do for the fiftieth anniversary of VE Day in the Mall. Millennium year was mostly memorable for the crass and wasteful Dome and the so-called 'entertainments' inside it, a triumph of questionable style over substance. Putting together another national celebration so soon after that fiasco was a real challenge. Again the 'experts' said, 'No one will come'. Again I didn't believe them. But I did believe that the nation had a huge affection and respect for the Queen, and couldn't imagine that the celebrations would not be massively supported.

When planning anything I go first to the agencies that really matter. Detailed planning for the Golden Jubilee had to start in 2000, so whilst producing the Royal Military Tattoo and Queen Elizabeth's hundredth birthday celebrations I held informal meetings with the Royal Parks, the police, the local council and licensing officials. These background meetings neatly removed all possible excuse for prevarication; if anyone said, 'We'll have to check with the police,' I could quite truthfully say that I had already done it. I had worked before with all these agencies, and they knew me well.

Only half listening to the Jeremiahs, I formulated a few extra rules for this special event. The most important was that it should involve as many participants from all over the country and from as many walks of life as possible. When worried about audience numbers we always worked on the principle that for every participant a 'Mum and Dad and an Aunty Glad' would come and support them. On that basis we should get at least sixty thousand people!

Secondly, it should be truly multicultural, rather than just featuring every culture except English.

The third was that we would make use of all the traditions, ceremonial and pageantry we possibly could. No 'Cool Britannia' for us. The *Daily Telegraph* had recently written in a leader, '*Major Sir Michael Parker... describes himself as a believer in "Warm Britannia". By that we take it that he means he has a deep respect for the history and traditions that have made these islands a bastion of liberty for centuries, and one of the foremost powers on earth... If Major Parker believes in Warm Britannia, then so do we.*' Well, this was certainly going to be 'Warm Britannia', if not positively 'Hot'!

Until then all the background work had been done unofficially. Then one day I received a call from Helen Bayne, the government official in overall charge of the celebrations, asking me to go and see her. Helen was very switched on, very thorough and had an excellent sense of humour. I took to her immediately, and we were to get along very happily over the year's work to come. Lord Levene, an experienced and expert businessman and a former Lord Mayor of London, had been appointed to chair the organising committee. The first thing I asked was if I could now make my meetings with the key agencies official, and they both agreed.

My first problem was to think up something totally different. I had got halfway there in various meetings, but now needed to sound out the Palace. There was obviously going to be a Thanksgiving Service in St Paul's, but we needed to keep large numbers of people interested and occupied over a longer period than just the State Procession. My first idea for an evening concert was to build a large revolving stage around the Queen Victoria Memorial. It wouldn't make the already poor view of the Palace from the Mall any worse, but it would mean we could play to crowds in the Mall, Constitution Hill and the areas around the Palace, and with large screens and a good sound system we could include Hyde Park, Green Park, St James' Park and Trafalgar Square in the potential audience.

A weekend in early June had been designated Jubilee Weekend. Peter Levene, who had been to some initial meetings at the Palace, told us that the Prince's Trust wanted to mount a concert in the gardens of Buckingham Palace at the end of June. This, I felt, would detract totally from what we wanted to do at the beginning of June. So I briefed Peter on my worries and sent him back into the fray.

By chance I sat next to the Princess Royal at a private livery dinner one night and chatted to her about my worries. I may have become a little too 'relaxed' and was probably rather more forceful than I should have been. But she in turn had some pretty strong views about anybody trying to spoil the Golden Jubilee. Shortly afterwards, the plans changed so that one Palace garden concert became two, a classical 'Prom at the Palace' and a pop 'Party at the Palace', to be held on the Sunday and Monday evenings of the Jubilee Weekend to benefit Jubilee charities. I was initially worried that so few people would be able to attend that they might be thought elitist, even with the big screens, but in the end the seats were balloted for and both events were a triumph.

In the meantime, we had to decide how to finance our events. Peter was of the opinion that the contracted production company should raise the money. However, in my experience production companies are much better at spending money than raising it, and I thought the money needed to be raised through Peter's city and business contacts.

'My' revolving stage did not seem to be going down well with the Palace so I progressed to another idea – to have two large stages and seating blocks in front of the Palace, with a beacon and later a Royal Box on the Queen Victoria Memorial itself. The programme for the weekend was shaping up well, with the BBC's classical 'Prom' on the Saturday night, and the pop 'Party' on the Monday night which would be followed by a major firework and projection display. The ceremonial procession to St Paul's on the Tuesday would be followed by 'my party'. I was still working on 'my party'!

* * *

At the same time I was working on a vast horse display at Windsor. Like so many things, it had come about by chance. Over the years Colonel Sir Piers Bengough and his wife Bridget had become great friends. Piers, Her Majesty's Representative at Ascot, was a splendid chap whose old-fashioned persona hid a penetrating mind combined with great attention to detail. He was always looking for ways to raise money and the profile of the racecourse. He had a brilliant way of squeezing considerable amounts out of unsuspecting people, and had raised large sums for various charities. At the Bodyguards' drinks party at St James' Palace he and I had met and chatted; we wanted to do something to celebrate the Queen's seventieth birthday, and horses seemed an obvious subject for any celebration and Ascot the ideal place. (Later the Palace suggested we move the tribute by one year to coincide with the Golden Wedding Anniversary, so that it included Prince Philip. This we did.)

After a few more glasses of champagne I suggested, 'What about the largest horse display ever – the story of the horse through history?' A thousand horses seemed a good round number. I immediately came up with a whole lot more ideas. Piers and I then 'trawled' the room and in a short time we had got the Major General Commanding the Household Division to agree to give us his bands including the Mounted Bands, plus the Household Cavalry Mounted Regiment and the King's Troop, Royal Horse Artillery. Sir Michael Oswald, in charge of Queen Elizabeth's horses, thought we could perhaps borrow some of hers. Lieutenant Colonel Seymour Gilbart-Denham, the Crown Equerry in charge of the Royal Mews, was also very keen, and later we approached the equine event organiser Simon Brooks-Ward.

I found my general ignorance of anything to do with horses a great help as my ideas were quite uninhibited by any considerations of what was practical or impractical. The idea was to use the stands at Ascot, with the show on the course itself and beyond. An excellent lunch given by Piers made the ideas flow more freely, and I started separate meetings and lunches with Rosemary Anne Sisson, the only person – I was sure – who could make something special of such a varied story line. I brought in Alan Jacobi of Unusual Rigging to build everything as he had so frequently in the past.

It was when we started bringing in the racecourse officials that things began to go adrift. At one meeting I was waxing lyrical about staging the Charge of the Light Brigade, with a hundred horses galloping down the course and into the cannon fire. 'Oh no,' the racing manager said. 'We can't have horses galloping down the course.' I replied that, limited though my knowledge of racing was, I thought that was precisely what racecourses were for. I was actually told that it would be 'the wrong kind of galloping'!

So many people wanted to take part that the show grew and grew, until it became clear that Ascot racecourse was not going to be big enough. We looked around for another site. The Queen Victoria Parade Ground in Windsor Great Park was suggested, not least because Seymour, who lived in the Royal Mews, had one of the Queen's paintings on his dining room wall which showed a splendid parade for the Shah of Persia accompanying Queen Victoria on the same site. By now our meetings had moved to the Crown Equerry's house, so this scene looked down on all our deliberations.

Alan had produced an initial budget for Ascot, but was keen for the event to go to the simpler site and assured us categorically that the cost would be the same. It was amusing to watch his technical and construction teams meeting with Piers; they clearly thought he was the woofly old cavalry officer he purported to be. They would make their pitch and sit back, and he would then clinically demolish everything they had said, much to their bemusement. Chuck Crampton, an excellent production manager, came on board at this stage and within a few days discovered that the budget was rubbish – the cost had more than trebled, and we were in dead trouble. Piers identified Prince Jefri, brother of the Sultan of Brunei and owner of Asprey's, as a possible supporter. In fact, Asprey's proved an outstanding sponsor and gave us great support. The remaining money came in bit by bit. All was going well until suddenly the military civil servants decided that they were going to charge us for everything. This amounted to well over £60,000, and was almost the straw that broke the camel's back.

Rosemary wrote an amazing script, with some input from me. The scenes ranged from the Four Horsemen of the Apocalypse right the way through the chivalry and jousting of the Middle Ages, through the Charge of the Light Brigade, and the First and Second World Wars. The music was arranged by Wing Commander Barry Hingley, and a marvellous cast of stars – Dame Judi Dench, Timothy West, Prunella Scales, Robert Hardy and Edward Woodward – read the different parts which John Del'Nero recorded especially for us. Construction started and BBC Television began planning in earnest. The director was Simon Betts whom we knew well (it was he who had thumped the television monitor at the Silver Jubilee celebrations), which made things much easier. A 'precious' television director can make life hell.

We had a full production meeting in Windsor the week before rehearsals started. Budgetary considerations had put paid to most of my designs and the setting was much simpler than I would have liked, but at least it was almost up. However, the weather had broken and the ground was very wet indeed. Alan Jacobi drove me around the site in a buggy and I was horrified that there was so little track discipline; everybody drove where they wanted and the practice areas were already very badly cut up and almost under water. It rained really hard during our meeting, and even as I tried to cheer everybody up with a stirring 'Dunkirk' type speech I think I knew in my heart that we were never actually going to do it.

The rain continued until the stables were more than a foot under water. Alan brought down the insurance company's representative, and one of the seating stands obligingly started to subside as he watched. Clearly we were going to have to cancel the whole thing. Easier said than done – the next day the first of a thousand horses would be setting out for the rehearsals. We had teams of people telephoning everybody around the clock. Some of those we talked to didn't believe us, so I asked the BBC to broadcast the news that the pageant had been cancelled, which they kindly did. The Queen was in Canada, so Piers telephoned her page to give her the message.

I was desolate; months and months of work from scores of people had gone down the drain, literally. Later we received some lovely letters from those who were to have taken part, telling us of their great disappointment. One that I loved was from a lady who said she had followed my instructions that everybody should get their horses used to light and loud noises. She said of her elderly horse, 'I've been playing him the 1812 Overture at full blast for a month – how am I going to tell him now that it has all been in vain?'

There was only one answer to the problem – my usual one. I knew that everybody would be free that night, so I would give a party. About fifty people came down to South Lodge and had a great dinner produced by my PA Catie Bland and her friends. We played the rehearsal CD of the show right through and I dissolved into tears as it became apparent what we had all lost. We had got so close. I still, even now, cannot quite believe we didn't actually do the show. It's just that I can't seem to find any photographs of it anywhere.

*   *   *

Five years later the second half of the pageant was reborn. 'All the Queen's Horses' had been the title of a chapter in our original souvenir brochure, and seemed a good one for a show. It would now be performed at Windsor, every evening after the Horse Show.

Rosemary rewrote the script starting at World War II, but we included as much as we could of the original. Again, there would be a thousand horses, stabled all around the Home Park. We took on as production manager Adam Wildi, who had done a brilliant job on the Royal Military Tattoo, with the rest of 'my' team of lighting, sound and stage management from the same event. The music was now handled by Mac McDermott and Ken Peers, former musicians in the Royal Marines who had also worked on the Royal Military Tattoo, and we asked the Windsor and Eton Choral Society if they would take part.

We recruited every conceivable type of horse you can think of, even though the 'experts' kept saying they would never work together. Racehorses were to prove a slight problem; I had asked the Queen's racing manager,

Lord Carnarvon, if we could borrow 'a couple of not-too-excitable racehorses' for the Ascot Gavotte from *My Fair Lady* for the previous 'Pageant'. When I met the Queen at the Royal Windsor Horse Show, she said, 'I hear you want to borrow two of my slow racehorses – I do not have any slow racehorses!' In the end we borrowed two of Queen Elizabeth's and put them in the Queen's colours. The Aga Khan was also one of our supporters, and he lent us a couple of his horses.

'All the Queen's Horses' was supposed to be launched at the Royal Windsor Horse Show in 2001, but the foot and mouth epidemic meant the Horse Show had to be cancelled. The Queen always had a large house party for the Horse Show so it was decided that year that the Stewards would give a 'Not the Windsor Horse Show Party' for the Royal house party and all involved with the Horse Show in one of the clubs in the Great Park.

The Queen arrived and said immediately, 'You're not a steward.'

I replied, 'I am, Ma'am, I'm the firework steward.' By then I had been running the Finale of the show for a number of years.

We had made a model of the proposed setting, and I took the Queen over to it to explain what we were going to do. She said, 'But you know nothing about horses!' I said, 'Ma'am, that's why I think I might be able to do all this, because I'm not distracted by too many inconvenient facts.'

Towards the end of my dissertation, I said, 'And here, Ma'am, the Gold State Coach will come out – the one you are to use for the Golden Jubilee Celebrations....' ...'

'Oh no, I'm not,' she said. 'I'm not going in the Gold Coach.'

I was completely taken off guard and did not know what to say. This was 2001; enthusiasm for the Jubilee had yet to materialise and I felt very strongly that we could not afford to miss a trick or be seen to be 'dumbing it down' in any way.

'But, Ma'am, the Gold State Coach only comes out every twenty-five years – you must use it.' I don't think the Queen is used to people saying she *must* do things but I had got slightly carried away.

She still said, 'No,' so I asked why. 'Because the clothes I will need to wear to St Paul's in the Gold Coach would not be suitable for your party in the afternoon.' She had obviously been briefed about my plans.

I was completely stumped. Then I suddenly had an idea born, I think, of desperation.

'Ma'am, you're going to lunch in the Guildhall after St Paul's and you will be there for some time. You could always change...'

The next morning came an outraged telephone call from the Private Secretary, Robin Janvrin. 'What the hell do you think you're doing, suggesting such a thing to the Queen?' I said that I just thought it was vital not to downgrade the celebrations. He was furious, and never forgave me. However, if you look at the photographs of the Jubilee you will notice that the Queen leaves Buckingham Palace in blue and returns in red.

*   *   *

Meanwhile, my plans for the Jubilee proper were progressing and a cast of over twenty thousand had been assembled.

I found dealing with the Palace a little difficult this time. Over the past twenty-five years I had been used to dealing only with the Queen's Private Secretary. Now the Keeper of the Privy Purse, Sir Michael Peat, was heavily involved and the two did not always seem to agree.

The two garden concerts, which were to be run by the BBC, were taking shape. This was the only time to my knowledge that the Palace had been directly involved in such events, and I was concerned about legal and health and safety issues, which we knew from experience could be a nightmare. It was clear, though, that Michael Peat had everything well in hand and all our concerns about elitism faded. The concerts were a complete triumph, and raised lots of money for Jubilee charities.

At about this time Lord Levene decided to step aside as Chairman of the Celebrations Committee and I looked around for his replacement. By now we had produced a fairly detailed budget and knew that we needed to raise about £5.5 million, a considerable sum but not astronomical. I had known for some time Jeffrey Sterling, Chairman of P&O who owned Earls Court and Olympia, who had also been a supporter of mine in the VE Day and VJ Day anniversary celebrations. I asked if he would be interested in coming in to raise the money. He was, and added to our existing working group a trade union representative, which proved a very good idea.

By this time we had gathered together the key departments whose support we needed. Helen Bayne had been a tower of strength and common sense throughout. The Government Minister in charge of the Celebrations, Tessa Jowell, could not have been more helpful. The Government did a great deal behind the scenes for which they were never given proper credit. Certainly the huge cost of running the Underground and buses over the holiday was something we could never have afforded ourselves.

The BBC producer of the main event was Dave Pickthall, whom I knew well from Royal Tournament days. Over lunch one day he wondered how he was going to keep the procession to St Paul's interesting enough. I was keen to get more and more participants on board, because I wanted every part of society to be represented, so I suggested commissioning a piece of multi-cultural music called 'Progress of the Queen' to include every sort of choir and musical combination we could think of. Dave thought this an excellent idea, and Barry Hingley wrote a brilliant twenty-minute piece as a tribute to all the nations of Britain and the music of fifty years. The BBC at that stage was very pleased.

Having recruited over five hundred musicians I turned my energies to the processions. Helen and I had been guests at the previous year's Notting Hill Carnival and found it fantastic if rather loud. I said we would be delighted if four thousand people in carnival costume could come but that we wouldn't be able to cope with trucks with huge amplifiers and speakers.

The year before, I had asked my old friend Patti Boulaye to gather together a gospel choir – six thousand seemed a good round figure – and had actually got them all together for a rehearsal in the Royal Albert Hall. They got completely carried away and performed the nearest thing to a musical riot that I have ever seen. Cliff Richard said it was the biggest backing group he had ever had, and the Albert Hall staff said they'd never seen anything like it. It was quite spontaneous; we could never have planned it.

The Services Parade would allow all those groups who constantly serve us to share in the limelight. There were about four thousand of them – Fire Brigade, prison guards, the RNLI, the Church Army, the Red Cross, St John Ambulance, the Jewish Lads' Brigade and the Girls' Brigade. At one stage they filled the entire Mall, and although they had had absolutely no rehearsal they had followed my instructions to the letter.

The Fifty Years Parade was put together by Helen Marriage and Hilary Westlake to give a flavour of the sights and sounds of the reign including fifty cars from Aston Martins to Robin Reliants. Jane Charlie, a freelance secretary who frequently came to the rescue, organised a Commonwealth parade of two and a half thousand including people from every country, and Keith Khan designed the Rainbow of Wishes. Thousands of children had sent in special wishes ranging from 'I wish for peace in the world' to 'I wish my father would stop beating my mother'. Some were very touching indeed.

In order to make the Palace look different for the balcony appearances, and so that even more children could contribute, I got Keith Khan to design a balcony hanging covered with the national flags of the Commonwealth, all made by the children, and painstakingly assembled by Jane Charlie.

National flags arrived from all over the world, signed *With love* by the children who had made them. They ranged from paintings to embroideries – one was even made out of old beer cans – and the Royal College of Needlework put them all together into a wonderful drape.

There were still some groups not represented in the parades that I was keen to have, in particular the Chinese and Far East contingents. Just as I was about to recruit them I was told that the BBC were no longer interested in covering the music in 'Progress of the Queen'. Typical BBC.

I remonstrated that they had specifically asked me to put it together, and I had done so. The Lord Mayor of London's Pageant Master Dominic Reed had also amassed a whole lot of brass groups to play a rolling fanfare as the procession went past – a good idea, though contrary to what we had originally agreed. Nick Vaughan-Barratt of the BBC said they would not now show either. I was furious, but got no support from the rest. So I stood down the Chinese and other groups that I was just getting sorted. The rest, by this stage, were too far committed, and I just prayed that they would not be too disappointed when they saw the television programmes afterwards.

*   *   *

The time was drawing near for the first event, 'All the Queen's Horses'. Catie Bland, my former PA who had worked on the last two Royal Tournaments, was now in charge of the administration and quite a headache it was too. We had to build stables in three different areas of the Great Park, and draw up complicated routes and timetables to ensure that the acts arrived on time, did not have to wait too long, and did not snarl up the limited backstage area.

We had briefed the Queen, unofficially, throughout the planning stages. I would tell Simon Brooks-Ward and he would tell the Stud Groom, Terry Pendry, who would get the message through and relay back any reactions. The heroes of the day were undoubtedly Colin Brookes, Brian Perry and their teams of stewards and marshals who devised a complicated but necessary series of checkpoints and timed everything to perfection.

Adam Wildi had built the stands, the hospitality boxes and the stage proscenium arch. John Pope had lit everything with his usual care and Paul Keating had produced excellent sound. All we needed now was to make the horse bit work. From all over the country, and from the continent, hundreds of horseboxes homed in on Windsor. The weather was quite good so we held our first acclimatisation programmes to get the horses used to strong lights, loud noises and music and also to being close to one another in large numbers.

The Queen, who was providing about forty horses under Terry Pendry, asked if she could come and watch because she wanted to see how they coped. They had come from London, Windsor, Sandringham and Balmoral, and like every other owner she was concerned about them.

I called them in, in their separate groups, slowly increasing the light and sound levels. They all gradually calmed down and were soon all taking it in their stride. We had virtually all the horses on by the end and it seemed to work surprisingly well. The Queen, like all the other owners, seemed very relieved. I was amused that I, who knew so little, surrounded by some of the most knowledgeable horse people in the world, was giving all the instructions.

The Gold State Coach was a big worry. It would be rather ironic if, having gone out on a limb to get it to take part in the main celebrations, we were to trash it at Windsor beforehand. Made for George III, it weighs four tons and has relatively narrow-rimmed wheels. Although it looks immaculate, no one really knows the state of the internal metal structure. We were going to have to be very careful. We toyed with the idea of having a different surface laid for it but in the end decided not to. The special surface of the arena , which we had perfected for the Royal Military Tattoo, was a twelve-inch layer of sand, fibre and wax which could take horses galloping, men marching and heavy vehicles. A lattice of drainage pipes underneath was to prove amazingly efficient in spite of some appalling weather.

The Gold Coach was brought down early one morning on a low loader, covered against prying eyes. Seymour Gilbart-Denham, who had been a stalwart support throughout the complications of the failed Ascot pageant, was to provide all the coaches and coachmen for this show. He and I watched as the amazing gold confection was gingerly wheeled down the ramp. We had built a special tent for it where the eight Windsor Greys could be harnessed up out of sight. They took up the strain and the coach rolled forward. The Queen's Head Coachman, Seymour and I looked carefully at how much it was sinking into our special surface. The answer, to our surprise, was hardly at all. We were delighted.

My original plan had been for the Coach to move only as far as the Royal Box, just over a hundred yards. I didn't think we dared take it any further. However, the Head Coachman was happy to try the complete circuit which meant many more people would be able to see it properly. This wasn't so popular with the grooms and the Yeomen of the Guard who had to walk alongside it. In fact, after a few laps the Yeomen gave up and stayed in front of the Royal Box and waited for the coach to re-join them.

Once again our 'voices' did an excellent job. Dame Judi Dench, Robert Hardy, Prunella Scales and Edward Woodward turned Rosemary Anne Sisson's clever words into a living story. And Mac McDermott and Ken Pearce had arranged all the music wonderfully to fit.

As I had first experimented on Horse Guards for the Royal Military Tattoo, the show would be continuous. There would be no pauses, no cues; everyone was expected to come on, perform and go off exactly in time with the voices and music. It was a tall order that was achieved brilliantly by the marshals and stewards. If you were late on your cue, you couldn't come on at all. There were no arguments. Under Dougie Squires' expert direction hundreds of dancers, children and actors all played their parts to perfection.

For me, the best part of the show was a display arranged by Jennie Loriston-Clark, with fifty-two dressage riders, all accompanied by Victoria Yellop on the violin.

It rained at the first performance, but the Earl and Countess of Wessex gamely arrived in an open carriage. The performance went well but all the participants got soaked. I felt sorry for some of the Pony Club who had at least forty minutes' hack home to their stables across the Great Park. But they dried out and were back the next day for more. By the time the Queen and the Duke of Edinburgh came on the Saturday night everything was fully rehearsed and worked pretty well.

At the end Simon Brooks-Ward and I went down to the car to say goodbye. The Queen looked radiant in a colourful sequinned jacket with an amazing zigzag diamond necklace. I longed to tell her how wonderful she looked, but didn't dare.

Afterwards, Staff Sergeant Baynes and I visited the stables where lots of parties were in full swing. Everybody was so elated that our tour took quite a time, and we became very 'relaxed'. I met many of the Commonwealth participants I hadn't been able to meet before, and also representatives from a number of the countries the Queen had visited in the past fifty years. Apparently my morning briefings to the head of each act had been passed on word for word, including my feeble attempts at jokes. They asked if I had really declared that if someone fell off they should get up; if they could get up, then they could ride; and if they could ride they could continue to do the act. There speaks someone who knows nothing about horses!

I went down to South Lodge for a day's rest before going up to London.

My heart had survived the strain pretty well but my permanent headache was getting worse and worse. Still, we had only a few weeks to go.

*   *   *

Whilst I was preoccupied with Windsor, Jeffrey Sterling had unilaterally changed the procession route in London, so it went past the Royal Box from right to left instead of from left to right. He said he had wanted to talk to me but couldn't track me down. I replied that I had been talking constantly to other people in his office who apparently had no difficulties. His alteration meant we had to change the way a number of the acts and groups were aligned and everything that had faced in one direction had to be moved to face the other. Robert Janvrin had been pressing me to make this change for some time but I had pointed out that it would mean at least twenty thousand people would be unable to watch the procession live.

Otherwise, all the preparations were going well. The big screens were up and working. I had two Portakabins on the site, one of top of the other, so that I could hide away and rest in the top one and no one would know I was there. I had done pretty well at Windsor and had not had to disappear more than once or twice.

The next period was going to be a problem, not least because of the aggro between the various parts of our team. I should have been used to people appearing out of the woodwork longing for Horlicks and looking proprietorial and ready to take all the credit, but it still annoyed me. However, dear Emma and the two Bayne(s), Helen and Staff Sergeant, kept me going.

Press interest was considerable, and I got so used to reporters being around that I didn't notice them. One day Malcolm Birkett, who was co-ordinating most of the work for Unusual Rigging, said, 'I'm afraid it's almost impossible to put the large Jubilee cypher on the top of the stages.'

I apparently replied, '*Almost* impossible is not impossible enough for me, so please do it!'

This was quoted verbatim in the *Telegraph* the next day. I had forgotten the reporter was there, and it caused some embarrassment both to me and to Malcolm. The Saturday before the classical concert, Jimmy Young interviewed me on his Morning Show and quoted the remark. I thought no more about it until the reception in the Palace after the concert.

The Countess of Wessex said, 'Your interview was so funny.'

'Really?' I said, surprised. 'I didn't think it was funny at all.'

'No, not the actual interview – what happened afterwards. Lots of people telephoned in to suggest you should run the Health Service or the railways, or even the country!'

I thought this was hilarious and even more so when scores of letters addressed to 'Sir Michael Parker, London' were later delivered to me via the Palace.

Emma and I went to the classical concert, which was laid on splendidly. Everyone was given a Waitrose cool bag with a delicious picnic. At a discussion beforehand everybody agreed that there should be water, but couldn't agree whether there should be a quarter-bottle or half-bottle of champagne. I said that I thought a quarter-bottle looked a bit mean. However, a half-bottle each turned out to be, in some cases, a little too much. The weather was fine and the concert was glorious. In the Royal Box, waiting for it to start, I remarked to Emma, 'Wasn't it nice to have Walkers shortbread in the picnic hamper?' The man in front of us turned round and said, 'I'm so glad – I'm Mr Walker!'

Afterwards we went down the Mall and were amazed at the huge numbers that had watched it all on the big screens. Jeffrey Sterling had suggested that the stars from the concert appear on a hastily-erected stage in the centre gate, a good idea which went down well.

The next day, Sunday, was our major preparation day. The Beacon that the Queen was to light was mounted on the steps of the Queen Victoria Memorial. After my less than perfect beacon-lighting for the Silver Jubilee and VE Day celebrations, I was determined to get this one right so I designed it myself. It consisted of a large perforated sphere, somewhat like a giant artichoke, which would produce a flame about thirty feet high; it used, I am told, one ton of liquid petroleum gas that evening. Rather than have a fuse that went along the ground, and so that the Queen would be as far up the Mall as possible, I thought it would be more impressive to have the beacon lit by a rocket guided down a line. It's fair to say that the Palace was not too keen on the rocket, but I persevered and eventually got agreement.

Early on I had decided that we needed fireworks on the roof of the Palace on a ten-times-grander scale than for the G7; Wilf Scott of Pyrovision, dependable as always, produced them. There would also be massive projections over the front of the Palace, done by Ross Ashton and Paul Chatfield. Large pumps would produce splendid thirty-foot fountains to liven up the dreary bit of water around the Queen Victoria Memorial which normally consists only of turgid pools with a few overflows. The video was done by Martin Jangaard and the lighting by Durham Marenghi who put fifty huge searchlights on the roof; they produced a marvellous effect but gave aircraft coming into Heathrow something to think about. The sound was by John Del'Nero.

On Sunday, during lunch with the crew in Green Park, someone rushed in to say that the Palace was on fire. Indeed, smoke was coming from the roof. My heart lost about four beats. We had tons of pyrotechnics up there and my first worry was whether all our boys were all right. I also had visions of being held responsible for burning down the whole Palace which, after the Windsor fire, would have been the final straw.

The police became hyperactive and closed the roads for miles around, and about fifteen fire engines turned up. One actually came speeding down Constitution Hill past the Palace, and continued down the Mall until it realised it was going the wrong way and turned back. I was very worried that the fire seemed to be near the Picture Gallery. Only the evening before I had walked down it with the Princess Royal, admiring the fantastic pictures there. I couldn't bear the thought that they might be lost forever.

The fire, in the end, was put out by one appliance, and to our huge relief it was in none of the areas where either we or the BBC had been working, so we were not to blame. It was caused by an electrical fault, and had actually done very little damage.

Our boys went back onto the roof to continue work. We had over fifty men up there, and it had been pointed out that they would need 'facilities'. There is a marvellous photograph, taken early one morning when no press were present, of a crane lowering a very obvious Portaloo onto the roof of the Palace. We sent a copy to the Queen, with the boys' caption: 'Installing a new throne in the Palace!'

That night was our only opportunity to rehearse, and we had got the press to agree not to photograph or film the rocket lighting the beacon. We fired a trial firework from the roof, one from the Palace forecourt, one from the Queen Victoria Memorial and one from Green Park where a lot of the very large mortars had been set up. That was all great – now for the rocket. I tried to brief the BBC, but they did not turn up for the rehearsal and consequently missed the rocket in the live programme. Fortunately one of our own cameras caught it perfectly, so it is on record.

The next evening the crowds arrived early so we kept them entertained with the big screens. The police said the crowd had reached a million. The police always underestimate, so the true figure was probably rather more. So much for those that had said no one would come!

I suddenly needed to go to the loo – but I was surrounded by a million people. 'No problem, Sir,' my friendly policeman said. 'Would Clarence House be all right?'

'Clarence House would be just fine,' I replied, so a large police escort pushed me through the crowd and then pushed me, much relieved, back again.

As the pop concert got underway I became aware of one of the worst decisions I had ever made. I had thought it would be nice if a mass of children carrying handmade lanterns accompanied the Queen and the Duke of Edinburgh from the Palace to the dais, about a third of the way up the Mall. The children themselves were lovely but most of the accompanying parents and minders were really badly behaved. There were three hundred children and, supposedly, a maximum of one hundred escorts, but in the end everybody brought their whole families. But there was nothing I could do about it, and when the children and the royal car arrived at the dais we had to shovel all the escorts as quickly as possible to the back.

The Queen mounted the dais, and Bruno Peek who had designed the ghastly torch handed it over. The Queen lit the fuse and the rocket went speeding off. Unfortunately, unlike at the rehearsal, it produced a thick cloud of smoke. Somebody had obviously done something to the rocket without telling me. We couldn't see a thing. No rocket, no beacon, no Palace even.

The Queen asked, 'What *are* you doing to me?'

'Ma'am, I'm terribly sorry. It wasn't like that in rehearsal,' was all I could say.

Eventually the smoke cleared and the fireworks looked tremendous. Wilf excelled himself and the music effects, lights and pyrotechnics were magical. The fact that we had all disappeared into the smoke was not at all apparent from the television coverage, but then neither was the rocket.

I had designed the projections to start with a red velvet curtain covering the front of the Palace that would 'rise' at the start of the show. The day before, a French reporter telephoned to ask how heavy the curtain was. I explained that it was a projection. She persisted. 'As it covers the whole of the front of the Palace it must surely be very heavy.' I tried once more. She hung up, still mystified.

After the stars' reception I walked back down the Mall with Staff Baynes, where the carpet of Commonwealth flowers was being put into place. I cannot look at any Union Flag without checking that it is the right way up, and after a while Staff Baynes had to lead me away, saying that I couldn't possibly check every flag in London.

The next morning was lovely. The choirs and orchestras were all there and Sir David Willcocks was having a quick rehearsal. Apart from the crowds, which the police said now totalled nearly two million, over twenty thousand performers were reporting in to Horse Guards Parade and the stages at Buckingham Palace.

The previous day I had tried to cycle up the Mall to Horse Guards without realising it was actually uphill. I collapsed and had to be rescued by Emma and Staff Baynes, who somehow got hold of a vehicle. But today I was obviously being kept going by adrenaline alone; my head was unbelievable, and I had to lie down for an hour. Nobody noticed.

The State Procession started forming up. Now came my first test. Barry Hingley's wonderful music started with 'Zadok the Priest' (or, as we called it, 'Zorba the Greek'). I had had a number of arguments with London District about whether the music would affect the words of command, and we had agreed a complicated technical solution. The sound system would ensure that the hundred yards in front of and behind the Coach would be quiet enough to hear words of command whilst the sound actually in line with the Coach would be at full volume. I'm not at all certain that it worked quite like that.

As the Gold Coach appeared, looking stunning, a tear formed in my eye. It was so right that it should have been used. By now, of course, having been pulling the coach at Windsor every day for a week, the horses were fit and pretty frisky. The Grooms and Yeomen had their work cut out keeping up and the Coach arrived at St Paul's slightly early.

The big screens worked well; it was probably the first time that a State Procession had been seen live by so many people. It must have been the first time, too, that a State Procession was accompanied by a massed steel band.

There had been a grand lunch at St James's Palace for the other members of the Royal Family and the sponsors and supporters. Afterwards they all walked down from the Palace to the Royal Box on the Memorial; the crowds were thrilled to have such a close view of, amongst others, Prince William and Prince Harry. Prince William told me, as we walked, how much he missed the Royal Tournament which pleased me no end.

Meanwhile on the Embankment, which we had closed for the day, four thousand Notting Hill carnival participants of all ages were helping each other into their fantastic costumes, some of them over twenty feet tall. The plan was for them to process to Whitehall, then down to Trafalgar Square, into the Mall and down to the Palace past the Royal Box. Everything had been timed to the last minute because so many groups were involved, from aircraft to horses and carriages, that we had to make certain that everything kept exact time.

But the procession didn't arrive. I got an exasperated radio message from the leader to say they had been stopped at the top of Whitehall.

'You can't come through here,' they were told. 'We're expecting a procession.'

'But we are the procession!' they said.

'No,' the police insisted. 'We're expecting a *proper* procession.' And they weren't allowed through.

I got hold of my friendly police commander. 'Oh dear,' he said, and got on the radio immediately. They were allowed through. A thousand children danced and sang their way down the Mall, largely made up of the Chicken Shed theatre group. It was very moving to see how the more able-bodied children looked after those of restricted ability. It was all done carefully and unobtrusively, just a hand here, an arm there, and a quick push of a chair. It was a total joy having them around.

From the Royal Box we could see what looked slightly like an invasion – Patti Boulaye was striding, Boudicca-like, at the head of her six-thousand-strong gospel choir. Many of the younger ones were from the Stagecoach acting school, who had also taken part in the frenzied rehearsal in the Royal Albert Hall the year before.

I had thought it would be rather fun to have six hundred or so children carrying gold streamers to make a 'river of gold' down the Mall in front of the Queen. She and the Duke of Edinburgh stood in the State Land Rover waving to the excited crowd. The Queen had changed at the Guildhall, and looked wonderful in bright red. Unfortunately the 'river of gold' children also got over-excited, and instead of preceding the Queen down the Mall they decided to mill around the car. I got a message from a protection officer telling me to get the children out of the way. I sent a message back which was brisk, bordering on terse, pointing out that I was half a mile away, and that as he was nearer than I was he should get the children out of the way himself. The Royal progress continued, swamped in gold foil which, although not exactly what I had planned, looked absolutely marvellous. When the Queen eventually arrived at the Memorial, she gave me a broad smile as if to say, 'Whatever was all that?'

The Royal Box was now full and the first of the main processions started.

Four thousand representatives from all the country's services, including the Armed Forces, Customs and Lifeboats, filled the Mall. They'd had no rehearsal but I had written detailed instructions as to length of pace, and how many paces to the minute. The Garrison Sergeant Major – the wonderful Perry Mason – and his team had sorted them all out and they advanced like toothpaste coming out of a tube. Even I was pretty impressed, but a sinking feeling came over me as I realised that there seemed to be no end to them. The whole Mall, as far as the eye could see, was full. This was the moment when I thought to myself hopefully, 'It will all be alright in the end... and if it isn't alright, it's not the end.'

Timing was becoming critical. The most pressing concern was the mass fly-past. Emma and Staff Baynes were trying to work out how many minutes we were adrift and we communicated the delay through our RAF Liaison Officer to some of the aircraft so they wouldn't take off until later. Others had to refuel over Essex.

The whole business of the fly past had been a bone of contention. The military had not wanted to do it because they were doing their own celebration for the Queen in a couple of weeks. I said, as politely as I could, that three men and a dog would watch their show, whereas the Jubilee Day was going to be watched by countless millions around the world. Jeffrey Sterling took up the cause and at one of our evening meetings announced that he had got them to agree. That was great; now, I said, all we needed were three Concordes to fly over at the end with the Red Arrows. Jeffrey said he would ask British Airways. The answer came back almost immediately – Concordes do not fly in formation, but they would provide one. We were able to contact all the aircraft by radio about the delay, except Concorde. We ended up asking London Heathrow if they had a Concorde standing by anywhere. They had – in fact, they had two in case there was a problem with the first – and the pilot was having a cup of tea. We invited him to get on the radio immediately!

The Fifty Years parade was being slightly precious, wanting to be completely ready before starting off. 'At this rate,' I told them, 'you'll probably be ready for the Diamond Jubilee. So get moving!'

Don't ask me why I thought it would be fun to start this section with the massed motorbikes of the Hell's Angels; I just did. A friend had said he knew a Hell's Angel and a splendid fellow came to see me in Collingham Place. He was known as Snob, he said, because he was posher than the others! Snob agreed to recruit fifty riders, and I learnt a lot about Hell's Angels. Snob's group did a lot of charity work and had raised considerable sums of money for the family of one of their members who had had cancer. Some groups in other countries have quite different reputations, and some Canadian broadcasters became quite irate about my lot because there had been trouble with Hell's Angels in Canada. Anyway, I sent the bikes off and hoped the rest would follow. They roared down the Mall and were thrilled when they got to the Memorial, as they started going around it the wrong way and just went on going round and round.

Fifty years of cars were followed by fifty years of musicals. Cameron Mackintosh allowed the cast of 'My Fair Lady' to take part, in costume. Cameron happened to be on the same float as Cliff Richard, and as they went past the Royal Box they shouted, 'Hello, Michael!' very loudly. Someone to my right remarked, 'I thought they had come to see us!'

The Commonwealth procession came next. It was a great tribute to my office staff that we had so many of them. However, it soon became clear that the various groups had slightly misunderstood why they were there, and seemed to think they were each to do a special performance for the Queen. So they all tried to stop in front of the Royal Box and do it. I tried to get Alan Jacobi to get the stewards to keep them moving but he didn't seem to be in 'receive mode' so I had to go down myself and try to move them on. I was not helped by many of the groups coming up to shake my hand and thank me for asking them.

I was still trying to get all the information together to adjust the fly-past timings. I made a final timing decision, and waited as Chicken Shed sang a short song about hope, and the Queen and the Duke of Edinburgh were accompanied from the Royal Box by two children who, with hundreds of others, were supposed to escort them to the South Centre Gate. Then a hundred and fifty Commonwealth children would take them on to unveil the balcony hanging. As we joined the first lot I suddenly realised they were all rather tall – not at all the little darlings I had had in mind – and we quite disappeared amongst them. When we actually got to the gate there were no Commonwealth children in sight. So I told the two who had brought us there to carry on. They were meant to ask the Queen if they could unveil the hanging. They just looked completely lost. I whispered to them to run towards the hanging in the hope that the riggers would take the hint. But they stood there uncertainly, and Prince Phillip remarked, 'They don't know what they're doing, do they?' Someone finally took the hint, the fanfare sounded and the cover came off to reveal the children's and the Royal

College's work. It did look splendid.

The Queen went inside, ready to come out on the balcony, and I returned to the Queen Victoria Memorial to cue the music and singing that would precede the appearances. I had agreed, or thought I had, a sequence of events on the balcony which would allow all our orchestras, bands, and choirs to contribute to the Final Salute.

Using a 'cherry picker', we had put James Edward, a young chorister from the Choir of the Chapel Royal, resplendent in his scarlet coat, high up in a tree. The plan was for him to start singing 'Amazing Grace' solo; it would be taken up by Patti Boulaye, then by the gospel choirs, and then by everybody including the massed military bands and pipes and drums. But the sequence went wrong almost immediately, so I had to ditch the whole plan, and over a thousand musicians and singers were totally confused.

The Queen and the Duke of Edinburgh came on to the balcony to thunderous cheers and applause. In desperation we played and sang 'Land of Hope and Glory'. We were going to do that in any event, though much later on. But it didn't seem to matter because everybody was having a great time. Sir David Willcocks was very understanding, as he tore up page after page of the script!

The aircraft were now roaring over group by group. In the distance I could just see Concorde with the Red Arrows on each wing tip. The crowd's excitement reached fever pitch and the roar that welcomed them was beyond deafening. The Queen said afterwards that it was the only time she had been unable to hear Concorde flying over. I was slightly miffed that they hadn't come down the centre line but I was probably the only one to notice.

The Royal Family went back indoors, then came out again. I managed to cue the National Anthem, and I doubt it has ever had a louder rendering.

*   *   *

It was over. I was completely shattered, my head was appalling, and I could not wait to lie down. It was only as I was walking back to the hotel that I suddenly remembered James Edward, the little boy up the tree. The poor fellow had been stuck up there for an hour. I later wrote to him saying how very sorry I was.

Back at the hotel Jeffrey Sterling seemed to be giving some sort of party. I was almost asleep on my feet so I sat down outside the room, where I could half hear what seemed to be a very long speech. Some of my team came out, fairly disgruntled, and said that everybody had been praised for contributing except for them. Apparently we had had nothing to do with the day that was worth mentioning.

I couldn't have cared less and went home to go to sleep, which I think I must have done for about two days.

A number of very similar letters came from the Palace to me and my staff. The ones from the public suggesting that I should take over the country were also still coming in dribs and drabs. Eventually, after about two months, another letter came from Robin Janvrin. In it he said that the Queen would like to give me a Parker pen set. That was very generous of her and it was very fine but I couldn't help feeling that it had been suggested by Janvrin as some sort of ironic put-down with some irony. I was thrilled for my team when some of them were mentioned in the Jubilee Honours List, though it was perhaps typical that the only person in Sterling's team who didn't get an honour was John Glanfield, who had done most of the real work.

Weeks later Jeffrey Sterling held a party at his home to say thank you to everyone. Robin Janvrin stood up and gave Jeffrey credit for absolutely everything. It was Jeffrey who had apparently conceived, designed, and produced the whole thing. Janvrin did not mention my team or me once. Jeffrey Sterling did mention me briefly – 'Well, of course, there was Michael Parker...' – then spent five minutes talking about the Concorde pilot.

But at least I had the satisfaction of helping to pay a tremendous tribute to the Queen, and proving all the Jeremiahs wrong, even if no-one acknowledged it. But no Jubilee Medal for me this time!

I did however receive a strange letter one day from the 'Spamies' to say that I had been awarded 'The Spam Life-time Achievement Award'! I received it at a very smart lunch at the Savoy. It consists of a tin of Spam on an engraved plinth. The tin has a sell by date 'best before end Feb 2005' Sic Transit Gloria !

I also was awarded a splendid Gold Medal from the Walpole Society, who promote British excellence. They told me I had also been nominated for 'The Cultural Award for 2002' and that my competitor was Julian Fellowes who had just won an Oscar for his script for 'Gosforth Park'. To my amazement and his huge feigned annoyance I won the Silver nodding Bulldog on its Union Flag Cushion. I think that The Lord Fellowes has more than trumped me now!

Alright in the End

It took me a very long time to recover from the Golden Jubilee. My years of 'overdosing' on extreme tension and stress were rapidly taking their toll and my future was looking dodgy.

Then suddenly, for me, everything started to go very right. In 2005, Emma and I had our marriage blessed in Chelsea Old Church, an occasion organised by Emma's aunt Gaby and taken by Peter Elvy. It was a wonderful service, with Patti Boulaye singing David Fanshawe's 'Lord's Prayer' in a special arrangement that he gave us as a wedding present, and Andrew Scott reading 'You're my cup of tea'. Oliver gave his mother away, part of his 'deal' for accepting me as stepfather, and gave an annoyingly excellent speech afterwards. Francis Gradidge was my best man and the remainder of my friends looked on in amazement, never having believed I would ever actually do it!

Emma and I have now moved to Wherwell, a delightful small village in Hampshire with a population of just over four hundred. We have wonderful neighbours, a pub and a small church, all on the beautiful banks of the River Test. We intend to live here happily ever after.

*   *   *

The best thing to come out of the Golden Jubilee was an invitation to speak on a Saga cruise ship. I was initially uncertain about this, but Emma persuaded me that it might be fun, and it was. Since then I have been a regular guest lecturer for them, and thoroughly enjoy the trips – luxurious cabin, great food, brilliant crew, no packing and unpacking, and dropping in to fascinating places all around the world. I try only to go on Saga, as they have small ships and are tremendously civilised and friendly.

I talk under the general heading 'Organised Chaos', about all the cock-ups that have happened during the hundreds of events that I have run over the years. There is no shortage of material!

One of my other joys in recent years has been producing events for the 'Not Forgotten' Association. Founded in 1920, it exists to entertain and cheer up wounded and disabled ex-servicemen and women. I became involved with them through a friend of mine, James Tedder, in the 90s. In the early days I used to find it almost unbearable to see the young men smashed and shattered by other people's ambitions. None of them ever complained, and as the years went on those we tried to cheer up seemed to become younger and younger.

From its earliest days 'Not Forgotten' has received unprecedented support from the Royal family. Even Queen Mary joined in to give tea parties for those horribly damaged by the First World War. It is the only charity to have its own private garden party at Buckingham Palace every year. I would organise a raft of stars to come to the garden party. They didn't have to perform in any way; their only job was to go round and talk to all the guests. This served a double purpose; the ex-servicemen got to meet the stars, and the opportunity to have a good look round the Palace gardens was a 'thank you' to those who had helped us with other events. However, although they weren't supposed to perform it did not take long for someone like Rolf Harris to commandeer the band and lead everybody in a sing-song of his well-known hits. Bruce Forsyth would be his normal inimitable self, and scores of other stars joined in. Dame Vera Lynn is always there and shows great patience posing for photographs and signing autographs.

One year we had the – then – only three surviving veterans from the First World War, marvellous old boys, all well over a hundred years old and as chirpy as anything. One of them, Henry Allingham, would sing continually, in fact it was almost impossible to stop him. The younger soldiers simply could not believe that they were meeting someone who was well over eighty years older than they were.

'Not Forgotten' also had a Christmas concert every year at St James' Palace. In fact, these concerts were really more like revues. Directed by Dougie Squires, they featured singers, dancers, conjurers, jugglers, ventriloquists, in fact every sort of entertainment you could think of. For me the best singer ever was Judy Campbell, then aged eighty-seven. She had been the first to sing 'A Nightingale Sang in Berkeley Square' in the 30s, and in 2003, the year before she died, though she was looking very frail with one of her arms bandaged, she sang it as I have never heard it before. Michael Mates, the MP, who was also performing his piano and song routine, stood with me watching her from the wings, and was mesmerised by her. He kept thanking me for asking him, and said he would not have missed it for the world.

We would also do one-off shows. Once we did one in the Painted Hall at Greenwich. Rolf Harris came on and, indicating the amazing ceiling and walls painted by James Thornhill over a period of nineteen years, he said, 'It's taken me all day to paint this, you know – can you see what it is yet?'

In the same show we had Engelbert Humperdinck, who looked as though he was on loan from Madam Tussaud's.

The boys hobbled in and out, some with no legs, some with no arms, some unable to see or speak. One lovely Royal Marine found he couldn't use artificial legs very easily so he used to run around on his stumps. 'I can cover the ground much quicker like this,' he would say.

In 2010, the Association's ninetieth birthday was on the horizon, and I was asked what I thought they should do. I suggested asking to use the Ballroom at Buckingham Palace, as it seemed the ultimate venue. The Queen agreed and the Princess Royal, Patron of the Association, was to be the Guest of Honour. As usual I decided to make the whole show as difficult as possible. As if the splendour of the Ballroom were not enough I decided to embellish the walls and ceilings with huge projections. We would tell the story of the ninety years in words and music. There would be a large military band, and 'my' Morriston Orpheus Choir, together with boys from the Choir of the Chapel Royal, would be joined by scores of stars from Robert Hardy to Judi Dench. The story would be 'told' by the founder, an American called Marta Cunningham. The projection boys had done the VE Day, Golden Jubilee and Sandhurst's 'Music on Fire!'; the images were chosen by Paul Chatfield and the mechanics were done by Ross Ashton. It was their masterpiece. Scenes of bucolic peace and hideous war flooded the room, and at one moment the whole ballroom was filled with masses of large swastikas with Hitler ranting in the distance. I thought ruefully it was a good job that Queen Elizabeth the Queen Mother was not able to walk in at that moment. In the Remembrance Scene everywhere one looked was filled with a sea of poppies fluttering down while Judi Dench read 'For The Fallen'. I was not the only one to have a tear in my eye.

Afterwards one of the young lads came up to me and said that it had been the best thing he had ever seen in his whole life, which made it all seem so worthwhile.

However during the day I had had great personal problems and I realised, probably not before time, that I simply could not cope physically or mentally with this sort of tension and exertion any more. Even what for me was a fairly simple show was too much. My head was getting worse and my pulse was alarmingly irregular. I realised that this would have to be the last big event I was going to do. So sadly, after just over fifty years, I had to pack it in. I could not think of a more wonderful and deserving last audience to have.

*   *   *

As I write, the Diamond Jubilee Celebrations are a recent memory. I was thrilled by how well they were done and received. I was also amused to see how many of my old ideas had been re-used but, as Emma says, imitation is a true compliment. I had put forward an idea for a stage around the Queen Victoria Memorial for the Golden Jubilee, but it did not find favour with the Palace. The design of the one used this year was infinitely better than mine, and made a tremendous performance space.

I thought it sad that the BBC treated the River Pageant with such a typical arrogance and lack of respect, and their audience with such disdain, disregarding the real efforts of so many people who went to great trouble and not a little personal expense to pay their tribute to the Queen. Otherwise, everything was magnificent and worked seamlessly. I think the fact that I was in no way involved was a great plus! It was also a great advantage to have the Marquess of Salisbury in charge. As Lord Cranborne he had presided so well over the Fiftieth Anniversaries of VE and VJ Day. Fortunately this time there were never any of the doubts about public lack of enthusiasm which had dogged the early days of both the Silver and Golden Jubilees. The country's huge enthusiasm for and gratitude to the Queen have always been there, but were now even more self-evident.

More recently, the 2012 Olympics were held in London and reminded me that in 1991 the International Olympic Committee met in Birmingham to 'award' the Winter Olympics some years ahead. Many luxurious 'gifts' were being bandied about – and because I had what looked like a very senior pass I was even offered a fur coat 'for my wife'! The Queen was coming to open both the Committee Session and the new Birmingham Conference Centre where it was being held. I laid on a large scale 'entertainment' with about seven hundred people. The President of the IOC was Don Juan Antonio Samaranch, whose team came to be briefed by me on how the ceremony would start. I told them that the delegates would enter first, then Mr Samaranch would enter, and then the Queen would arrive. They said that was quite unacceptable, as Mr Samaranch took precedence over all Heads of State. 'Not in my country' I replied – the Queen would enter last. And I stood firm. One of the British minders hissed in my ear that I should give in, or 'Britain will never ever be awarded the Olympics now!' But I persisted and won the day.

The minder was not very accurate in his prediction as Britain won the 2012 Olympics after what I thought was an excellent pitch. I had never wanted to be involved, firstly because I knew that 'my sort of thing' would not have been politically acceptable, and secondly because I had no desire to struggle with the massive bureaucracy that was being put in place. From my – happily – detached position I watched with great interest. To my mind, things did not start well. The Logo looked as if it had been designed by some schoolchildren with a pot of paste and some square bits of paper. The Take Over/Hand Over Ceremony in Beijing had been embarrassing and very amateur, and the Mascots would not have won a prize at a small village fête. Then things started to look up. The Park was obviously going to be great, with some wonderful buildings and even more brilliant landscaping. (Pity about that pile of red scrap metal, though.) The enthusiasm generated around the country and the dedication, hard work and commitment of all the participants were a joy to behold.

After a lot of hype (and a serious budget) the Opening Ceremony was both impressive and fun. Some wonderful images – the chimney stacks, the fiery Olympic Rings and the masterpiece of the cauldron – were brilliant. It was a pity about the none-too-subtle political posturing and the quality of the television commentary. Such visual poetry needed people who can speak in full sentences and not make it sound like the weather forecast. After the brilliance of the Flame, Paul McCartney's geriatric anti-climax also was sad. The thing I will remember most is the rendering of 'Abide with me' by Emeli Sandé, in spite of the frantic dancing trying to spoil it.

The sport was amazing and brilliantly done, and the results stunning. The volunteers restored one's faith in the country. The Closing Ceremony, although not a patch on the Opening, had some great moments. All in all, Great Britain should indeed feel very proud of itself. The Para-Olympics were also a triumph and very moving.

*   *   *

As Leonardo da Vinci said, *'You do things. Most of them fail. Sometimes they work. If they work really well, others will copy them so you have to do them differently again. The trick is doing something different.'* Well, if it's alright for Leonardo, who am I to disagree?

I have created many things, some good, some quite good, some bad and some plain awful. As Herman Melville said, *'It is better to fail in originality than to succeed in imitation.'*

As I look back over thirty-eight years during which I was lucky enough to do some extraordinary events, I have only one real regret, and that is that they were all so ephemeral. They have never really been fully captured for posterity; they only live on in the audiences' memories. Television coverage or recordings, no matter how good, cannot quite capture the atmosphere, or the roar of two million people around the Palace when Concorde flew over, or the audience at the Royal Tournament during a Field Gun run, or the sound of two thousand military musicians in Wembley Stadium.

No matter – they actually happened. And I was there, and they live on in my imagination. As it is now all over, it must have all been 'alright in the end'!

List of Productions

1961   Revue 'Son of Sandhurst', Royal Military Academy Sandhurst

1962   Taj Mahal party, Detmold

1963   Produced and played Thomas à Becket in *Becket*, Detmold

        1812 party, Detmold

1964   Produced and played Richard III in *Richard III*, West Berlin

1965   My First Tattoo, Olympic Stadium, West Berlin

1967   Berlin Tattoo, Olympic Stadium (1812)

        British Week, Brussels

1970   Battle of Trafalgar, Schloss Bredebeck, Hohne

1974   My First Royal Tournament

1975   Royal Tournament

Aldershot Army Display

Massed Cavalry Bands, Horse Guards

Berlin Tattoo

1976   Royal Tournament

Tidworth Military Tattoo

1977   Royal Tournament

HM the Queen's Silver Jubilee Beacon
Lord Hunt • Sir Edmund Hillary • Gloria Hunniford

Rolls—Royce Parade, Windsor Castle

Royal Variety Show, Home Park, Windsor
*Bruce Forsyth • Leo Sayer • Dame Edna Everage • Elton John
Olivia Newton John • Mikee Yarwood*

Air Tattoo, White Waltham

Household Division Beat Retreat, Horse Guards

Aldershot Army Display

Berlin Tattoo, Deutschlandhalle

1978   Royal Tournament

Household Division Beat Retreat, Horse Guards

1979   Royal Tournament

First Great Children's Party, Hyde Park, International Year of the Child

Household Division Beat Retreat, Horse Guards

Aldershot Army Display

Wembley Musical Pageant

Brighton Festival Tattoo

SSAFA Tattoo, Aldershot

Berlin Tattoo

'Carols for the Queen', Buckingham Palace
Cliff Richard

1980   100th Royal Tournament

Queen Mother's 80th Birthday, Earls Court

Household Division Beat Retreat, Horse Guards

Brighton Festival Tattoo, Brighton Centre

Royal Artillery Massed Bands, Horse Guards

HMS *Excellent* 150th Anniversary Celebration, Portsmouth

1981   Royal Tournament

Royal Fireworks for the wedding of HRH the Prince of Wales and Lady Diana Spencer, Hyde Park

Household Division Beat Retreat, Horse Guards

Aldershot Army Display

Wembley Musical Pageant
Dame Vera Lynn

Berlin Tattoo

'The Story of Christmas', St George's, Hanover Square
Dame Judi Dench • Sir Robin Day • Robert Morley
Sian Phillips • Robert Hardy • Michael Williams
Prunella Scales • Timothy West • Edward Fox

1982   Royal Tournament

Household Division Beat Retreat, Horse Guards

St John Cadets Celebration, Royal Albert Hall

Berlin Massed Bands, Waldbühne
Cliff Richard • Leo Sayer

Naming Ceremony for *Victory '83* (America's Cup)

'Story of Christmas', St George's, Hanover Square
Anthony Andrews • Cecil Parkinson • Dame Judi Dench
Peter Barkworth • Frank Muir • Rowan Atkinson
Hannah Gordon • Michael Williams • Edward Fox
Jeremy Paxman

1983   Royal Tournament

Aldershot Army Display
Household Division Beat Retreat, Horse Guards

Son et Lumière, 'Heart of the Nation', Horse Guards
Sir John Gielgud • Paul Sccofield • Keith Mitchell
Hannah Gordon • Anthony Andrews • Prunella Scales
Edward Woodward • Barbara Windsor • Michael Cochrane
Isobel Dean • Gordon Jackson • Maxine Audley
Robert Hardy • Timothy West • Maurice Denham
David Langton • Patrick Holt • Christopher Good
Penelope Keith • Peter Barkworth • Clive Panto
Frances Cheater • Gerard Green

Royal Ball for America's Cup, Newport, Rhode Island

TA Celebration, Lord Mayor of London's Parade

Berlin Tattoo

'The Story of Christmas', St George's, Hanover Square
Sir Michael Hordern • Anthony Quayle • Joanna David
John Timpson • Anna Massey • Anthony Andrews
Andrew Cruickshank • Selina Scott

1984   Royal Tournament

Household Division Beat Retreat, Horse Guards

Rotary International Tattoo, Birmingham

Gatcombe Park Horse Show (entertainment)

'Milk Cup Final' (entertainment), Wembley Stadium

Opening of St James's Club, Antigua

St John Ambulance Banquet, Hampton Court

'The Story of Christmas', St George's, Hanover Square
Alec McCowen • Jan Leeming • Gordon Jackson
Dame Judi Dench • Tim Piggott Smith Dulcie Gray
Michael Denison • Richard Stilgoe • Sebastian Coe

1985   Royal Tournament

Regimental 300th Anniversary Celebrations, Royal Albert Hall

'Milk Cup Final' (entertainment), Wembley Stadium

Wembley Musical Pageant

Rhine Army Horse Show

St John Ambulance Fireworks, Osterley Park

Son et Lumière, Horse Guards (as for '83)

50th Birthday Celebrations for HM King Hussein of Jordan,
Amman

'Story of Christmas', St George's, Hanover Square
Tim Piggott Smith • Dame Judi Dench • Brian Johnston
Anthony Andrews • David Dimbleby • Jan Leeming
Sir John Mills • Geraldine James

Berlin Tattoo

1986   Royal Tournament

BAEE Tattoo, Aldershot

Opening Ceremony, World Chess Championships, London

100th Anniversary Celebration of Olympia Show Halls

'The Story of Christmas', St George's, Hanover Square
Timothy West • Prunella Scales • Nigel Hawthorne
Jan Leeming • Bob Monkhouse • Peter Bowles • Hayley Mills
Angela Thorne • Barbara Leigh Hunt • Richard Pasco

Olympia Horse Show , Finale

1987   Royal Tournament

Second Great Children's Party, Hyde Park

Household Division Beat Retreat, Horse Guards

P&O Centenary Celebrations, Greenwich-, *Richard Baker*

'The Queen's Shilling' for SSAFA, Royal Albert Hall
Roslind Ayres • Peter Bowles • Max Bygraves • Jonathan Cecil
Charles Collingwood • Judy Cornweall • Bernard Cribbins
Isobel Dean • Hannah Gordon • Garrard Green
James Grout • Martin Jarvis • TP McKkenna
Virginia McKenna • Sir John Mills • Richard Morant
Julia Osborne • Murray Watson

Wedding of HRH Prince Feisal and Alia al Tabbaa, Jordan

Wedding of Shaker bin Zaid, son of Commander in Chief,
Royal Jordanian Armed Forces

'The Story of Christmas', St George's, Hanover Square (my last
one)
Barbara Leigh-Hunt • Edward Fox • Brian Johnston
Angela Thorne • Gordon Jackson • Joanna David
Michael Williams

Olympia Horse Show, Finale

1988   Royal Tournament

            'Joy to the World', Royal Albert Hall
            Anthony Andrews • Harlem Boys Choir • Ossian Ellis
            *Peter Bowles *Tristan Fry • James Grout • Penelope Keith*
            Ben Kingsley • Cliff Richard • (President Reagan)

            Coronation Anniversary Celebrations for HM King Hussein
            of Jordan

            Olympia Horse Show, Finale

1989   Royal Tournament

            SSAFA Massed Bands, Horse Guards

            300th Anniversary Celebrations of Royal Welch Fusiliers,
            Powys Castle

            Westminster Cathedral Flower Show (centre piece)

            100th Royal International Horse Show, Birmingham

            Finale and 'Around the World in 80 Hours Competition'
            Ernie Wise

            'Joy to the World', Royal Albert Hall (the Queen's Christmas
            Broadcast)
            Edward Woodward • Mollie Sugden • George Segal
            Cliff Richard • Nicola Pagett • Anthony Andrews • Roy Castle
            Stafford Johns

            Olympia Horse Show, Finale

1990   Royal Tournament

The Queen Mother's 90th Birthday Celebration, Horse Guards
Sir John Mills

Berlin Massed Bands Concert

National Day Celebrations, Oman

'Fortress Fantasia', Gibraltar

Finale, World Equestrian Games, Stockholm

'Joy to the World', Royal Albert Hall
Benjamin Luxon • Robert Ttear • Suzi Quatro • Leo Sayer
Wayne Sleep • Bertice Reading • Diane Leighton
Chris de Burgh • David Copperfield • Paul Daniels
Anthony Andrews • Jane Asher • Peter Bowles
Evelyn Glennie • Bonnie Langford

Olympia Horse Show, Finale

1991   Royal Tournament

G7 Summit Celebration, Buckingham Palace
James Galway

SPAR Celebrations, Royal Albert Hall
Lulu • Bob Monkhouse • Angela Rippon

Opening Ceremony, XCVII Session of International Olympic

Committee, Birmingham

'Joy to the World', Royal Albert Hall
Paul Scofield • Prunella Scales • Cliff Richard
Gloria Hunniford • Robert Powell • Angharad Rees
Geraldine James • Penelope Keith • Anton Rodgers
Anthony Andrews • Wilhelmina Fernandez • Hannah Gordon

Olympia Horse Show, Finale

1992   Royal Tournament

Edinburgh Military Tattoo

HM the Queen's 40th Anniversary Celebrations, 'The Great
Event', Earls Court2
Sir Ian McKellen *Garrard Green • Lord Hunt
Sir Edmund Hillary • Julian Slade • Chris Biggins
Norma Pank • Patrick Green • Timothy Bentinck
Felicity Finch • Peter Dimmock • Brian Johnston
HRH Prince Edward • Darcy Bussell • Zoltan Solymosi
Lonnie Donegan • Wendy Craig • Oliver Samms
Dame Vera Lynn • Original Tiller Girls • Petula Clarke
Dame Gwyneth Jones • Cliff Morgan • Robert Tear
Raymond Baxter • Larry Adler • Cliff Richard
Dame Judi Dench • Simon Brown • Tony Britton
Liz Robertson • Evelyn Laye • Felicity Lott • Cilla Black
Michael Ball • Norma Burrowes • Anna Massey
Sir Roger Bannister • Henry Cooper • Bobby Charlton

United Grand Lodge of Masons of England, Earls Court

British National Day, EXPO Seville

The Last Berlin Tattoo
Status Quo • Roger Whittaker • Bonnie Tyler

'Joy to the World', Royal Albert Hall
Cliff Richard • Lon Satton • Ruby Wax • Gloria Hunniford
Geraldine James • Roger Moore • Peter Bowles
Patricia Hodge • Anthony Andrews • Patti Boulaye

Olympia Horse Show, Finale

1993   Royal Tournament

Edinburgh Military Tattoo

The wedding of HRH Prince Abdullah and Rania al-Yassin

Memphis Tattoo, Tennessee

Pavarotti International Horse Show (Opening and Finale),
Modena
Luciano Pavarotti

National Celebration, Jordan

Opening of Queen Elizabeth the Queen Mother's Gates, Hyde
Park

'Joy to the World', Royal Albert Hall
Anthony Andrews • Patti Boulaye • Stephanie Cole
Graham Crowden • Patricia Hodge • Cliff Richard
Anton Rodgers • Ruby Wax • Frank Bruno • Colin Welland

Olympia Horse Show, Finale

1994   Royal Tournament

Edinburgh Military Tattoo (my last one)

Opening Ceremony, Thurrock 'Lakeside'

D-Day 50th Anniversary Commemoration, Normandy
Veterans, Royal Albert Hall
Dame Vera Lynn • Charlie Chester • Hannah Gordon
Raymond Baxter

Duke of Gloucester's 50th Birthday Celebration, Kensington
Palace

Army Benevolent Fund 50th Anniversary Drumhead Service, Royal Hospital Chelsea

Pavarotti International Horse Show (Opening and Finale), Modena
Luciano Pavarotti

Naming Ceremony for P&O ship *Shenzhen Bay*, China

RNLI Ball, Hilton Hotel, London

Royal Scots Dragoon Guards, Celebration Concert, Usher Hall, Edinburgh
Mark Knopfler

Sothebys' 250th Anniversary Celebration

Memphis Tattoo, Tennessee

'Joy to the World', Royal Albert Hall
Larry Adler • Jean Boht • Lesley Garrett • Bob Holness
Benjamin Luxon • Paul Nicholas • Nanette Newman
Clarke Peters • Diana Rigg • Jimmy Tarbuck • Lon Satton

Olympia Horse Show, Finale

1995   Royal Tournament

VE Day 50th Anniversary Celebrations, Hyde Park

RBL Concert
Dame Vera Lynn • Douglas Anderson • Colin Baker
Michael Ball • Lionel Bart • Honor Blackman • Gaye Brown
Dave Clarke • Wendy Craig • Michael Denison
Michael Elphick • Gretchen Franklin • Hannah Gordon
*Dulcie Gray *David Jacobs • Lesley Joseph • Ute Lemper*
Annabel Leventon • Dame Vera Lynn • John Nettles
Elaine Paige • Cliff Richard • Dorothy Tutin

Buckingham Palace, Balcony Appearance
Dame Vera Lynn • Harry Secombe • Cliff Richard
Bob Holness

Heads of State Ceremony
Sir Ian McKellan • Patricia Hodge • Sir David Willcocks

VE Night Party
*Colin Baker *Michael Ball • Chris Biggins • Dora Bryan*
Bernard Cribbins • Lorna Dallas • Barbara Dickson
Peter Duncan • Barbara Ferris • Rosemarie Ford
Mark Greenstreet • Robert Hardy • Anita Harris
*Melvyn Hayes *Hinge and Brackett • Patricia Hodge*
Basil Hoskins • Gloria Hunniford • Polly James
Grace Kennedy • David Kernan • Ross King
Bonnie Langford • Diane Langton • Cast of 'Les Miserables'
Celia Lipton Dame Vera Lynn • Ruth Madoc*
Ami McDonald • Robert Meadmore • Ron Moody
Original cast of 'The Boyfriend' • Julian Slade
Original Tiller Girls • Billy Pearce • Clarke Peters
Kate Rabette • Liz Robertson • Norman Rossington
Anthony Way • Elisabeth Welch • Sandy Wilson

VJ Day 50th Anniversary 'Final Tribute', Horse Guards
Iain Cuthbertson • Dame Judi Dench • Maria Ewing
Edward Fox Garrard Green • Saeed Jaffrey • Mark McCann*
Keith Mitchell • Sir John Mills • Joan Plowright
Denis Quilley • Viscount Tonypandy

SSAFA Beat Retreat, Horse Guards

Kempton Park Gala

50th Anniversary of Liberation of Jersey

Naming Ceremony of P&O ship *Oriana*, Florida

Kempton Park Gala

60th Birthday Celebrations for HM King Hussein of Jordan, Amman

Pavarotti International Horse Show (Opening and Finale), Modena
Luciano Pavarotti

Santa Barbara Horse Show, California

'Joy to the World', Royal Albert Hall
*Anthony Andrews *Chris Biggins • Sarah Brightman*
Fascinating Aida • Nickolas Grace • Patricia Hodge
Gloria Hunniford • Grace Kennedy • Sian Philips
Anthony Way • Cliff Richard

Olympia Horse Show, Finale

1996   Royal Tournament

Fireworks for P&O ship *Oriana*, Sydney Harbour

Kempton Park Gala

Royal Windsor Horse Show, Finale

Not Forgotten Association Christmas Show, St James's Palace

'Joy to the World', Royal Albert Hall
Anthony Andrews • Michael Ball • Honor Blackman
Patti Boulaye • Johnny Dankworth • Cleo Lane
Christopher Gable • Nickolas Grace • Patricia Hodge
Ben Kingsley • Dennis Quilley • Angharad Rees
Liz Robertson • Issy van Randwyck • Anthony Way

Olympia Horse Show, Finale

1997 Royal Tournament

    Countryside Rally, Hyde Park

    Kempton Park Gala

    Royal Windsor Horse Show, Finale

    Fireworks for the Ruby Wedding of HM the Queen and
    HRH the Duke of Edinburgh, Luton Hoo

    Naming Ceremony of P&O ship *Dawn Princess,*
    Fort Lauderdale, Florida

    The last 'Joy to the World' Royal Albert Hall
    Anthony Andrews • Peter Bowles • Grace Kennedy
    Nickolas Grace • Dame Diana Rigg • Chris Biggins
    Patti Boulaye • Gloria Hunnifrod • Suzi Quatro • Leo Sayer
    Hannah Gordon • Derek Nimmo

    Not Forgotten Association Christmas Show, St James's Palace

    Olympia Horse Show, Finale

1998 Royal Tournament

    SSAFA Beat Retreat, Horse Guards

    Kempton Park Gala

    Royal Windsor Horse Show, Finale

    Re-Opening The Albert Memorial, Hyde Park
    Dame Judi Dench • Peter Bowles • Michael Williams

    Naming Ceremony of P&O ship *Dawn Princess,*
    New York Harbor

Jessye Norman • Harlem Boys Choir

Not Forgotten Association Christmas Show, St James's Palace

Olympia Horse Show, Finale

1999   The Last Royal Tournament
Rowan Atkinson

Centenary of King Abdul–Aziz al Saud, Saudi Arabia

Royal Windsor Horse Show, Finale

Kempton Park Gala

Not Forgotten Association Christmas Show, St James's Palace

Olympia Horse Show, Finale

2000   The Royal Military Tattoo 2000, Horse Guards
Anthony Andrews • Peter Bowles • Dame Judi Dench
Nickolas Grace • Robert Hardy • Martin Jarvis
Keith Michell • Dennis Quilley • Prunella Scales
Viscount Montgomery • Timothy West • Michael Williams
Edward Woodward • Kate Adie

Queen Elizabeth the Queen Mother's 100th Birthday, Horse Guards

Royal Windsor Horse Show, Finale

Re-opening of Somerset House, and the Gilbert Collection

Not Forgotten Association Christmas Show, St James's Palace

Olympia Horse Show, Finale

2001 Royal Windsor Horse Show, Finale

    Kempton Park Gala

    Not Forgotten Association Christmas Show, St James's Palace
    Alisdair Malloy • Hannah Gordon • Dillie Keane
    Lia Kristenson • Choloe Hanslip • Esther Rantzen

    Olympia Horse Show, Finale

2002 Golden Jubilee Celebrations, Weekend Festival

    Fireworks and Beacon Lighting, Buckingham Palace

    Massed Parades, Fly Past, Mall and Buckingham Palace

    'All the Queen's Horses', Home Park, Windsor

    'Reaching out for Africa', Royal Albert Hall
    Boney M • Patti Boulaye • Gabrielle • Uri Geller
    Cliff Richard • Rick Wakeman

    Not Forgotten Association Christmas Show, St James's Palace
    Barry Cryer • Bill Pertwee • Judy Campbell • Pam Cundell
    Michael Mates MP • Honor Blackman • Vince Hill

    Olympia Horse Show, Finale

2003 Opening of Cannon Center Concert Hall, Memphis, Tennessee

    Naming Ceremony for *Minerva II*, Tower Bridge
    Kiri te Kanawana • Stephen Fry

    Not Forgotten Association Christmas Show, St James's Palace
    Gyles Brandreth • Alasdair Malloy • Honor Blackman
    Fay Presto • Robert Meadmore

Olympia Horse Show, Finale

2004   'Music on Fire!' Royal Military Academy Sandhurst
        Timothy West • Kathryn Nutbeam • Laurie Brock

        Royal Welsh Agricultural Show 100th Anniversary Cavalcade,
        Builth Wells

        Not Forgotten Association Christmas Show, St James's Palace
        Angharad Rees • Victoria Yellop • Honor Blackman
        Nickolas Grace • Liz Robertson • Robert Meadmore
        Keith Barron • Clare Sweeney • Boney M • Hannah Gordon

        Olympia Horse Show, Finale

2005   60th Anniversary of Liberation of Jersey

        200th Anniversary of Battle of Trafalgar, Royal Yacht
        Squadron, Cowes

        'Glory of Wales', Denbigh

        Not Forgotten Association Christmas Show, St James's Palace
        Richard Stilgoe • Surrey Harmony • Cilla Black • Robert
        Meadmore • Jemina Phillips • Charlie Green •   The Drifters

        Olympia Horse Show, Finale

2006   100th Anniversary Celebration, Central School of Speech
        and Drama, Old Vic
        Graham Norton • Lynda Bellingham • Emma Watson
        David Robb • Cherie Lunghi • Rufus Sewell
        Amanda Donohoe • Tony Robinson • Jennifer Saunders
        Catherine Tate • Terence Stamp • Dominick Gerard
        Martyn Ellis

Not Forgotten Association Concert, Tower of London
Joan Hind • Gordon Cree • Jane McDonald • Chris Biggins
The Drifters

'Music on Fire!' RMA Sandhurst
Myleene Klass • Patti Boulaye • Sir Donald Sinden
Dame Judi Dench • Honor Blackman • Robert Hardy
Kate Adie • Shelley Katz

Not Forgotten Association Christmas Show, St James's Palace

2007   Not Forgotten Association Concert, Painted Hall, Greenwich
Rolf Harris • Engelbert Humperdinck • Sarah Jones
Kate Adie • Edward Woodward • The Drifters • Robert Hardy
Michele Dotrice • Original Tiller Girls

'Football, Reaching out for Africa', Royal Albert Hall

Not Forgotten Association Christmas Show, St James's Palace
Barry Mason • Pam Cundell • Hannah Gordon
Eddie Devine • Kate Adie • Adrian Nash • Honor Blackman
Simon Callow • Dillie Keane • Nickolas Grace • The Drifters
Jivers

2008   Not Forgotten Association Concert, Tower of London
Lesley Joseph • Anthony Stuart Lloyd • Paul Zerdin
New Seekers

'Music on Fire!' RMA Sandhurst
Sir Trevor McDonald • Rowan Atkinson • Peter Bowles
Hannah Gordon • Joanna Lumley • Prunella Scales
Timothy West • Jonathan Ansell • Hayley Westenra • Teatro

GOSH Carol Concert, St Paul's Knightsbridge
Sir Trevor McDonald • Catherine Tate • Thandie Newton
Rhydian

Not Forgotten Association Christmas Show, St James's Palace
Liz Smith • Paul Zerdin *Boney M • Steve Rawlings

2009   Not Forgotten Association Christmas Show, St James's Palace

2010   Not Forgotten Association 90th Anniversary Celebration,
Buckingham Palace
Dame Judi Dench • Lorna Dallas • Terence Stamp
Nickolas Grace • Peter Duncan • Simon Williams
Robert Hardy • Rick Wakeman • Anton du Beke • Erin Boag
Blake • Hannah Gordon • David Copperfield
Not Forgotten Association Christmas Show, St James's Palace
(my last show)
Kate Adie • Harry Patch (aged 108) • Jean Martyn
Hannah Gordon • Carl Scofield • The Soldiers • Rolf Harris
Swingtime Sweethearts

Acknowledgements

This book would not have been possible without the vital assistance of many thousands of people, not least because without them the events would never have happened and there would have been nothing to write about.

I seem to have done more than 230 events all around the world, so sadly some – both events and people – have had to be left out, for which I apologise.

I would particularly like to thank:

Firstly, certain people who have played a key role in shaping my whole life: Gordon Fairley, Major Delmé Seymour-Evans, Major General Sir Philip Ward, Major General Sir John Nelson, General Sir Patrick Howard-Dobson, Major General Harry Dalzell-Payne, Colonel Dan Reade, Colonel Iain and Margaret Ferguson, Sir Christopher Aston, Margaret Parker, Gina Phillips, Francis and Liz Gradidge, and Guy and Sarah Norrie – without them I would never have achieved anything.

Some of those above are, very sadly, no longer with us but my gratitude to them lives on.

Then all my friends in the Regiment and the Army who were my first real family.

Rosemary Anne Sisson who first dragged a 'thick Army officer' into the professional world of the theatre and wrote for me so many marvellous scripts that made my scatty ideas work.

I am also deeply grateful to the scores of Stars and Personalities who have very generously given of their time and talent to support the multitude of charity and other events that I have run over the years. My gratitude is also due to Sir Donald Gosling and Sir Ronald Hobson for their outstanding generosity in supporting so many of my events and charities that have benefited so many thousands of people.

All the talented professionals who have been mystified by the strange way that I do things: Dougie Squires (a patient genius), Gary Withers (an unsung genius), George Douglas (Uncle George), Maureen Mele, Catie Bland ('Catie dear'), Robert Ornbo ('Prince of Darkness'), John Del'Nero ('Silence is golden'), Jon Pope, Paul Keating, Wilf Scott (pyromaniac), Adam Wildi, Chuck Crampton, Alan Jacobi (for a while), and hundreds of other very hard-working designers, production staff, riggers, technicians, projectionists and pyro-technicians.

My grateful thanks also go to all the tens of thousands of (mostly) uncomplaining soldiers, sailors and airmen who have been forced to take part in my events and suffer under me. Their patience and great good humour have been more than I deserve.

In that respect I would also like to thank my twenty-eight orderlies, who know better than most what a nightmare I am to work for.

Last, but most certainly not least, my gratitude is due to all the Directors of Music, Conductors, Musicians and Choristers who have put up with my ignorance and stubbornness with kind resignation for well over forty-five years.

*   *   *

To Anne Dewe of Andrew Mann Ltd, who gave me much early encouragement with this book.

To my publisher, Anthony Weldon of Bene Factum, for much sound advice and for taking it all on.

To Mary Sandys who has edited my ramblings into a coherent whole and made me seem a much better writer than I really am.

To Jennifer Holmes who typed up all my rubbish in the first place.

*   *   *

And lastly - to my lovely god-children: Lucinda Wakefield (née Pipe), James Norrie and Andrew Norrie (honorary), George Cordle and Pandora Brooks-Ward, who have always been such a joy and given me the excuse over the years to do all the childish things that I so love doing.

And of course to my darling Emma and Oliver and their family (now mine!) who have kept me sane and made me so happy.

Index